MW00607911

MICS, CAMERAS, SYMBOLIC ACTION

NEW MEDIA THEORY
Series Editor, Byron Hawk

The New Media Theory series investigates both media and new media as a complex ecological and rhetorical context. The merger of media and new media creates a global social sphere that is changing the ways we work, play, write, teach, think, and connect. Because this new context operates through evolving arrangements, theories of new media have yet to establish a rhetorical and theoretical paradigm that fully articulates this emerging digital life.

The series includes books that combine social, cultural, political, textual, rhetorical, aesthetic, and material theories in order to understand moments in the lives that operate in these emerging contexts. Such works typically bring rhetorical and critical theories to bear on media and new media in a way that elaborates a burgeoning post-disciplinary "medial turn" as one further development of the rhetorical and visual turns that have already influenced scholarly work.

BOOKS IN THE SERIES

MICS, CAMERAS, SYMBOLIC ACTION

Audio-Visual Rhetoric for Writing Teachers

Bump Halbritter

Parlor Press
Anderson, South Carolina
www.parlorpress.com

Parlor Press LLC, Anderson, South Carolina, USA

© 2013 by Parlor Press
All rights reserved.
Printed in the United States of America

SAN: 254-8879

Library of Congress Cataloging-in-Publication Data

Halbritter, Scott K.
   Mics, cameras, symbolic action : audio-visual rhetoric for writing teachers
/ Bump Halbritter.
      p. cm. -- (New media theory)
   Includes bibliographical references and index.
   ISBN 978-1-60235-336-7 (pbk. : alk. paper) -- ISBN 978-1-60235-337-4
(hardcover : alk. paper) -- ISBN 978-1-60235-338-1 (adobe ebook) -- ISBN
978-1-60235-341-1 (ibooks) -- ISBN 978-1-60235-339-8 (epub) -- ISBN
978-1-60235-340-4 (mobi)
   1. English language--Rhetoric--Study and teaching--Data processing.
2. Mass media--Authorship. I. Title.
   PE1404.H332 2012
   808'.0420285--dc23
                              2012019812

                         1 2 3 4 5

Cover design by David Blakesley.
Cover image created by Bump Halbritter
Printed on acid-free paper.

Parlor Press, LLC is an independent publisher of scholarly and trade titles
in print and multimedia formats. This book is available in paper, cloth and
eBook formats from Parlor Press on the World Wide Web at http://www.
parlorpress.com or through online and brick-and-mortar bookstores. For
submission information or to find out about Parlor Press publications, write
to Parlor Press, 3015 Brackenberry Drive, Anderson, South Carolina, 29621,
or email editor@parlorpress.com.

Contents

Preface

We view language as a kind of action, symbolic action. And for this terministic perspective we have proposed the trade name of 'Dramatism' precisely because we would feature the term act.

[A] Dramatistic approach to the analysis of language starts with problems of terministic catharsis (which is another word for "rebirth," transcendence, transubstantiation, or simply for "transformation" in the sense of the technically developmental, as when a major term is found somehow to have moved on, and thus to have in effect changed its nature either by adding new meanings to its old nature, or by yielding place to some other term that henceforth takes over its functions wholly or in part).

—Kenneth Burke

WHY ALL THE DRAMA?

Terministic Catharsis: the expression itself sounds dramatic. Terministic suggests the linguistic—logos, the word; however, it seems also to resonate with reference to crisis, urgency, and finality—telos, end or purpose. Catharsis suggests, as Kenneth Burke claims, rebirth, transcendence, and transformation (*LSA* 367). As such, the expression, terministic catharsis, at once suggests death and rebirth: a lexical phoenix bursting into flame and rising again, anew, from the ashes of its previous manifestation. *Logos* sheds its skin to escape the constraints of a definition that is too tight—a word who has grown too big for its britches.

This book was written at a time of terministic catharsis and its author assumes that the particular instance of terministic catharsis examined in this book is not a relic of history, a momentary event like a tsunami wave that forms, crashes, and dissipates. This terministic catharsis remains in flux, like the ongoing ebbs and flows—the tugs and pushes—of the tides themselves: always moving, always changing, always effecting movement and change. This book explores the terministic catharsis of *writing*, and it will argue for the terministic catharsis of that ancient term, *telos*, as it is applied to the teaching of writing transformed. Our goal, our *telos*, will be to question the goals of writing instruction and to match those with the writing goals we assign, asking, when is *a* work of writing done and when is *the* work of writing done? As such, we will attend to writing as a verb primarily and we will access that by way of the production of writing as a noun. The noun is the vehicle. The verb is the goal.

Mics, Cameras, Symbolic Action will attempt to expand the territory of writing by way of symbolic action. It will amass and test theory, terminology, and both writing and teaching practices that will aid our progress into that expanded territory of writing. This pedagogical approach will remix the old with the new: the pious with the impious. What will help us make the new stick to the established? Duct tape.

Let me explain.

In my years spent as a working musician, I learned the essential, practical value of duct tape. Little, at the time, did I realize the full scope of its rhetorical value. That dawned upon me at a conference for writing professionals. I was presenting on a panel devoted to a discussion of electronic publishing opportunities for undergraduate writers and researchers, with emphasis on the publishing of multimedia products. When I arrived at the room where our panel would present (one hour before the first presentation of the day—as always—to scope out what we would need in order to use the room), I found a table covered with pitchers of water and drinking glasses, six round tables with chairs for attendees, and a long narrow table for the presenters. All of the tables had white tablecloths and the venue had supplied notepads and pens for participants. However, there were no presentation materials: no overhead projector, no digital projector, no speakers, and no projection screen. None. Of course, I was showing a movie—not only as usual, but as promised. And, of course, I was prepared—or nearly prepared. You see, I'm used to showing up at academic conferences that are ill-equipped or, as in this case, completely un-equipped for the sort of media I will be presenting. I brought my own computer, digital projector, speakers, and extension cords—oh yeah, and a roll of duct tape, as always—just in case. However, as you may imagine, I was unable to travel to this conference with a projection screen—and *this* room did not have one. Yet with all I had brought, I was unprepared to conduct my presentation.

Venues usually charge exorbitant prices for presentation media. I understand that. However, *reading* the rhetoric of the situation, the conference organizers communicated this decision: for a conference of writing professionals, who according to formal position statements value audio-visual writing, tablecloths are necessary, but presentation media are not. In other words, it is perfectly reasonable, even if un-desirable, to conduct a conference on writing without presentation media. Audio-visual writing is the parsley on our disciplinary plate. Writers and writing professionals read papers and take notes on paper at their conferences. What they need is a room, some drinking water, a few notepads and pens, chairs, tables, and tablecloths. The basics. The pious materials of our work. We say we value audio-visual writing, for our students, but we do not expect that it will be essential to the work that writing professionals *do*. Even if that *is* what they do.

Well, I am grateful that white tablecloths were deemed to be worth the investment, because with my roll of duct tape, we were able to make a screen. Duct tape made audio-visual writing stick in this ses-sion at this conference. Duct tape. Now, it wasn't pretty. The duct tape signaled an obvious case of jury-rigging. It said quite clearly, "This is NOT what we do here." Even in the few rooms that *were* equipped with screens and projectors, ones that didn't need duct tape and in which tablecloths were tablecloths, there were no speakers. Audio, even if it is incorporated in audio-visual media, is absolutely not what we do. We do text and bullet points and still images—not only at this conference, but at essentially every professional conference in our field. I recently attended a presentation by one of my graduate students who had to have her session attendees huddle around the speakers of a lap-top to hear her movie—the one announced in the program. We appar-ently, as a discipline, don't recognize that these media are really ours. We write *about* them, not *with* them. That's not what we *do*. Even if that *is* what we do.

So I call our attention to the *duct tape*: a visual and practical indicator of the hypermediation—the impiety—of audio-visual media. Duct
tape: a medium symbolic of our attempts to jury-rig audio-visual writing to our pedagogy. An *ad hoc* fix. Something stuck on and not integrated. A thing awaiting a more permanent fixing. In this book, *Mics,
Cameras, Symbolic Action: Audio-Visual Rhetoric for Writing Teachers*,
we will listen and look for what is already here, even if we don't recognize it as our own—even if it is duct-taped in place, for now. Where
we notice duct tape, we will listen and look carefully for more permanent solutions to the temporary adhesion it facilitates. The presence
of duct tape has always indicated *use* to me: Duct tape is symbolic of
purposeful, motivated, necessary action. Duct tape is used to correct
infrastructures and protocols that were not designed for emergent actions. Musicians play shows in venues that were not designed for them
or for the equipment unique to each musical act that performs at the
venue. Even if a particular venue was designed for *a* musical act, it
likely was not designed for *the* musical act on any given night. Invari-
ably there will be cords and cables that need to be run across floors
where the musicians or others will need to walk. These potentially
dangerous obstructions will be secured with duct tape. Duct tape will
facilitate the emergent action. Duct tape will help the musical act fit
the scene—for now, at least.

Our emergent action in this book is to situate the new work of
twenty-first century writing within a pedagogy for the teaching of academic writers. Some of our work will be realized as expansion: We will
add some new terms, tools, and practices. For that we will turn to discussions about music and audio recording, visual arts design, and film
and video production. However, some of our work will be realized as
reduction and reallocation—by way of terministic catharsis: We will
reevaluate some of our terms and their associated concepts in play to
determine what is most and least conducive to realizing twenty-first
century writing.

This book will embark on a quest for terministic catharsis: to move
intellectual property law professor Lawrence Lessig's claim that audio-visual media making is *writing* into use by those of us who teach
writing—for those of us who participate in *acts* of writing. For even
if we share Lessig's view that audio-visual media making *is* writing,
that does little more than point to the duct tape holding audio-visual writing to our syllabi (or syllabuses, as Erika Lindemann has ad-

vised). Terministic catharsis—paradigm shifting—must pursue piety through impious means. The pious must be made impious in order to be rendered pious anew. In this book, the vehicle for terministic catharsis of our pious term *writing* will be Burke's term, "symbolic action." *Action* is established as the lens through which we investigate the things that rhetoric *does*: what it accomplishes, how it moves people to participate purposefully with their animate and inanimate surroundings. Through this lens of rhetorical action, we will consider distinctions between poetry and prose and reconsider the static notion of *rhetorical stance* as the always moving and shifting steps of a multidimensional, *rhetorical dance*. We will employ Burke's *dramatistic pentad* (act, agent, agency, scene, and purpose) as a terministic filter for examining how authors may be motivated to perform types of rhetorical dances for realizing a variety of rhetorical outcomes—outcomes always fitted to specific scenes of rhetorical action (*Grammar*). We will also visit the educational theories of John Dewey to situate and *retune* Donald Murray's process-based approach within a pedagogy for teaching audio-visual writing, and we will see how Robin Williams's indelicate C.R.A.P. principles for visual design may help us talk about audio-visual writing as well. *Symbols* will be examined according to two types, aural and visual, and will be considered throughout the three primary phases comprising the operation of writing: collection (mics and cameras), correction (editing on computers), and connection (sharing edited products with various audiences). These become the building blocks for positing *multidimensional rhetoric*: rhetoric that is crafted in layers of media, motives, and appeals; and play will become the motivator for helping our writing students express intrinsic value for the hard work of crafting multidimensional rhetoric by way of audio-visual writing assignments—hard work that will translate into instrumental values for using their new, audio-visual writing skills and habits of mind to solve real problems in their lives.

We undertake this mission for two reasons: because our discipline and the world around us has said that we must and because we are largely un- or underprepared to do so. The National Council of Teachers of English (NCTE), released its "Resolution on Composing with Nonprint Media" in 2003. That resolution states, "Teachers need both the theoretical and pedagogical base to guide their students in the best educational uses of multimedia composition." In the service of this position, the organization offers the following four resolutions:

Resolved, that the National Council of Teachers of English

- encourage preservice, inservice, and staff development programs that will focus on new literacies, multimedia composition, and a broadened concept of literacy;
- encourage research and develop models of district, school, and classroom policies that would promote multimedia composition;
- encourage integrating multimedia composition in English language arts curriculum and teacher education, and in refining related standards at local, state, and national levels; and
- renew the commitment expressed in the 1983 Resolution on Computers in English and Language Arts to achieve equity of access to the full range of composing technologies.

These resolutions call for education and curricular integration of multimedia composition; and while the NCTE resolution uses the term *multimedia*, this book pursues a specific subset of multimedia writing: *audio-visual writing*. However, NCTE's position comes one step short of adopting Murray's thesis that a writer teaches writing (*Writer*). This book adopts Murray's thesis in earnest—a position I came to embrace when I was a graduate student: A multimedia writer teaches multimedia writing; an audio-visual writer teaches audio-visual writing.

It was the end of fall semester of 2001. I was a TA in the Department of English at UNC-Chapel Hill. TAs primarily taught one of the two required first-year composition courses. I had spent the semester planning to teach my first section of the second course in the sequence. Then I was called to the office of our Writing Program Administrator (WPA), Erika Lindemann. She needed someone to TA in the big Film Criticism class and wondered if I might be interested in taking the assignment. I told her that if she was asking, I was accepting. Erika could have asked me to cut her lawn and I would have accepted—I still would—and that's essentially what I thought she was asking. I did not want to TA in this film class. I had never even taken a film class. I knew nothing about film. I was a writing teacher. I wanted to teach writing classes. I took the section as a favor to Erika.

As it turned out, Erika had done me the favor, as usual.

Of course, I didn't see this immediately. I was struggling to learn as much as I could about film as quickly as possible so that I didn't fall flat on my face as a discussion leader for twenty-five undergraduates. I read our book carefully and watched each and every film before our in-class screenings, taking pages and pages of notes. It helped. What helped even more was being assigned mini-lectures for the big section (about 150 students). My first major assignment was to give a mini-lecture on the opening sequence of *Citizen Kane*, a film I had never seen prior to this class. I watched those opening minutes at least a dozen times. I read everything I could about *Citizen Kane* and Orson Welles's approach to filming and directing the work. I had pages and pages of notes. I was most amazed by just how much there was to say about these three minutes. I was overwhelmed by how much information Welles was able to present in such a brief period of time. This, and all of the stuff I'd read about Welles's tour-de-force of moviemaking, made me ask, how? My training as a writing teacher made me ask, what were the rhetorical effects of the many choices that Welles had made? In order to see and hear those choices, I had to break apart the scenes into types of choices—into layers of information—a move that was familiar to me from my many years of experience with multitrack, music recording. I started paying careful attention to the camera positioning that Welles employed, not as a matter of mechanical fascination (or fetishism), but as a window to Welles's attention to audience. In other words, I asked, why does Welles want the audience to see the scene/actor/action from here? What's to be gained or lost from this perspective? What other options may have been considered? I asked questions about Welles's editing choices, paying careful attention to the efficiency with which Welles walks the audience through Kane's lifetime of achievement even as he attempts to build the audience's appetite for the story that will follow.

At the same time, I was taking a semester-long seminar on the works of Kenneth Burke, and as luck or fate would have it, we were reading *A Grammar of Motives* at just about the same time we were reviewing *Citizen Kane* in the film class. Burke's pentad remediated perfectly onto the concerns that were surfacing as relevant in the *Citizen Kane* analysis: camera angles, music, and editing choices became Welles's means—his *agency*—for regarding the *actors*, *acts*, and *scenes* of action. By studying Welles's choices of means, I could posit the rhetorical *purposes* that were driving the story as a whole and in individual scenes of action. Furthermore, these elements worked together to form a window to Welles's *attitude* toward (or perspective on) the work.

Years later, Stuart A. Selber would give me language to better understand the literacies involved in these analytical skills I was developing. Reading the means that Welles employed, in and of themselves, is an act of *functional literacy*: It's a look under the hood of the rhetorical machine. Reading and interpreting Welles's text itself, the narrative and the film transporting it—the film's *aboutness*, is an act of *critical literacy*: An act that, as Selber argues, is greatly enriched by understanding the functional options available to the author (*Multiliteracies* 234-35; "Reimagining" 481, 497-98). Or in keeping with the automotive metaphor, it's a ride in the rhetorical machine. Most importantly for our concerns, reading and interpreting Welles's actions as an *audiovisual writer*, the relationship between his choices of means and the corresponding *aboutness* that emerges from them, is an act of *rhetorical literacy*: It's a conversation with the maker and driver of the rhetorical machine—it's learning from Henry Ford himself.

I realized that what I was doing was not reading the film as a reader, but reading the film as a writer. Go figure. This film criticism course, contextualized within the larger academic scene in which I was participating, was moving me to see criticism as a means for not only writing *about* movies, but as a means for writing movies of my own. I left this class saying, "I wanna make a movie!" Suddenly, all of the movies we watched came to rhetorical life for me. Director Alex Cox and cinematographer Roger Deakins present an intoxicatingly beautiful and deeply disturbing sequence in *Sid & Nancy*. In this sequence, the hotel room in which the protagonists of the story are staying catches fire. Nancy, under the influence of heroin intoxication, watches from bed as the flames dance and dive about the room even as Sid nods off beside her. The functional literacy that allows us to interpret the means by which these filmmakers deliver the scene allows us to gain a critical perspective on the character's, Nancy's, perspective on the scene. Furthermore, the attention that the filmmakers devote to this scene indicates just how important it is to *them*. In other words, we *see* the scene through Nancy's eyes, and as we do so, we *hear* the rhetorical voice(s) of the audio-visual author(s). In doing so, we are now in the presence of author(s). We now are studying their *language* as surely as we study the language of Nathaniel Hawthorne when we do a close reading of *The Scarlet Letter*. Only the language of Welles or of Cox or of any audio-visual authors involves more, and often a lot more, than language *per se*. When we attend to the ways the audience is being directed to encounter the story, we are attending to rhetorical concerns—to the concerns of writers.

Of course, these words will probably sound like heresy to those who consider works of film to be best understood as works of *art*, which they most certainly are. However, art is directed by artists who have any number of purposes for creating the art they do in the way(s) they do. I do not mean to rob artists of their magic. I do not wish to merely expose the "wizard" behind the curtain. However, I do want to pay attention to what is going on behind the curtain in relation to the magic that emerges—not as a means for explaining what did happen, but as a means for modeling what may happen, and not as a means for being in the heads of other authors, but as a means for liberating what is inside of our heads—as a means for reading like writers, not necessarily as the writers that we read, but as the writers we may become.

Paulo Freire discusses a liberatory pedagogy. In Freire's discussions, *liberatory* is meant as a remedy to political and social oppression. I mean no disrespect to Freire's intentions or his most noble mission when I say that audio-visual rhetorical literacy is liberatory. It is. Its mission is just quite different. With few exceptions, audio-visual authors, especially those who work in digital technologies, are not "oppressed" in the way Freire's Brazilian contemporaries were. The students with whom we are concerned are, in many ways, already liberated—they are, after all, college students. While college students in the United States span an enormous range of socio-political positions, they are all, by virtue of their enrollment, already liberated from the type of oppression that apparently motivated Freire. Our work is a liberation of degrees—quite literally—but, as with Freire, this is a liberation of voices, and more importantly, of the ideas they carry.

I also noticed, back in that film criticism class, I was seeing and hearing things my fellow TAs for the course, graduate students specializing in a variety of English language literatures, apparently did not. I began to realize that this, quite possibly, could be due to the simple fact that they didn't *do* this—they were not audio-visual writers. I was that. I *did* that. I didn't make movies—yet; however, I had been a recording musician for many years, and that experience led me to envision doing the type of audio-visual writing I was studying and teaching. So I began to make movies—and ask my writing students to make them too; and I'm still doing so. This is a book about *doing* audio-visual writing, and about the things it will help you see and hear and value and *do*, so that you may help your students do the same.

This book, *Mics, Cameras, Symbolic Action: Audio-Visual Rhetoric for Writing Teachers*, grows from these perspectives. It pursues inquiry into the technologies and tools—the *agency*—of audio-visual writers: mics, cameras, and symbolic action. Bethany Tomaszewski, a former student in one of my audio-visual writing classes (you'll learn about her work in Chapter Five), concluded her final reflection of the semester with these words:

> This class has made me curse technology and count my blessings. It has changed the way I watch commercials, music videos, TV shows, and movies. Instead of being a passive viewer, I'm now thinking about the process of creation: how many cameras were used, what kinds of B-roll were incorporated, why is this video cut this way, etc. I've begun to analyze the composition of film—the camera angles, framing, timing, sequencing, music, audio effects, and how all of these things are layered and mixed to make a piece of multimedia art. I now have the skills and knowledge to make that art.

Bethany articulated this position at the end of the semester, after she had spent fifteen weeks in my class playing around *doing* the hard work of audio-visual writing—after she had become an audio-visual writer. She learned the lessons she claims above by writing. A writer learns writing.

This book asks that you and your students do the same and provides the theoretical and practical guidance to direct your progress.

Acknowledgments

I could not have written this book without all of the students who have been kind enough to allow me to be their teacher. Thanks to each and every one of you.

Next, I must thank the wonderful and inspiring Erika Lindemann. I arrived at the University of North Carolina at Chapel Hill as a graduate student in linguistics with a TA position in Erika's writing program. When my wife, Jules, picked me up after the first day of TA training (a.k.a. Lindemania), I told her, "Erika Lindemann is without a doubt the smartest person I've ever been around." Two years later, supercharged by what I was learning while teaching in Erika's program, I entered the PhD program in English. Erika was kind enough to give me her blessing to write this book, which I have always imagined as a companion to her *A Rhetoric for Writing Teachers*. Thank you, Erika, for your support and for continuing to be among the most impressive, inspiring, and generous people on this planet.

My move to the English department was inspired not only by Erika but also by Todd Taylor, with whom I had had the great fortune to take "Teaching with Technology." I made my first movie with Todd and taught my first moviemaking assignment while I was writing my dissertation under Todd's direction. Todd introduced me to the work of Jim Berlin, Joe Harris, and just about everyone in the field. Todd became my mentor, my teacher, my writing partner, and most importantly my best friend. Thank you, Todd, Jill, Max, and Jake for welcoming me into your lives.

I also must thank Bill Balthrop, who introduced me to Kenneth Burke, Jane Danielewicz, who introduced me to John Dewey and Paulo Freire, and Daniel Anderson, who asked me to say more about how music could serve as a thesis statement. However, I must also backtrack a bit and thank a few people who got me to UNC-CH. I had exceptional models and mentors of teaching at Indiana University of Pennsylvania. I first met Donald Murray, Mike Rose, and Patricia Bizzell while studying with Lynne Alvine, who is one of the first teachers I had as a graduate student and who remains one of the very best. Thank you, Lynne. Also, Mike Vella and Jeannine Fontaine helped me transition from the rock club circuit to the academy. Thank you, both, for your patience and tolerance. ☺

My first teaching position after graduate school was in Andrea Lunsford's Program in Writing and Rhetoric (PWR) at Stanford University. Thank you, Andrea, for allowing me to develop the pedagogy of this book within your program. Your influence helped me see inquiry as the fuel of the writing curriculum. Thank you, also, to my colleagues in PWR who helped me grow into the profession—which is to say, thanks for being such a bunch of smarty pants! Thank you, especially, to Christine Alfano and Eric Miraglia for your inspiration, and to Laura Roman, who, literally, introduced me to the great documentarian Les Blank. Andrea is also responsible for introducing her new hire with the funny name to her recent graduate, Jenn Fishman. I don't know where I'd be without the mind, wit, patience, friendship, and adult beverages of Jenn Fishman. Cheers, Jenn!

I thank my generous and amazingly impressive colleagues in the Department of Writing, Rhetoric, and American Cultures at Michigan State University. I am fantastically fortunate to work with you and learn from you. Though, could we slow the pace, just a bit? I mean, come on already. I'm kidding, of course. Kinda.

Special thanks to my friend and writing/research partner, the relentlessly kind and disarmingly brilliant Julie Lindquist. Julie was kind enough to read all of the very first drafts of this book—and that had to hurt. Julie has also been the other half of my brain since my arrival at MSU in the fall of 2006. Everyone should have the good fortune to work with Julie—but back off, 'cause we won't be done with the mountain of work ahead of us for a long, long time to come. Lucky me. Thank you, Julie. Your ock!

Crystal VanKooten, Casey Miles, Heather Hill, Steven Lessner, Guisseppe Getto, Minh-Tam Nguyen, Rachel Seiderman, Dean Holden, Ann Lawrence, and Kathy Schoon-Tanis all helped me in a variety of ways as I moved this book from concept to product(s). Thank you! And thanks to my partners and crew at the Documentary Lab (The DocLab): Noah Blon, Ben Froese, Jim Jansen, Tristan Johnson, Dan Nufer, and the amazing Scott Schopieray. Thanks, fellas! And thanks to Janet Swenson and Dànielle DeVoss for helping me realize that dream.

Thank you to my friends, colleagues, and fellow editors at NCTE: especially, Kurt Austin, Dana Driscoll, Joe Harris, Kelly Ritter, John Schilb, Kent Williamson, and Kathi Yancey. Thanks also to the editorial board of *CCC Online*.

Thank you, Parlor Press: David Blakesley, Byron Hawk, and our iPad guru, Turner Vaughn. Y'all rock!

Speaking of rock, thank you to my many musical collaborators and co-writers from my first life. Y'all are as responsible for this book as anyone. I loved every minute of it. Thank you. Social!

And finally, speaking of love, I must thank my most patient, supportive, and loving family: Robert Halbritter (Dad), Dianne Halbritter (Mom), Greta Halbritter (Li'l Sis), Ernie Lorelli (Ernie J), Vicky Lorelli (ViVi), and Laura, Scott, Kelsey, and Kira Cunningham. I love you.

But most of all, thank you, Jules, Sawyer, and Bennett to whom I dedicate this book and my life.

Mics, Cameras, Symbolic Action

1 Twenty-First Century Writing as Symbolic Action

> *[A] definition so sums things up that all the properties attributed to the thing defined can be as though "derived" from the definition. In actual development, the definition may be the last thing a writer hits upon. Or it may be formulated somewhere along the line. But logically it is prior to the observations it summarizes. Thus, insofar as all the attributes of the thing defined fit the definition, the definition should be viewed as "prior" in this purely nontemporal sense of priority.*
>
> —Kenneth Burke

It may seem obvious that a book called *Mics, Cameras, Symbolic Action: Audio-Visual Rhetoric for Writing Teachers* (*MCSA*) will begin with a definition of *writing* that entails possibilities for *audio-visual rhetoric*. It must. However, it does so in the spirit of Kenneth Burke's attitude toward definitions expressed in the epigraph above. Burke gives us three important concepts for framing the work of this book: logical priority, temporality, and the acts of writers (*LSA* 3). I will argue that when offering a definition of *writing*, it is the last of this triad that is most important to keep in mind. Writing, as engaged by writers, is far from being *done*. As such, we have to consider that established definitions of *writing* express logical priority that corresponds to situated temporality; that is, these definitions were "hit" upon at times when the acts they described seemed most to be "derived" from the definitions themselves. Definitions are written. They are the products of writers. However, the *project* of writing continues, and, as it does so, we can expect that the act of writing its definition—as it continues through time—will teach us new things about the acts we hope to define. Thus, the *definition* of "writing," which as Burke suggests, must be logically prior to the *discussion* of "writing," may indeed still be in the process of being "hit upon" by those attempting to write the definitions. Why? Because, in the words of Bill Condon, "no piece of writing is ever finished, it's just due" (Taylor, *Take 20*).

At this time, writers are claiming definitions of *writing* that are derived from their acts—acts that consequently seem to be derived from the definitions they offer. I am one such writer, and I am in the company of millions of writers whose actions define the term. In this first chapter, we will listen to some prominent voices in the ongoing project of writing in order to hear reasons for reconsidering the logical priority of established definitions of writing, definitions that feature the terms *language* and, at least in Western cultures, *alphabetic script* to the exclusion of other types of symbolic action. This book emerges from its author's dissatisfaction with established definitions of writing, definitions that did not allow him to derive all of the properties of his own writing and writerly actions. In 1968, Donald Murray reminded us that *A Writer Teaches Writing*. Murray introduces the second edition of the book, offered in 1985, as a complete rewrite, stating that he "did not want to view the subject through the lens of old language and old ideas" (xi). What emerges from Murray is an approach to writing, to teaching writing, and to thinking about writing—because "writing is thinking" (3)—that is both informed by experience and founded upon newness. Murray writes in the second edition,

> This book is not the end for me, but another beginning I have learned from writing it, and having written it I will learn how to depart from it. It is the sum of what I know today, but fortunately it is not the sum of what I will know at the end of next semester or the next year or the next years of writing and teaching. (5)

Murray knew in 1985 that he was still writing his definition of writing, and trusted that the process of writing that definition would continue to teach him about writing—that he would continue to learn about writing by way of writing.

Murray's perspective expresses the epistemic value of writing defined by James A. Berlin. In *Rhetoric and Reality: Writing Instruction in American Colleges, 1900–1985*, Berlin writes, "The epistemic position implies that knowledge is not discovered by reason alone, that cognitive and affective processes are not separate, that intersubjectivity is a condition of all knowledge, and that the contact of minds affects knowledge" (165). Applied to our act of defining *writing*, Berlin helps us see that the logical priority of a definition must not *define* or limit our thinking about writing. It recognizes that knowledge is a product of experience: of affect and reason. It also recognizes the intersubjectivity or *rhetorical value* of knowledge creation: that definitions emerge from individuals in dialogue with other individuals. As Burke claims, "Identification is compensatory to division. If [individuals] were not apart from one another, there would be no need for the rhetorician to proclaim their unity" (*Rhetoric* 22). Writing not only produces knowledge by way of its process, it argues for *common* knowledge by way of its product. Murray offered his "personal book by a single writer" (5) as a contribution to a common knowledge about writing and the teaching of writing. Through his book, Murray models how other writing teachers may use their experiences to both produce, convey, and inspire the production of common knowledge. It moves from personal knowledge (*A Writer*) by way of social action (*Teaches*) to common knowledge (*Writing*). Writing is compensatory to division. Or, as I often tell my writing students, *when it comes to writing, you're often on your own, but you're never alone.*

I am a writer, and I am a writing teacher. My experience of writing has traveled though many genres and many media. I am a musician who has written and recorded many musical compositions. My knowledge of song writing has been informed by my experiences of sitting alone on the edge of a bed with a guitar, a pen, and a pad of paper. It has been informed by the act of continuing to write songs in rehearsal with groups of performing and collaborating musicians, and informed still by continuing to write those same songs in the recording studio in collaboration with musical producers, recording engineers, and music business executives who want it to have more "boom, boom, boom." It is also informed by my wish to claim ownership of my writing and the potential revenues that may result from my ownership as defined by copyright laws that value *invention* more than they value *editing*.

I also am a writer of academic and professional prose who understands academic research and inquiry as facilitated by, realized through, and conveyed by way of highly specific forms of written language, among them essays, surveys, reports, and personal reflections. These forms of writing are the forms most commonly discussed in writing texts and among the writing professionals I have known and studied. My experience as an academic and professional writer is informed by my wish to claim ownership of my academic writing and the potential vitae lines it will provide, some of which are more valued than others by my peers, which will ultimately affect whether or not I may advance in or even retain my employment.

Further, I am a documentary movie maker who has learned that my acts of capturing, inventing, and editing the audio-visual information that comprise the movies I make draws from the range of experiences I have had with my other forms of authoring, my experience with reading other types of texts, and the possibilities that I can imagine as a result of all I know (or think I know). My experience as a movie maker is informed by my experience as a recording musician. Consequently, I not only *write* movies with this perspective, I *read* them with this perspective as well. As Selber has offered, my critical (reading) and rhetorical (writing) literacies have been enriched and informed by my functional literacy: my knowledge and experiences of musical composition and the techniques and technologies of sound recording. Furthermore, my experiences with moviemaking have informed what I value as data in the interview-based literacy research I do, which yields not only things people say—the kind of data that fits well in academic articles and books in the form of quoted statements—but also performances, contexts, and a variety of actions and interactions that further shape the things people say. Those forms of data do not remediate as cleanly to traditional forms of scholarship; however, they are the kinds of data that can really make or break a *scene* in a movie.

I am, as well, a writing teacher whose teaching has been informed by my experience collaborating with hundreds of student writers on thousands of pieces of student writing. I am informed by my experiences of being a student writer and of observing and training dozens of other writing teachers; I am informed by an extensive corpus of published and unpublished conversations about writing and the teaching of writing; and I have been at this long enough to recognize that my experiences with writing have produced a personal knowledge of writing that does not always appear to be *common* with the experiences or knowledge of my colleagues nor with those of many of my students. I realize with increasing regularity that while each of us is writing—and according to Andrea Lunsford's "Stanford Study of Writing" students today "are writing more than any previous generation, ever, in history"

(Haven)—the writing products we generate often look and sound *uncommon*. That said, our *common* knowledge base is more likely to be comprised of process experiences—as mine are through my experience of writing across many genres and media—than of product experiences. It has been attending to those *process* experiences that have helped me move my own teaching from being product-oriented to process-oriented.

That brings us to the heart of this discussion: exploring and establishing means for realizing *common* writing goals. This is a pedagogy for developing writers, not for perfecting forms of writing. It acknowledges openly that definitions for what writing *is* are in rapid flux. It also acknowledges that writing may be understood as the various actions and products of *writers*. By looking and listening to what writers *do*, we may be able to "hit upon" a definition of writing, eventually, that "so sums things up that all the properties attributed to the thing defined [*writing*] can be as though 'derived' from the definition" (Burke, *LSA* 3). This pedagogy for developing writers recognizes that a writer teaches writing—that *writers* both self-identify (I am a writer, I am writing) and argue for the commonality of their writing both in and with the texts they produce. Berlin writes, "in studying the way people communicate—rhetoric—we are studying the ways in which language is involved in shaping all the features of our experience. The study of rhetoric is necessary, then, in order that we may intentionally direct this process rather than be unconsciously controlled by it" (166).

In this text, I ask that we extend Berlin's use of the term *language* by way of Burke's discussion of *symbolic action*. Burke writes, "We view language as a kind of action, symbolic action. And for this terministic perspective we have proposed the trade name of 'Dramatism' precisely because we would feature the term 'act'" (*LSA* 366). Burke continues, "'Action' encompasses the realm of entities that respond to words as such (not just to the mere physical vibrations of the syllables, as with electrically discriminatory devices, which have taken a big step forward recently, in the direction of Cybernetics). And 'motion' encompasses the realm of entities that do not respond to words as such" (*LSA* 366). Like Berlin, Burke here limits his discussion of symbolic action to a discussion of language; however, Burke explains elsewhere the relationship between language and symbolic action:

> Action, as so defined, would involve modes of behavior made
> possible by the acquiring of a conventional, arbitrary symbol

system, a definition that would apply to modes of symbolicity as different as primitive speech, styles of music, painting, sculpture, dance, highly developed mathematical nomenclatures, traffic signals, road maps, or mere dreams (insofar as a dream is interpretable as "symbolic" of the dreamer's "psyche," or whatever such term a psychologist might prefer to work with). ("(Nonsymbolic) Motion" 809)

While Burke concentrates his attention on language, he clearly distinguishes that "language is an example of symbolic action in which we variously participate by means of a 'conventional, arbitrary symbol system'—this particular brand of English" ("(Nonsymbolic) Motion" 810). So, as our thinking about *writing* is being influenced by a variety of writers engaged in, apparently, unprecedented numbers of writing acts, I suggest that we embrace the larger territory of Burke's *symbolic action*: a territory that includes language as only one of the conventional, arbitrary symbol systems at a *writer's* disposal.

REMIXING LAWRENCE LESSIG'S *REMIX* OF WRITING

With the yoke of language, *per se*, lifted, *writing* may not only be and do new work, it may live and breathe in scenes of symbolic action that we may not have been recognizing as scenes of writing. In *Remix: Making Art and Commerce Thrive in the Hybrid Economy*, Lessig makes it his project to claim the audio-visual work of contemporary media remixers as *writing*. Lessig defines two major trends in American mediated culture, Read Only culture (RO) and Read/Write culture (RW), and argues that emerging digital technologies are enabling RW culture in ways that older analog technologies did not. Lessig states, "The 'natural' constraints of the analog world were abolished by the birth of digital technology. What before was both impossible and illegal is now just illegal" (38). It's predictable that Lessig, a Harvard law professor who specializes in intellectual property and copyright law, is concerned with the legality of contemporary RW culture. What may be less predictable is Lessig's claim that remix—"an essential act of RW creativity" (56)—is a form of writing:

> Writing, in the traditional sense of words placed on paper, is the ultimate form of democratic creativity, where, again, 'democratic' doesn't mean people vote, but instead means that

everyone within a society has access to the means to write. We
teach everyone to write—in theory, if not in practice. We understand quoting is an essential part of that writing. It would
be impossible to construct and support that practice if permission were required every time a quote was made. The freedom
to quote, and to build upon, the words of others is taken for
granted by everyone who writes. (52–53)

By claiming remixing as *writing*, Lessig asks us, his largely college-
educated audience, to consider the ethical infrastructure of our own
writing. Our stock in trade, especially in the academy, is built on the
ethos gained by way of reference to the larger academic conversation—
evident in my own references, thus far, to Burke, Murray, Condon,
Selber, and Lessig. As a law professor, Lessig knows this and, apparently, knows his audience because he summons an example that college
writing teachers can truly take to heart. In doing so, Lessig can ask us
to consider *his* laws—those of copyright—as *our* laws—the conventions defining plagiarism. We will discuss remix, intellectual property,
copyright, and Fair Use in Chapter Six; however, for now, I want to
concentrate on Lessig's direct appeals to our community of college
writing teachers. Following this logic, imagine if I had to contact not
only Professors Lessig, Condon, and Selber for permission to engage
their work as I am doing at present, but that I also had to track down
the heirs of Burke, Berlin, and Murray to obtain their permissions to
engage the intellectual property to which they hold copyrights. Lessig
asks us to consider, by extension, that failure to do so would constitute
a breach not only of ethics, but of law. Consequently, Lessig can forward the logical backbone of *Remix*: "Even the good become pirates in
a world where the rules seem absurd" (44).

Lessig's use of the term "democratic," published in the election year
at the end of George W. Bush's (Republican) presidency, packs both
political punch and ethical power for writing teachers like myself, who
are studied in the democratic pedagogies of Dewey and Freire. Lessig's
disclaimed statement, "We teach everyone to write—in theory, if not
in practice" (52) carries potential resonances both for fans of the "No
Child Left Behind" policies of the Bush era and for educators alike. ☺
Lessig seeks legal footing on some of the most common ground among
us: concern for our children and their education. As Lessig claims out-
right, "this is a matter of literacy" (114). In defining his argument as

one concerning RW culture, Lessig fixes his stance to two thirds of the three Rs of education. He reasons,

> While writing with text is the stuff that everyone is taught to do, filmmaking and record making were, for most of the twentieth century, the stuff that professionals did. [. . .] But what happens when writing with film (or music, or images, or every other form of "professional speech" from the twentieth century) becomes as democratic as writing with text? (54)

Lessig here claims real estate within the expanded territory of symbolic action that Burke surveyed but did not develop. In claiming these forms of symbolic action as *writing*, and not as "writing" (i.e., something other than writing as signified by scare quotes), Lessig may define his titular term, *remix*, not in terms of technologies and types of texts, but in terms of the rights of people: of *writers*. Lessig states, the "right to quote—or as I will call it, to remix—is a critical expression of creative freedom that in a broad range of contexts, no free society should restrict" (56).

It is here that Lessig makes the dangerous, paradoxical turn that I will ask us to make as well, namely, linking democratic education principles to an economy of costly technological products—ones that frankly replace themselves so quickly that discussion of them in a book such as this one would render the text out of date before it could ever go to print. Yet, our (American) system of higher education is systematically undemocratic. We impose admissions standards, charge tuitions, and give grades. We distinguish, sort, promote, and refuse. In short, we are a judgmental lot. And yet, we are—in theory, if not in practice—motivated by democratic principles that attempt to give all of our students (once they are admitted, of course) access to the means to write. In this way, we are relatively democratic. Lessig, in a turn of logic that only a lawyer should attempt at home, aligns the potentially least costly writing technology, the production of text—and by *text* Lessig clearly refers to words on pages—with the most elite, exclusive, and schooled social circles in the history of Western culture. Lessig outlines Latin as the language of elite European cultures in the Middle Ages and claims, "Text is today's Latin" (68). Lessig can then claim computer-based literacies such as "TV, film, music, and music video" as the "vernacular of today" (68). *Text* is elite, Apple's iLife is democratic. I know, I have trouble swallowing it as well.

However, it's all relative. In our various filtered communities of higher education, iLife can be a vehicle for democratic expression because the forms of writing it enables ("TV, film, music, and music video" [68]) are increasingly vernacular in that the texts they enable users to *write* are the texts most commonly *read* in American culture(s). Writing with these technologies, Lessig argues, has been exceedingly elite. Only professionals specializing in media creation could participate in making—*writing*—these media in years past, yielding a RO culture of consumption for the vast majority of members of the culture at large. The advent of relatively cheap and ubiquitous technologies (compare the capabilities of thousands of today's $1,500.00 MacBooks, equipped with standard software such as Garage Band and iMovie, to a million-dollar audio-video editing studio in the 1980s) have made RW culture relatively democratic for a relatively huge number of formerly RO consumers. In other words, the same people who can buy flat screen high-definition TVs, can now buy the technology to make and broadcast programming to be played on those TVs. Lessig claims, "Whether text or beyond text, remix is collage; it comes from combining elements of RO culture; it succeeds by leveraging the meaning created by the reference to build something new" (76). With remix, Lessig claims that students can write in forms of symbolic action most familiar to them, be they music, images, movies, text, or some combination of any or all of these forms of writing.

Lessig claims, "When kids get to do work they feel passionate about, kids (and, for that matter, adults) learn more and learn more effectively" (*Remix* 80). Here Lessig's form of relative democracy sounds most like Dewey's doctrine of interest as expressed in his *Interest and Effort in Education*: "Genuine interest is the accompaniment of the identification, through action, of the self with some object or idea, because of the necessity of that object or idea for the maintenance of a self-initiated activity" (14). Dewey adds, "Persons, children or adults, are interested in what they can do successfully, in what they approach with confidence and engage in with a sense of accomplishment. Such happiness or interest is not self-conscious or selfish; it is a sign of developing power and of absorption in what is being done" (35–36). Consequently, Dewey advises educators that "The doctrine of interest [. . .] is a warning to furnish conditions such that the natural impulses and acquired habits, as far as they are desirable, *shall obtain subject-matter and modes of skill* in order to develop to their natural ends of achievement and efficiency" (*Interest* 95). Lessig does not refer explicitly to Dewey in *Remix*; however, ninety-five years after *Interest and Effort in Education* was published, Lessig's recognition of democratized writing leverages the implicit reference to build something new. A writer teaches writing and continues to learn about writing in doing so.

REMIXING DEMOCRATIC WRITING AND LITERACY

> *How an individual mind processes ideas is difficult to say. But it is possible that the synthesis of thought necessary for writers to make meaning need not come exclusively from work with pen and paper.*
>
> —Patricia A. Dunn

Writing is not just a transaction between rhetors, auditors, texts, symbol systems, a shared world, and material reality; as Berlin contends, writing is a way of knowing. This epistemic view of writing must correspond to an epistemic pedagogy, expressed best, I think, by Freire:

> For me, teaching is a form or the act of knowing so that the student will not merely act as a learner. In other words, teaching is the form that the teacher or educator possesses to bear witness to the student on what knowing is, so that the student will also know instead of simply learn. (Torres 101–02)

Freire's liberatory pedagogy is an epistemic pedagogy, where the goal is not learning, but knowing. I stated earlier that mine is a pedagogy for developing writers, not for perfecting forms of writing. In this way I think it is most like Freire's pedagogy, which is designed to help people develop knowledge—to search for and find answers—not to help people acquire knowledge. How do our students come to *know*—how do they *write* knowledge? If, as Thomas Kent suggests, there is no generalizable process for writing, (*Post-Process*) then we should expect that there is no generalizable process of knowing, and consequently, no generalizable process for teaching or learning. However, that does not always appear to be the pervasive attitude toward writing theory and instruction.

Patricia A. Dunn writes, "It is assumed that all people have more or less the same ability to use language and that students will develop facility with academic discourses and conventions as they have opportunities to use them" (7). Since this assumption apparently applies to all "normal" people, Dunn asserts, "Trouble with written language becomes a 'disability' only in a society that values a certain kind of literacy. To insist that everyone think the same way is to truncate the thoughts of those who may be the most creative people" (42). Adopting this attitude toward literacy has profound impact upon writing pedagogy because it considers all communicators to be normal, just differently-abled. Furthermore, all of these normal communicators demonstrate a similarly broad and normal range of interest in the course-related activities they encounter. As Todd Taylor describes, we have a pedagogical obligation to develop instructional methods that counter student "narcolepsy" ("Design"), a concept that also owes much to Dewey's doctrine of interest. Disinterest in course-related activities must not be confused with "disability," even though ability and interest so often seem to go hand-in-hand. Thus, we should expect a variety of rhetorical abilities and interests from our students and be prepared to engage and develop those abilities and interests.

A liberatory/democratic pedagogy for writing must imagine and target a variety of forms for legitimate rhetorical action that correspond to the variety of rhetorical situations that our students will encounter. Freire states, "My great preoccupation is method as a means to knowledge. Still we must ask ourselves: to know *in favor of what* and, therefore, *against what* to know; *in whose favor* to know, and *against whom* to know. Those are the questions that we must ask ourselves as educators" (Torres 99). Insisting that there is a normal way of knowing through language favors those in the academy and our pious[1] means of expression. Text *is* today's Latin. Furthermore, this normative view disfavors the impious—the vernacular. Consequently, only those able to write by pious means will be able to argue among the pious for the realities they envision. Dunn's discussion of linguistic learning disabilities is indeed a discussion of literacy: "I mean by *learning disability* or *dyslexia* the inexplicable difficulties some people have in learning to read and write" (5). As J. Elspeth Stuckey maintains, "Literacy legitimizes itself. To be literate is to be legitimate" (18). A narrow definition of literacy violently silences the illegitimate. Dunn states,

> As instructors, we need to believe that people think in many ways. We need to break out of binary categories regarding right and wrong ways of learning, and to challenge ourselves and our students to change classroom culture from over-re-

liance on single-modality teaching. Questions about writing need to be recast, with ideas regarding what it means to compose solicited from people with a variety of learning styles. Composition specialists, who are for the most part people who like to write, may have a hard time tolerating or even imagining unconventional ways of writing, much as they might want to include and respond fairly to all students. Incorporating multisensory options into regular coursework and assessment will expand educational opportunities for everyone and reveal talents that many students, LD [Learning Disabled] or otherwise, may not have known they had. (201)

Dunn's terms *single-modality teaching* and *multisensory options* resonate with a pedagogy for writing with multiple and integrated media. Audio-visual writing gives teachers and students a variety of options for *multimodal* learning. Both rhetors and auditors may use a variety of senses and means of engaging the world to argue for the realities they compose. Furthermore, Dunn finds that writing instructors' strengths with traditional literacy perpetuate single-modality teaching. In teaching what they know, instructors reinforce that students may only know by way of what they are taught. This may coincide with some students' ways of knowing; however, it is nearly certain to exclude others—possibly many others. Dunn adds, "Reforming general education and broadening ways of learning will not only benefit all students. It will *re-able* those whose substantial talents have been underused for too long in a linguisto-centric educational system" (8). For Dunn, being *able* is essentially being recognized as someone who *knows*.

Kathleen E. Welch suggests that we amend our definitions of literacy by unifying literacy with orality. She states, "literacy has to do with consciousness: how we know what we know and a recognition of the historical, ideological, and technological forces that inevitably operate in all human beings" (67). She adds, "the false and ubiquitous separation of literate consciousness from oral consciousness leads to dangerously simplistic ideas of literacy, which has entered a new phase after one hundred years of electric communication" (104). Welch supports her claims by listening not to film or cinema, but to an even more academically impious medium: television. She writes,

It is no accident that the term 'sound bite,' a central metaphor of television culture, is aural and not visual. [. . .] Television is

more acoustic than visual, and so is attached strongly to oral-
ism/auralism. One can turn one's gaze away from the television, but one cannot turn one's ears from it without leaving
the area where the monitor leaks its aural signals into every
corner. (101–02)

Welch notices that television contributes substantially to the soundtrack
of American lives and households. She argues, "Our HUTs, households using television, need to be theorized from the point of view
of the humanities in general and of rhetoric and composition studies in particular" (131). This scene of rhetorical action, the American
household, has been impacted by the sounds of television. Making
and hearing meaning in this type of rhetorical situation, referred to as
electric rhetoric by Welch, thus constitutes a legitimate form of literacy.
She adds,

> The ubiquity of television machines accounts for part of the
> consciousness, or mentality, changes that characterize our
> end-of-the-millennium era of radical change and that recon-
> struct the nature of literacy into something that it has never
> been before.
>
> The hegemony of mechanical print now concludes after
> four centuries. Alphabetic literacy, however, remains en-
> trenched, crucial, and even more important than it used to
> be. However, print now co-exists with other communica-
> tion forms, all of which are rhetorically as well as electrically
> charged. (131)

Welch concludes, "electric rhetoric is not a destroyer of literacy, as it
is commonly thought. It is, instead, an extension of literacy, a thrill-
ing extension" (157). Welch's "electric rhetoric" extends *literacy* by way
of the expanded territory of Burke's *symbolic action*, and Welch's assertion that alphabetic literacy remains "entrenched" resonates with
Burke's discussions of piety and terministic screens. For Burke, terministic screens "filter" ideas by directing attention in discourse-specific
ways (*LSA* 45). Terministic screens shape world views; they determine
what is discussable and what is not. Burke compares them to colored
lenses on cameras that allow different views of the same object (45).
They make certain things observable and render others unobservable.
Welch argues that impious forms of communication and literacy are
presenting legitimate challenges to the pious paradigms of alphabetic

composition and the arguments that they have, until recently, effectively silenced by refusing to acknowledge them.

Welch's redefinition of literacy has been inspired, especially, by Walter J. Ong's description of "secondary orality"[2] in which she suggests "there is a new emphasis on the ear and a change in the emphasis on the eye" (58). Marvin Diogenes and Andrea Lunsford describe secondary orality as "a form of communication that appears to be oral but is actually 'planned and self conscious'[3] and deeply inflected by writing and print" (142). Diogenes and Lunsford also rely upon Ong to offer their "secondary literacy": "a form of communication that still looks a lot like traditional print literacy but that is deeply inflected by other media, including spoken words and sounds, video, and images of all kinds" (142). This secondary literacy leads them to offer a "tentative rewriting" of the definition of *writing*:

> A technology for creating conceptual frameworks and creating, sustaining, and performing lines of thought within those frameworks, drawing from and expanding on existing conventions and genres, utilizing signs and symbols and incorporating materials drawn from multiple sources, and taking advantage of the resources of a full range of media. (144)

This admittedly "clumsy" definition, they suggest, begins to capture the sense of writing "as epistemic, as performative, as multivocal, multimodal[4], and multimediated" (152). Diogenes and Lunsford understandably want to retain *writing* as a key term of composition. However, in doing so, their definition—one that I feel resonates with the definition of writing that Lessig offers and that I am pursuing— is screened by the preceding discussion of secondary literacy which "looks a lot like print literacy" and is deeply inflected by "images of all kinds." In other words, their use of secondary orality seems to be more visually directed than Welch's aurally attuned discussion.

However, the definition offered by Diogenese and Lunsford names the "nature" of writing as primarily technological: Writing is "a technology for . . ." I am pursuing writing as symbolic action. Burke writes, "To define language simply as a species of tool would be like defining metals merely as species of tools. [. . .] Language is a species of action, symbolic action—and its nature is such that it can be used as a tool" (*LSA* 15). I prefer to think of writing as fundamentally verby: as action (a verby noun made of the verb "to act"). Following Burke's lead, we can recognize that writing's nature is such that it can be used as a tool—as a technology—as an *object* of study—as a nouny thing. Also I think it's important to recognize that, as an act, it *selects* technologies appropriate to its purposes. Of course, acts don't select anything, actors do, but since all acts need actors—i.e., people—focusing on symbolic action necessarily focuses on the purposes and decisions of people[5]. By making this move, the technology doesn't run the show, the agents, the actors, the *writers* do. A writer *defines* writing.

Is This Writing, "Writing," or Composition?

Kathleen Blake Yancey states: "Composition is not writing anymore, it's composition" (Halbritter and Taylor). She continues, "I think composition is a more promising word because composition brings into play other kinds of issues, that I think are in play and will increasingly be in play, that writing, even used metaphorically, does not evoke." Yancey finds that *composition* is the more appropriate term for evoking "issues like design, issues like weaving together disparate elements, [and] issues like the connection to art." In fact, hybridity and the connection to visual arts (especially storyboarding) are among Mary E. Hocks's primary concerns in her "pedagogy of writing as design" (632). However, Yancey points out a critical connection to art that the term composition exposes: music—aural art. Yancey, after attending a discussion broadcast on National Public Radio of the process of composing employed by musical composers, determines that "so much of that is applicable to what we do in the writing classroom" (Halbritter and Taylor). Of course, this realization is not so shocking to those of us who are songwriters, for we have been merging text with music, the verbal with the non-verbal, and the visual with the aural, all along.

Hocks's metaphorical use of the term *writing* has facilitated her visual digital rhetoric. I am fortunate to know Professor Hocks—a magnificent singer and musician—and her subsequent work on sound. However, at least at the time of her writing of "Understanding Visual Rhetoric in Digital Writing Environments," Hocks's metaphoric use of *writing* had not yet expanded to include the aural elements glossed in her analysis of hybrid digital documents. Yancey argues that *composition* is a more appropriate term for multimedia/hypermediated/hybrid works because it does not privilege any of their rhetorical elements. The traditional mediations of writing have privileged the visual elements, especially the alphabetic (in texts written in Western languages), and our terminology for discussing *writing* in the abstract has done little to counter the visual hegemony of composition theory. Frankly, as Yancey claims, when we start to get too far away from alphabetic text (and it doesn't take too long to get too far away), it starts to *sound* a lot less like *writing* and a lot more like *composition*. Yet, call it what you want, apparently, Yancey *claims* that territory as "promising" since the *composing* acts found there are "in play and will increasingly be in play" in *writing* classrooms and pedagogy (Halbritter and Taylor).

When we move to Chapters Two and Three, the distinction between product/noun and action/verb will become more important. For now, let's recognize the impetus being generated to think of writing as more than exclusively linguistic—as drawing from the expanded resources of symbolic action. If we think more about what writers *do* and less about what writing *is*, the similarities between composing and writing are much easier to recognize. As Yancey says about the description of what a musical *composer* does: "so much of that is applicable to what we *do* in the writing classroom" (emphasis added). A writer teaches writing.

TRANSPOSING THE NEW KEY OF WRITING

Regardless of the subtle differences between Lessig, Berlin, Freire, Dunn, Welch, and Diogenes and Lunsford, it is important that we hear the pedagogical resonances in these discussions. All of these scholars seem to suggest that if our pedagogy concerns literacy, and ours most certainly does, we must adjust our teaching philosophies and practices to accommodate the multiple forms of legitimate literacy that our students encounter and practice—a statement that echoes, essentially, the thesis of Yancey's address to the 2004 Conference on College Composition and Communication—one remediated in her essay later published in *CCC*, "Made Not Only in Words: Composition in a New Key." Yancey asserts, "Literacy today is in the midst of a tectonic change. Even inside of school, never before have writing and composing generated such diversity in definition" (298). She asks,

> What do our references to writing mean? Do they mean print only? That's definitely what writing is if we look at national assessments, assuming that the assessment includes writing at all and is not strictly a test of grammar and usage. Accord-

ing to these assessments—an alphabet soup of assessments, the SAT, the NEAP, the ACT—writing IS "words on paper," composed on the page with a pen or pencil by students who write words on paper, yes—*but* who *also* compose words and images and create audio files on Web logs (blogs), in word processors, with video editors and Web editors and in e-mail and on presentation software and in instant messaging and on listservs and on bulletin boards—and no doubt in whatever genre will emerge in the next ten minutes. (298)

Yancey's emphasis here is on the uncommon perceptions of the nature of the products of writing. Her concerns and observations point to differences, not similarities. Differences that writing scholars and writers are beginning to see as surface details, not deep, structural details. As I stated earlier, it is in the verby nature of writing—the parts described as *process*, as *symbolic action*—where we can start to detect *common behaviors* of writing and of writers. Of course, the alphabet soup of standardized tests that Yancey indicates are not designed to test the results of a pedagogy of knowledge; they are designed to test the results of a pedagogy of learning. Until the fundamental missions of pedagogies of knowledge and assessments of learning are aligned, the perceptions that emerge from each will likely continue to be uncommon.

Composition scholar Erika Lindemann begins the preface of the fourth edition of *A Rhetoric for Writing Teachers* by claiming that "for all teachers, new technologies present both problems and possibilities that we could not even have imagined a generation ago" (xi). The rest of this book, *MCSA*, addresses these technological concerns by adopting a conception of writing and reading that also could not have been imagined by many writing teachers when Lindemann's text was first conceived. While the text looks forward to these emerging writing technologies, it finds its theoretical foundation by looking back to Burke's discussion of symbolic action, which both complements and casts a wider net than the attention to linguistics and cognitive science so important to composition pedagogy a generation ago. In late February 2009, NCTE Past President, Kathleen Blake Yancey, addressed the field's critical need for such a resource in "Writing in the 21ˢᵗ Century: A Report from the National Council of Teachers of English," published on behalf of the organization. Yancey both introduces and concludes her "call to action" with "three challenges that are also opportunities: developing new models of writing; designing a new curriculum supporting those models; and creating models for teaching that curriculum."

The rest of *MCSA* takes up these challenges in earnest, situating a pedagogy for writing and reading what I call the "multidimensional rhetoric" of twenty-first century writing, an approach I hope will help new and experienced writing teachers alike select, create, and engage productive models for designing and negotiating audio-visual writing assignments and curricula. In Chapter Two, we will glory in the present-progressive, unfinishedness of audio-visual writing and, in Chapter Three, we will read like writers and examine the layers of multidimensional rhetoric in works of audio-visual writing. In Chapters Four and Five, we will listen to and look at the world around us in order to hear and see possibilities for shaping how others hear and see it in our works of audio-visual writing. In Chapter Six, we will explore how the terministic catharsis of (audio-visual) *writing* may begin to be realized as pedagogical catharsis—a transformation that draws its power from its foundational metaphor: Work is play. As this first chapter has done, the rest of the book encourages writing teachers to carry forward what they have learned and what they know about teaching writing into a pedagogy for teaching the new work of writing in the twenty-first century.

Most of all, the chapters that follow build upon the model of Murray by listening to and looking at the ongoing project of *writing* and by anticipating that next semester, next year, and in the years thereafter we will come to understand writing anew—again and again, and that we will determine, again and again, that *writing is* what *writers do*. As Murray disclaimed his project as simply *a* way to teach writing, not *the* way to do so, *Mics, Cameras, Symbolic Action: Audio-Visual Rhetoric for Writing Teachers* presents *a* way to approach the teaching of twenty-first century writing. It acknowledges that all rhetoric—all writing and all teaching—is situated. Consequently the goals driving the lessons of this book will always look for direction to the learning goals for the courses that would employ them, not to the production of types of texts, *per se*. Some courses will, by design, be geared toward the perfection of types of writing: They will be courses in web design, or grant writing, or play writing, etc. Other courses will be geared toward the development of writers: courses that aim to help writers respond effectively to a wide variety of always changing writing situations. I would like to think that this book will make important contributions to courses at all points along the spectrum of possibility between these equally legitimate ends. However, at its heart, this book and its author are motivated more by the latter aim than the former. This is a people-first book that proposes a people-first pedagogy for twenty-first century writing instruction. A book that accepts as its foundational perspective that a writer *knows/teaches/learns* writing.

2 Learning Goals: The Unfinished Works of Twenty-First Century Writing

> *Most of us are trained as English teachers by studying a product: writing. Our critical skills are honed by examining literature, which is finished writing: language as it has been used by authors. And then, fully trained in the autopsy, we go out and are assigned to teach our students to write, to make language live.*
>
> —Donald Murray

REFLECTING ON RHETORICAL ACTION

As we established in Chapter One, Kenneth Burke proposes that we think of language use—speaking and/or writing—as symbolic action. In each case of language use, a person accesses artifacts or ideas by way of symbolic representations of those artifacts or ideas. In the case of language proper, the symbols are either the sounds of speech or the visual indicators of traditional literacy. A discussion of symbolic action seems to want to begin with symbols—as that's what comes first. In *symbolic action*, symbols are temporally, sequentially, prior to action. However, since *symbolic* is employed as a modifier, *action* is logically prior: Action is genus, symbolic is species.

OK. Action is logically prior to symbolic action. So what?

Well, in 1972, Donald Murray encouraged that we "Teach Writing as a Process Not Product." Murray reminded us that it is the verby nature of writing—a term that is realized as both a noun and a present-progressive verb—that is the more productive thing to teach. This

makes great sense if what we are teaching is students and not subjects, as verbs, especially action verbs, belong to people. Burke says
of actions, "Though the concept of sheer *motion* is non-ethical, *action* implies the ethical, the human personality" (*LSA* 11). And Burke
elaborates elsewhere,

> we do make a pragmatic distinction between the "actions" of
> "persons" and the sheer "motions" of "things." The slashing of
> the waves against the beach, or the endless cycle of births and
> deaths in biologic organisms would be examples of sheer mo-
> tion. Yet we, the typically symbol-using animal, cannot relate
> to one another sheerly as things in motion. Even the behavior-
> ist, who studies man in terms of his laboratory experiments,
> must treat his colleagues as *persons*, rather than purely and
> simply as automata responding to stimuli. (*LSA* 53)

Consequently, Burke maintains that "though there can be motion
without action [. . .], there can be no action without motion" (*LSA*
366). Action is to square as motion is to rectangle. The determining
characteristic that sets action apart from its motion kin is sentient and
socially-infused choice. As such, action is not entirely human. Nonhu-
man animals act as well. However, by tying action to the ethical, Burke
separates human action from animal instinct, for an ethic is often determined by how it counters rather than adheres to instinct. Whereas
an instinct may be an individual possession that may be shared with
others, an ethic is a set of rules that has been articulated with the
purpose of governing others. In other words, whereas an instinct may
be entirely encoded in the DNA (i.e., motion) an ethic is inherently
rhetorical (i.e., action). To *follow* an instinct may or may not be ethical. To *fight* an instinct—i.e., to make a behavioral *choice*—is ethical.
Murray writes:

> Instead of teaching finished writing, we should teach unfin-
> ished writing, and glory in its unfinishedness. We work with
> language in *action*. We share with our students the continual
> excitement of *choosing* one word instead of another, of search-
> ing for the one true word.
>
> This is not a question of correct or incorrect, of etiquette
> or custom. This is a matter of far higher importance. The
> writer, as he writes, is making *ethical* decisions. *He doesn't test
> his words by a rule book, but by life.* He uses language to reveal

the truth to himself *so that he can tell it to others*. It is an excit-
ing, eventful, evolving process. ("Teach" 4, emphasis added).

Murray's articulation shares much with Burke's. Murray's process-oriented approach is a pedagogy of socially-situated choice. It is driven by
the purpose of revealing personal truth and sharing it with others; the
articulation of that truth is motivated and crafted by a person who is
engaged in the dangerous business of having to live with those other
people and their reactions to her articulation of the truth. Meeting,
exceeding, challenging, or shattering their expectations may have consequences that far outstrip breaking a rule; it may break something far
more important: their trust—their support—their acceptance.

The term *process* represents a thing; it's a noun. However, it's a
noun whose very *being* depends upon some form of *doing*. A process
is a noun that describes either a course of motion (e.g., how a piece of
sand becomes a pearl) or a course of purposeful action (e.g., how pearls
are harvested and brought to market). An active process, the only kind
of process that will concern us, is employed with the intention of making something happen; it is goal directed. As such, a process needs a
few things in order to be a process: (1) it needs *an action* or a series of
discernable actions, (2) it needs *a person* who has designed/employed/
participated in these specific actions, (3) as a *means*, (4) and in a particular *context* or *scene* of action, (5) for accomplishing a particular
purpose. Burke's dramatistic pentad supplies a fit heuristic for revealing
the pragmatic value of *process*.

At the turn of the twentieth century, Charles S. Peirce articulated
the maxim of pragmatism: "Consider what effects, that might conceivably have practical bearings, we conceive the object of our conception to have. Then, our conception of these effects is the whole of our
conception of the object" (*Pragmatism* 231). Let's plug *writing* into
this maxim as the "object of our conception": "Consider what effects,
that might conceivably have practical bearings, we conceive [*writing*]
to have. Then, our conception of these effects is the whole of [*writing*]." Consequently, writing *is* not only what writing *does*, writing *is
everything that might conceivably have practical bearings* on what writing *does*. One glance back to Burke's pentad can help reveal categories
for a host of practical effects of writing.

Burke's *agency* (means) is an especially fertile category that can seem
to fuse with *scene* (context). Here, means are not only technologies of
production (e.g., alphabetic text, computers, static images, music, etc.)

but also the host of genres that shape that production, the ideas to which the writing responds, the artifacts and ideas that are remixed (quoted), and technologies that will carry the finished products of the writing, and potentially—at least for this writer—things like walks around the block and hours of listening to Jimi Hendrix's music. And more. In short, all of the means at a writer's disposal. So *writing*, according to the maxim of pragmatism, must be all of that. And more. All of that is generated from a very quick look at simply one of the categories of the pentad. Adopting this *attitude* (the first player off the bench on Burke's dramatistic basketball team) toward the process of harnessing the pragmatic power of writing is far more complex than autopsying the artistic effectiveness of portions of the text alone—which remains one of the means at a writer's disposal.

In Chapter One, we learned how Lessig has leveraged the pragmatic maxim to define writing and remix anew by looking to the effects that he has conceived writing to have. Burke claims, "Every perspective requires a metaphor, implicit or explicit, for its organizational base" (*Philosophy* 152). Lessig's perspective on twenty-first century writing grows from the following metaphor: Remixing is quoting. Lessig defends his perspective by knowing the process of remixing—both the functional knowledge of the technical processes by which remixed products are made and the functional knowledge of the social/ethical processes that have governed the uses of these and similar products. Lessig has asked that we reconsider the effects of writing in the twenty-first century, and when we do, then writing will be the whole of those effects. Lessig's approach for understanding those effects is a process approach. Lessig must defend a perspective that moviemaking is writing, not by comparing the products of films and alphabetic texts—things qualitatively and *symbolically* distinct—but by comparing the effects of those products and their production: distinct things with many shared *symbolic* actions. In short, Lessig asks us to understand symbolic action by first attending to the action—what people are purposefully doing—and then to look to the symbols through which they accomplish their work.

In asking us to teach writing as a process not product, Murray, widely associated with expressivist writing—and expressly so by Berlin—offered an approach to writing instruction that was *pragmatic*, according to the maxim articulated by Peirce, the founder of pragmatism. Regardless, expressivist or pragmatist, it seems far less productive to claim what Murray *was* than to interpret what his writing *does*. What it does is remind us to be mindful of the whole of the effects that we conceive to have practical bearing upon the object of our conception: teaching the present-progressive process of writing.

Processes are inherently pragmatic; they are defined by the very things they are designed to accomplish, whatever they may be. Murray claimed to offer a process for teaching writing; however, it could be argued that his process was better suited to teaching writ*ers* than to teaching writ*ing*. Yet something about that doesn't seem right to me. As a moniker, *writer* seems to me to have a weighty past. It is a title that one earns through completed action, much as people earn the titles doctor, singer, mother, or Olympian. It represents past action, accomplishment, and identity. Certainly, this is how Murray means for us to interpret the subject of his mantra, "A Writer Teaches Writing." It is the pool of amassed knowledge that emerges from autopsying the process, not the product of writing, that is to be taught to students of writing—writing, the noun born of the always present-progressive action verb; writing, the unfinished process of getting it right; writing, the living, organic action verb engaged by writers, not the finished, past-tense material noun that is autopsied by literary critics. Murray's "writing" is to be apprehended in its act of becoming, not in its state of being, and so he asks us to "glory in its unfinishedness" ("Teach" 4).

In Chapter Three, we will explore the particulars of what I call *multidimensional rhetoric*: rhetoric that integrates a variety of modes, media, and genres—sound, images, language, music, etc. My use of the term was inspired by years and years of experience as a recording musician, and so, in this chapter, we will follow a similar path. When recording music, there are two distinct products that are made. The first is usually a multitrack recording—layers and layers of independent tracks of musical recordings. These tracks may have been recorded simultaneously, or possibly at different times completely. For example, and for simplicity's sake, let's imagine a four-track recording of a rock song (I say simplicity because it is not uncommon for musical recordings to employ upward of fifty tracks—really): on Track One, we may have the rhythm section (the drums and the bass); on Track Two, we have the rhythm guitar; on Track Three, the lead vocal; and on Track Four, harmony vocals and the guitar solo. Each of these tracks, once recorded, may be played in isolation or blended in any combination. As such this multitrack product represents unfinished writing, as it demands many choices to be made in terms of the arrangement and performance of its content. Much of that work is inventive as well, as the mixing of the work, even in the simple four-track example we are considering, can change the character of the final product dramatically. That final mix is the thing with which we all are most familiar. The final mix is the two-track stereo (left and right) version of the song that appears on our CDs and iPods. The final mix is finished writing—the mix that was *due*. The final mix is identical for every listener. That is, the mix itself does not change from CD to CD. That's not to say that every listener hears the same thing, however. We'll talk more about audible differences in playback in Chapter Four.

First, let's take a little music break. Go get your copy of "Little Wing" by Jimi Hendrix—the original studio version from 1967. You know you have a copy of this song. And if you don't, yet, you'll thank me momentarily. Once you've located a copy (in your music library or online), let me know.

Everyone ready? Good. OK, here we go. Let's talk again in about thirty-five seconds. And, play. Ahhhhhh . . .

. . . Thirty-three, thirty-four, thirty-five, and press pause. Sorry to interrupt, but in this second, we just heard something that may or may not have thrown up a listening flag for you. At this second, The Jimi Hendrix Experience, a three-piece, power-trio rock group (Jimi on guitar and lead vocals, Noel Redding on bass, and Mitch Mitchell on drums) has just gone four-piece with the addition of the bass and drums to the guitar and bells we have been listening to. Hmmm . . . OK, so someone else is playing bells (widely reported on blogs across the Internet to be not bells, but a glockenspiel). I'm not sure who is playing those bells, but I can live with that—for now, at least. Let's go back to listening for another minute or so. Sing it, Jimi.

. . . Ninety-eight, ninety-nine, one hundred, and press pause, again. OK, so who is playing lead guitar now? Dude, that's Jimi Hendrix, of course! Who else could it be? Alright, then who has been playing the rhythm guitar throughout the song? Dude, that's Jimi Hendrix, of course! Who else could it be? How can this one-of-a-kind guitarist be in two places at once? That's accomplished with the "magic" of that four-track recorder we discussed above. With a little bit of the functional literacy that Selber has talked about, my critical literacy can now hear the same person in two places at once. What, without this functional literacy, is simply impossible, is now not only possible, it's downright simple to explain by way of our newly-expanded functional literacy. Furthermore, I can now start to listen more carefully to determine how six pieces of musical information (drums, bells, bass guitar, rhythm guitar, lead guitar, lead vocal) were recorded on what was likely (in England in 1967) only four tracks.

Now, let me say this: I don't *know* how they did this any more than I know who played the glockenspiel—if that's what it was; I only *know* that the instrument I hear sounds like bells. However, with my functional literacy of four-track recording, I know that bass and drums were likely to be mixed together to one track by way of a process called *bouncing*, where several independent tracks are *bounced* to a single track. Recording engineers, especially when working with relatively few tracks (for example, four) bounce tracks so that additional music may be recorded over the tracks that are now freed up. One of the prices to pay for the benefit of bouncing is that once tracks are combined, you are stuck with the mix on that track. Actually, it's my critical literacy telling me that the bass is way too quiet throughout. That critical response triggers my functional guess that early in the recording process the bass was combined with the drums on a single track, preventing the bass from being turned up in the final mix without turning up the drums as well. Fig. 2.1 and Fig. 2.2 show what a bounce such as the one I am describing may look like.

Track One		Drums
Track Two	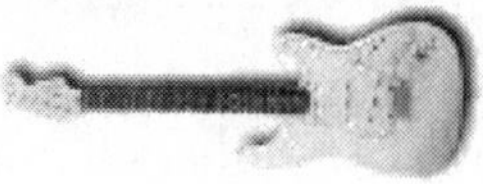	Rhythm Guitar
Track Three		Bass Guitar
Track Four		

Fig. 2.1: Three basic tracks.

Track One		
Track Two		Rhythm Guitar
Track Three		
Track Four	  +	Bass Guitar + Drums

Fig. 2.2: First "bounce" combining Tracks One and Three onto Track Four and clearing Tracks One and Three.

The prominence of the rhythm guitar throughout makes me believe that it started out on its own track; however, I'm guessing that it was eventually combined on a track with the bells. Fig. 2.3 and Fig. 2.4 show this second set of moves.

Track One		
Track Two	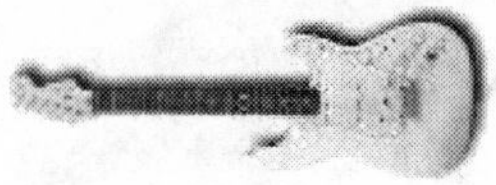	Rhythm Guitar
Track Three	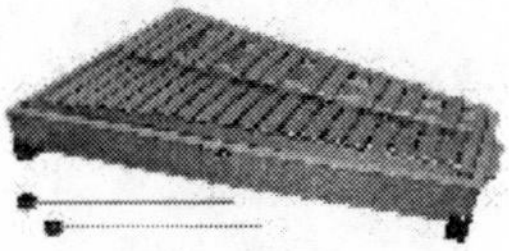	Glockenspiel
Track Four	  +	Bass Guitar + Drums

Fig. 2.3: Glockenspiel added to Track Three.

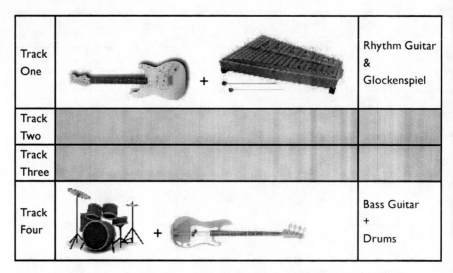

Track One	<image: electric guitar + glockenspiel>	Rhythm Guitar & Glockenspiel
Track Two		
Track Three		
Track Four	<image: drums + bass guitar>	Bass Guitar + Drums

Fig. 2.4: Second "bounce" combining Tracks Two and Three onto Track One and clearing Tracks Two and Three.

That leaves us with two tracks left—one each for the two most prominent pieces of musical information on this recording: the lead vocal and the lead guitar. Four tracks, six instruments—and probably three musicians. See Fig. 2.5.

Track One	<image: electric guitar + glockenspiel>	Rhythm Guitar & Glockenspiel
Track Two	<image: microphone>	Lead Vocal
Track Three	<image: guitar>	Lead Guitar
Track Four	<image: drums + bass guitar>	Bass Guitar + Drums

Fig. 2.5: Tracks Two and Three refilled with lead vocal and lead guitar—six instruments on four tracks.

Again, I don't *know* any of this, but knowing the facts is not ultimately important here. This is not an exercise in establishing historical record. This is an exercise in writerly listening—in listening for traces of unfinished writing in finished writing. What is important here is that my functional literacy allows me to make informed guesses about *the process* of how this was done. My functional literacy fuels my critical literacy to allow me to make a hypothetical roadmap for how this multitracked musical work may have been composed—not merely as a musical composition, but as an aural composition. This informs my rhetorical literacy—one that I can now use to make my own recordings; one, in fact, that I *have* used to make my own recordings; one that was developed by way of learning to listen in a writerly way. A recording musician teaches music recording.

But enough of my yackin'. Let's listen to the final forty-six seconds of "Little Wing." Play it, Jimi!

See, you're thanking me now, aren't you? Jimi Hendrix will do that for you.

You're welcome.

Why are we talking about multitrack music recording here? Because the unfinished writing of music recording may give us an important filter for (re)viewing the form of unfinished writing that Murray discusses. In many ways, Murray's form of unfinished writing—traditional text—is in the same form as its finished partner. It begins as a linear sequence of text on a page and it ends as another version of the same. However, music recording is qualitatively different in that it often integrates many layers of temporally linear sequential and synchronic information into just two layers. In fact, those two stereophonic layers are often reduced further into one monaural layer, as was the original mix of The Beatles's *Sgt. Pepper's Lonely Hearts Club Band*—another work *written* on a four-track recorder in 1967. The final mix is music that is all there at once. As such, it represents what the writer/recorder *did*. However, unless we understand the process by which the music was recorded, we may not have a window to the writer's writerly choices—the things the present-progressive writer/recorder *is doing* and the nature of the things with which the writer works. To view those choices, we need a familiarity with the process of recording—a functional literacy—so that we can begin to hear the layers of the music separately. Once we can do that, we can begin to hear—to read—as a writer/producer and not solely as a reader/consumer. We can begin to hear in layers, not just to hear music that is all there at once. In Chapter Three, we will explore this multidimensional functional literacy in more depth. For now, we need to keep in mind only that the nature of the multiple tracks of music recording are more like the individual ingredients in a cake than they are like the individual paragraphs in an essay. They mix/combine/integrate to make something else. Only when you know something about baking will you likely identify the presence of baking powder in the taste of the red velvet cake, otherwise, it will likely be hard to get much past the chocolate, flour, sugar, and butter. A baker teaches baking.

The autopsy of literary criticism—critical literacy—is most often a practice of reading like a consumer—albeit a connoisseur consumer. A literary critic reads as a jazz aficionado listens, noticing nuances of content that flavor the interpretation of the text as it appears—all there at once. This is an effort to complicate or enrich the all-there-at-onceness of the texts themselves. To use Murray's autopsy metaphor, they complicate the singular thing by either carving up the body of the text to identify its internal components, or by uniting the singular body with others. I'll call these moves the claiming of multiple readerly tracks—historical background, biographical information, genre analysis—that serve to give a window on how we are to interpret the final mix—the finished work under consideration. They are interpretive filters that help distinguish the readers of texts more than they help to distinguish the writers of texts.

Please, let me be perfectly clear here: This is a tremendously valuable critical skill to develop. I do not mean to set out an intellectual hierarchy for valuing readerly and writerly autopsy. My appeal throughout this text is not either/or, but both/and: that the functional, technical skills required to create new media inform critical engagement with new media and vice versa. However, as we begin to recognize social values for rhetorical action that engages emerging technologies, we may need to shift the lion's share of our attention to the functional concerns of using these media, at least initially, in order to engage that emergent rhetorical action most robustly as both readers and writers. As Selber states, "I do not necessarily place a higher value on it [rhetorical literacy]: There will be times when an attention to functional or critical concerns should be paramount" (*Multiliteracies* 25). That said, even though we shift our attention to the functional, it is equally paramount to remember *our* ultimate goal in this scene of rhetorical action: delivering twenty-first century writing instruction.

In attending to functional concerns, we must remember that we are not training students to become audio-video engineers (unless, of course, we are). Rather, we looking and listening for the kinds of functional lessons that resonate most with our goals as writing teachers. While some of those lessons will be portable among most of us, many of them will be specific to just a few of us as our pedagogies and the learning goals with which they are partnered are always rhetorically situated—they are contextually and *scenically* unique. Let's recall from Chapter One that Burke writes, "Identification is compensatory to division. If [individuals] were not apart from one another, there would be no need for the rhetorician to proclaim their unity" (*Rhetoric* 22). Not only are individuals divided but identified groups of individuals are apart from one another as well; and while this book attempts to compensate for *our* division—*our* apartness—it does so by recognizing openly that our pedagogies must diverge as much as they merge. This book asks that we identify with a theoretical foundation that is concrete enough to support the weight of our unified body and flexible enough to accommodate the demands of our independent actions. This book, as well as its author, assumes we are unified by our goal— delivering twenty-first century writing instruction—even as we are divided by precisely what that goal means to each of us and to each of the learning communities we serve. Our teaching and our students' learning happens by way of symbolic action that is fitted to the pedagogical scenes that contain those actions. Or not.

Selber claims, "While I have no doubt that many teachers take a rhetorical approach, there is still much to be done to conceptualize the praxis required to help students become reflective producers of technology" (*Multiliteracies* 27). It is *the process of reflection* that is really at the heart of this pedagogy's portability. The process of reflection profits from dramatistic inventory: How effectively did/does an *agent* employ symbolic *action*(s) and *agency* (means) within a particular *scene* in order to fulfill her rhetorical *purpose*? In other words, how well did/does the writer's efforts fulfill her desires? Those desires *may* be to produce a finished work that looks and sounds like that of Zana Briski and Ross Kauffman (directors of *Born Into Brothels*). However, those desires may materialize, instead, as unfinished work— as a knowledge-building activity rather than a symbol—a product—of acumen. Dewey claims, "To reflect is to look back over what has been done so as to extract the net meanings which are the capital stock for intelligent dealing with further experiences" (*Experience* 87). The rhetorical act of reflection is pragmatic in that it is pedagogical. If we are to accept Murray's premise that a writer teaches writing, then it is the practical wisdom—*phronesis*—that comes of making writerly moves and writerly decisions that is to be the vehicle of this teaching, not merely an appreciation for moves made well (or poorly) by others. The former deals in the performance of pragmatic effort, the latter in the performance of schooled awe. Or, we could say that the former studies how to perform magic, and the latter studies how magic is performed—even as we just studied above, via functional literacy, the four-track recording magic that—POOF!—cloned Jimi Hendrix. A magician teaches magic.

A Magician Teaches Magic

I remember going to see Disney's *Fantasia* when I was a boy. Mom took me to the Blair Cinema in Hollidaysburg, Pennsylvania for a Saturday matinee during the film's rerelease run in 1969. As I reflect on that experience now, I realize that the highlight of that film to my five year-old self—and of Disney in general , I suppose—was in the display of magic. The part of *Fantasia* I remember most is "The Sorcerer's Apprentice." As the sorcerer's apprentice, Mickey Mouse knows what magic does; however, he doesn't really know how to do the magic. He knows the tricks, just not the process of how to perform or control them. The success he has is from performing the bits of magic that he's seen the sorcerer do. The trouble is magicians do a lot of things specifically to make those watching think that the observable actions are somehow responsible for the observable outcomes—and the trick lies in the fact that they are not. The real process of magic goes unobserved, right under the noses of those observing. I remember, clearly, Mickey in the swirling vortex of water brought about by his misappropriation of magic, desperately riding the book of magical incantations to his doom—the book that contained page after page of formulas for the magic that he could not do. The hatless sorcerer comes to Mickey's rescue in the nick of time, parting and dissipating the magical seas with the wave of his hands. A contrite Mickey surrenders the hat—the symbol of the sorcerer's power, if not the true source of his power.

This film, released originally in 1940, worked its magic by making mushrooms and pink elephants dance, an ostrich perform ballet, and brooms fetch pails of water. More importantly, though, Disney reinforced the most important lesson of magic: A magician performs magic. Not you, kid. You can watch the magic, but you can't make it happen. Leave the magic making to the professionals.

Of course, Walt Disney wasn't teaching magic; he was selling it. Consequently, Disney sold finished magic: magical product, animated magic that only animators could render in their imaginations as unfinished animation. In 1940, there were precious few who could see the wizard behind the curtain making that magic happen. By 1969, little had changed in that regard. The making of media was not for the common laborers, the Mickey Mouses (Mickey Mice?) of the world. The making of media was for media wizards, and the unfinished work of media making was as invisible to the naked eye as the rabbit prior to emerging from the hat in the grasp of the magician's hand. Magic.

I've seen that look on my writing students' faces too: the schooled awe of writing done well that appears only in the grasp of full-blown sorcerers—not in the grasp of apprentices. They are certain to flood the studio with their efforts; they will need to be rescued by the hand of the sorcerer who runs this class—the magician who may not even return for his hat. Why bother? The magic's not in the hat.

It takes time, sometimes, to convince my students that *this* sorcerer isn't interested in selling magic; he's interested in teaching it. Not because he wants to run a wizard mill—each semester turning out dozens and dozens of sorcerers each equipped with a handful of foolproof tricks for pulling finished essays and websites and documentaries out of their course-issued hats, but because he wants to watch unfinished magic happen. He wants to help students find their ways to forming the habits of magicians, not to schlep about with buckets of water but to see the moves that actually make the magic happen—even if the magic itself doesn't happen, . . . this time, to see the rabbit all along, not only in the instant that it emerges from the hat in the grasp of the magician, to glory in the unfinishedness of their nascent, evolving, present-progressive acts of magic.

Glorying in the finished magical act may require little more than perception and a leap of faith: a belief that what seemed to be is what indeed was. Glorying in the unfinished act of magic, however, is an exercise in intelligence. "Intelligence," claims pedagogue and pragmatist, John Dewey, "is associated with *judgment*; that is, with selection and arrangement of means to effect consequences and with choice of what we take as our ends. A man [*sic*] is intelligent [. . .] in virtue of his capacity to estimate the possibilities of a situation and to act in accordance with his estimate" (*Quest* 213). "Intelligent activity," Dewey says, "is distinguished from aimless activity by the fact that it involves selection of means—analysis—out of the variety of conditions that are present, and their arrangement—synthesis—to reach an intended aim or purpose" (*Experience* 84). Dewey's aimless/intelligent distinction shares much with Burke's motion/action dyad. Both intelligence and action are imbued with means that an agent has selected for purposes.

However, Dewey awards the title *intelligent* not to those who espouse truth, but to those who exercise "judgment," who make choices, who act on informed *guesses*—"estimates." For Dewey, the measure of intelligence is not in what is known, it is in what follows from an agent's best guesses. Intelligence is associated with the ability to form and test hypotheses, and hypotheses, for Dewey and his mentor Peirce, are the purposeful, goal-directed, problem-solving seeds of all knowledge. Intelligence or intelligent action is directed by purpose. Dewey writes, "A genuine purpose always starts with an impulse. [. . .] A purpose is an end-view. [. . .] Foresight of consequences involves the operation of intelligence" (*Experience* 67–68). What does Dewey claim to be the impulse of a genuine purpose? Well, that's a problem. Literally. According to Dewey, "problems are the stimulus to thinking. That the conditions found in present experience should be used as sources of problems is a characteristic which differentiates education based upon experience from traditional education" (*Experience* 79). Dewey asks us to look to the unfinished business of our students' present-progressive lives as a source of purpose for intelligent action—to unsolved problems that demand the unfinished work of hypotheses and purposeful courses of action that follow from those hypotheses. Dewey's pedagogical answer is the student's questions—each student's questions.

THE INTELLIGENCE OF GUESSING

Ability to frame hypotheses is the means by which man is liberated from submergence in the existences that surround him and that play upon him physically and sensibly.

—John Dewey

Let's take a moment to glory in the unfinishedness of hypotheses. Dewey distinguishes hypotheses from "final truths" by virtue of their meaning-making capacity. "Fixed truths," says Dewey, "must be accepted and that is the end of the matter" (*Experience* 86). However, "ideas or hypotheses are tested by the consequences which they produce when they are acted upon" (87). Accordingly, truth (once established), like magic, becomes a matter of faith.

- Question: How does Santa Claus enter houses?
- Answer: By way of the chimney.
- Result: True.

Hypotheses, however, are process building, for hypotheses ask to be tested—to generate knowledge by way of experience and empirical evidence. Hypotheses are pragmatically designed to respond to a perceived problem. They are composed. They are epistemic. They are unfinished magic, because even as final drafts, their work remains unfinished. They are calls awaiting response. They are opening acts.

- Problem: But our house has no chimney!
- Hypothesis: Maybe Santa has a master key.
- Course of action: Watch the front door.

Hypotheses, since they are composed in response to perceived problems, are themselves the products of a goal-directed, logical process, one that Peirce has named *abduction*. Peirce explains, "Abduction is the process of forming an explanatory hypothesis. It is the only logical operation which introduces any new idea; for induction does nothing but determine a value and deduction merely evolves the necessary consequences of a pure hypothesis" (*Pragmatism* 230). Consequently, Peirce claims, "every single item of scientific theory which stands established today has been due to Abduction" (*Pragmatism* 230). Abduction is a process of symbolic action—the manipulation of ideas—that leads to practical courses of action: symbolic or otherwise. As Dewey said above, intelligence is demonstrated by an *agent*'s selection (*act*) of present (*scene*) means (*agency*) and the *purpose*ful arrangement of those means. Hypotheses—also called "ideas" by Dewey above—are the things that drive intelligent action.

Burke eventually expanded his dramatistic pentad to a hexad with the addition of the motivator for his *A Grammar of Motives*: *attitude*, which he defined as "an incipient act" or the "substitute for an act" (476). Attitudes, essentially, are hypotheses about scenes; they guide how an agent *reads* the situation at hand. Attitudes are problem finders—or problem overlookers. For example, a student may approach a particular class meeting with an attentive attitude, with an eager, interactive attitude, with a resistant attitude, or with a narcoleptic attitude. Depending on her attitude, she will read the scene—and, consequently, the acts, purposes, and selection of means it suggests—in potentially very different ways. Furthermore, depending on her attitude, she will be any one of a great variety of agents: a listener, a speaker, a leader, a follower, a rebel, a hibernator. Burke says, "an attitude is a state of emotion, or a moment of stasis, in which an act is arrested, summed up, made permanent and total" (476). An attitude is a movie poster: a still frame that, in an instant, freezes and encapsulates the entire action. Burke would later name such an attitude-directed *summing up* an act of *entitlement*. In Chapter Three we will see how attitude may be expressed through the symbolic act of *entitlement*. For now, it is important that we realize that these emotional snapshots of attitude can entitle either courses of action or states of being, that is, a sympathetic attitude may be "incipient" for consequent acts of sympathy (sending flowers, embracing, sharing emotion) or by way of a "substitute for an act" of sympathy realized as a state of being or feeling: I am sympathetic; I have sympathy. We can sum up, with our present attitude, Burke's *A Grammar of Motives* as a grammar of problem-solving intelligent action—a grammar of hypothesis making and responding—a grammar of abduction.

OK, let's all take a deep breath.

How did we just go from Jimi Hendrix to Mickey Mouse to Santa Claus to Peirce, Dewey, and Burke by way of Murray? Better yet, why?

Because our ultimate aim here is pedagogical. Our purpose is to establish reasonable courses of action for writing instruction. Pedagogies, to be pedagogies, must bring together two things: (1) a foundational theory about teaching and learning in general, and (2) implications for local implementation of teaching and learning (praxis). Pedagogies—while clearly *not* hypothetical themselves—are global hypotheses about local hypotheses, and vice versa. Why hypotheses? Well, this book discusses motivations for all of our courses. It attempts to address *any* writing course. As such, it addresses *no* specific writing course. It is motivated by a problem that its author sees as common: What on earth should writing instructors do with audio-visual information? In other words, I have made a best guess about at least one of our shared interests and concerns. The product of my symbolic action, this book, is meant to speak to many of you (I hope). However, it is now in the hands of just one of you—i.e., *you*. Should *you* actually come to be sympathetic with my attitudes about audio-visual writing, you may be moved to incorporate audio-visual text production into your syllabus(es). Each syllabus represents a localized hypothesis that (with hope) follows from the general pedagogical hypothesis: It says, essentially, *what follows is the instructor's best guess about exactly what it will take to teach (each and every one of) the enrolled students the promised content of this course.* Next (or sometimes mid-) semester, we will each likely revise our hypotheses—goaded by a sense of perfection, motivated to solve problems that we realized while testing our hypotheses.

Teachers, we are in the business of hypothesis making and testing.

Burke's Grammar—act, scene, agent, agency, purpose, and attitude—is consequently a fitting grammar for pedagogical reflection. It can help us reflect upon and revise our hypotheses about both our global and our local concerns, about both our shared and our individual situations, and about our motives and our students' motives. Pedagogies are unfinished magic because even as final drafts, such as the one you are reading, their work remains unfinished. They are calls awaiting response. They are perpetual opening acts. They are composed in response to perceived problems, and are, themselves, the products of a goal-directed logical process. They are directed by universal aims but look ultimately to local applications. They are operations designed to generate processes. Dewey distinguishes global *operations* from local *processes*: "Processes are local and temporal, particular. But the relation of means and consequence which defines an operation remains one and the same in spite of these variations. It is a universal" (*Quest* 162). "An operation," Dewey claims, "determines any number of processes and products all differing from one another; but *being* a telephone or a cutting tool is a self-identical universal, irrespective of the multiplicity of special objects which manifest the function" (163). This book takes as a foundational premise that *writing*, too, is a self-identical universal, irrespective of the multiplicity of special objects that manifest the function. A pedagogy—of writing—calls for both operations and processes.

When Murray tells us to "Teach Writing as a Process Not Product," he speaks specifically to each of us. He asks us to act locally. However, to do so, he (and we) must think globally. As such, the seeds for Kent's Post-Process theory were sown in Process theory itself. Writing students take writing classes that are situated in programs of study within departments and colleges and universities that operate within peer groups that embrace or refute certain types of pedagogical missions. Teachers within this system, such as yourself, both respond to operational needs by teaching courses and shape operational direction by designing courses and sharing scholarship. For teachers of writing, teaching and scholarship are two sides of the same coin. When informed by a shared pedagogy, teaching processes exemplify teaching operations. Dewey writes, "an operation[,] as a relation which is grasped in thought[,] is independent of the instances in which it is overtly exemplified, although its meaning is found only in the *possibility* of these actualizations" (*Quest* 163).

Now let's take a moment to glory in the unfinishedness of Dewey's last statement because the operation is not defined by the actual instances that comprise it but by the *possibility* of instances that may comprise it. Operations are unfinished. Operations are open to improvement. Expanding our definitions of writing does not bust the system, it helps it realize its potential as long as the act of expanding participates in the overall attitude that describes the operation. Dewey writes, "The more adequately the functional relation can be apprehended *in the abstract*, the better can the engineer detect defects in an existent machine and project improvements in it. Thus *the thought of it* operates as a model" (*Quest* 163, emphasis added).

The *thought* of it.

As we saw in Chapter One, Lessig and Yancey, among others, are expanding *the thought of* writing, i.e., writing in the abstract. The mission of our current project is, accordingly, to detect defects (a.k.a. identify problems) in and suggest improvements to the functions of writing instruction by establishing a more adequate theoretical (i.e., abstract) understanding of our attitudes about writing, teaching, and learning. Improving writing instruction begins with better apprehending the ideas of both writing and instruction. With our foundational expansion well underway, we will now return to one of our field's foundational texts to see how the thought of twenty-first century writing may help us both detect defects in an existent, pedagogical machine and suggest improvements to it.

Co-Operating Donald Murray's Unfinished Pedagogical Machine in the Twenty-First Century

[A] Composition stripped of its methodological pluralism, and with its back turned more firmly than ever on the potential of practice as knowledge-making, promises to be a feeble Composition indeed.

—Stephen M. North

Donald Murray offers ten implications of glorying in unfinished student writing—that is, of teaching writing as a process not product ("Teach" 5–6). Murray's four-page essay from 1972 makes no overt reference to educational or philosophical scholarship. Of course, we would not expect it to, following from his earlier, 1968, thesis that *A Writer Teaches Writing*. Murray's *ethos* is composed of *phronesis*: practical, acquired, situated wisdom—knowledge acquired by way of experience gained by engaging the pragmatic, intelligent, situated symbolic action we have encountered in the philosophies of Peirce, Dewey, and Burke above. While Murray does not discuss Peirce, Dewey, or Burke, he clearly speaks with and from them. Murray's process approach enacts their scholarship. I am reminded of two musical metaphors when I think of Murray's essay. The first is from the mock/rockumentary, *This is Spinal Tap*. Lead guitarist Nigel Tufnel (Christopher Guest) is showing filmmaker Mary DiBergi (Rob Reiner) his wireless guitar transmitter, which allows him to "play without all the mucky muck" of obvious, tangible, hardwired connecting cables. Murray plays without all the theoretical mucky muck. Of course, as anyone who has ever used a wireless device (especially from the 1980s) knows, it takes a lot of wires to run a wireless system. In other words, wireless technologies obey a theory of greater and lesser entropy—disorder or mucky muck—where instances of less mucky muck exist at the expense of instances of greater mucky muck in a universe of general mucky muck.

All mucky muck aside, Murray's essay reads more like an editorial column than a piece of scholarship—which probably accounts for its popularity. It *sounds* like a piece of pop music. Which brings me to my second musical metaphor—technically, a simile: Claiming that Murray's essay is theoretically thin (as I've heard it described) is akin to claiming that the Beatles's music is theoretically thin. The fact that neither "artist" makes overt references to the theoretical underpinnings in their works makes those works no less theoretically inspired or complex. Unlike NASCAR drivers, they do not wear their sponsors on their sleeves. They are not theorists. They are practitioners.

Murray, a practitioner, writes to practitioners—us. Stephen M. North says that "Notions like Macrorie's learning-to-lie developmental sketch or Elbow's cooking and growing metaphor for writing work for Practitioners because they are grounded in a common experience and framed in a language of *doing*" (52). In fact, it has been reported widely that Paul McCartney, one of the most successful song*writers* in the history of popular music, cannot read or write down music. Now, if that alone doesn't call for a reexamination of "the thought of" writing, I don't know what does. McCartney and Murray are writers, writers who know writing by way of the present-progressive experience of doing it. While writers may *sell* writing as a product not process, writers *teach* writing as a process not product.

Why, then, do we need Murray if we already have Peirce, Dewey, and Burke? Because Murray does something that his scholarly predecessors do not: He speaks directly to our discipline. Let's look again at the opening paragraph of "Teach Writing as a Process Not Product." I say again because this is the epigraph I've chosen to begin this chapter:

> Most of us are trained as English teachers by studying a product: writing. Our critical skills are honed by examining literature, which is finished writing: language as it has been used by authors. And then, fully trained in the autopsy, we go out and are assigned to teach our students to write, to make language live. (Murray, "Teach" 3)

Us, our, we: Murray addresses an audience of English teachers, abducing, in 1972, that since the people he knew who were teachers of writing had degrees in English, and since he was addressing teachers of writing (whom he did not know), that those people—we—were most likely to be the products of traditional English literature programs. A strong hypothesis—in 1972. The reasonable course of action that followed from such a hypothesis was for Murray to teach us— folks not trained in composition or rhetorical theory, but in literary criticism—what to do as quickly as possible. As a good teacher and Pulitzer award-winning editorial journalist, he chose to teach us by talking *with* us. Four decades or so later, Murray's hypothetical audience is a bit more academically heterogeneous. However, even though we, as a field, have been trained in an increasingly diverse variety of programs—many of which do not feature the term *English*—Murray's words resonate with a homogeneity akin to that from 1972: Most of us were not trained to teach audio-visual writing. It is with this critical attitude, informed by my functional and rhetorical knowledge of being both an audio-visual writer and a teacher of audio-visual writing, that we return to 1972, unified and estranged anew, a retrofitted audience of writing teachers who need to learn about the process of audio-visual writing so that we may teach it.

First, a critique. Murray identifies three distinct phases of the writing process ("Teach" 4):

- *Prewriting:* everything that takes place before the first draft— choosing and focusing on a subject, spotting an audience, choosing a form.
- *Writing:* the act of producing a first draft.
- *Rewriting:* reconsideration of subject, form, and audience. It is researching, rethinking, redesigning, rewriting—and finally, line-by-line editing, the demanding, satisfying process of making each word right.

Murray goes so far as to tell us how much of the process may be slotted to each of these three steps of the writing process: 85%, 1%, and 14% respectively. These figures seem contradictory and counterproductive to the claim that the process changes to fit the needs of individual writers and situations and that "there are no rules, no absolutes, just alternatives" (6). Murray's entitlements introduce a temporal linearity to the process that defines distinct phases—phases that *this* author has noticed do not align so neatly with *his own* process(es). Of course, I am hardly the first to recognize or address this inconsistency. The Post-Process movement that grew from the works of scholars such as Thomas Kent, Gary A. Olson, Sidney I. Dobrin, and Nancy DeJoy, among others, specifically rejected the notion of a generalizable Process (with a capital "P"). I agree; however, as we will see, Murray's ten Implications reveal that he, too, doubted the utility of proclaiming a

Process, for there is a sense in which Process—the thing we are *all* to teach—becomes an operation: a type of machine, "a self-identical universal, irrespective of the multiplicity of special objects which manifest the function" (Dewey, *Quest* 163). That is, Process (with a capital "P") is a shared concern or attitude that transcends local, applied action, even as process (with a small "p") becomes a *special object*—an individualized, localized, *special action*. Consequently, I have entitled three pedagogical themes, rather than phases, that identify types of special actions in Murray's ten Implications for the operation of teaching writing as a process:

- Cooperative Learning: Student Choice and Ownership
- Variation of Processes and Products
- Course Content Management and Assessment

Ultimately, I offer these entitlements to defeat a translation of Murray's phases that would devalue pre-writing as mere planning and rewriting as mere fixing. In my experience with audio-visual authoring, invention and revision are often part of the same act of writing, and they rarely coincide with distinct areas along the production timeline of any piece of writing. We will review Murray's Implications, according to my revised themes, listening closely to hear where Murray's instrument continues to resonate and to determine where it may need to be retuned. I use the metaphor of retuning to follow a musical metaphor of instrumentation. I remember first hearing guitarist Michael Hedges and wondering how on earth he was able to make a guitar sound the way he did. It was clearly a guitar—it sounded like a guitar—but then again, it didn't. Hedges was able to facilitate his virtuosic instrumental catharsis of guitar playing, in part, by retuning the standard instrument. He was able to communicate the music in his head by retuning his instrument. Thus, in memory of the great Michael Hedges, we will retune Murray's instrument to realize the new music of audio-visual writing. However, we will revisit Murray's instrument, first, with an ear for resonance, as we may not have to retune every string. One string that will be retuned throughout is that I will retune Murray's generic singular masculine pronouns to resonate with gender-neutral sensibilities.

THEME I. COOPERATIVE LEARNING:
STUDENT CHOICE AND OWNERSHIP

Murray's first three Implications mark the operation of writing instruction as a decidedly *cooperative* machine:

> *Implication No. 1.* The text of the writing course is the students' own writing [. . .] they study writing while it is still a matter of choice, [. . .].

> *Implication No. 2.* Students find their own subject.

> *Implication No. 3.* Students use their own language.

Resonance: Murray's words continue to resonate within a field that has authored and touted position statements and resolutions such as NCTE's "Teaching Composition: A Position Statement" (1985), NCTE's "Resolution on Students' Right of Expression" (2004), "NCTE Beliefs about the Teaching of Writing" (2004), and Conference on College Composition and Communication's "Students' Rights to Their Own Language" (1974 and 2003). These documents have made disciplinary policy of Murray's points above about process-oriented student-centered learning, concepts about education, in general, forwarded in the early twentieth century by Dewey. Dewey writes, "there is no defect in traditional education greater than its failure to secure the active co-operation of the pupil in construction of the purposes involved in his studying" (*Experience* 67). The spirit of Murray's first three Implications is clearly cooperative with Dewey's warning. In fact, the first three Implications seem to emerge directly from Dewey's "doctrine of interest." As we considered in Chapter One, Dewey states,

> The doctrine of interest [. . .] is a warning to furnish conditions such that the natural impulses and acquired habits, as far as they are desirable, *shall obtain subject-matter and modes of skill* in order to develop to their natural ends of achievement and efficiency. Interest, the identification of mind with the material and methods of a developing activity, is the inevitable result of the presence of such situations. (*Interest* 95)

Murray's second Implication speaks explicitly about subject matter to Dewey's doctrine of interest; however, it speaks implicitly about something only hinted at by Dewey: Burkean scene. Burke states that "scene is a fit 'container' for the act, expressing in fixed properties the same quality that the action expresses in terms of development" (*Grammar* 3). If our classrooms, institutions, and pedagogies do not "furnish conditions"—that is, not only the *methods*, but also the *materials* of a developing activity—for students to *act* upon their "natural impulses and acquired habits" for engaging audio-visual writing, then it will matter little what our assignments invite them to do. Their acts will develop from scene-appropriate interests. In other words, if there is no operational retuning that makes the bold statement, *take a look around you—this IS what we do here*, then we should not expect to see retunings at the level of individual processes. So, by recognizing a process-level resonance for cooperative learning, we recognize an invitation for the operational retuning of the scene of cooperative learning.

Retuning #1: Scene must be a fit 'container' for symbolic action. Dewey states, "The problem of educators, teachers, parents, the state, is to provide *the environment* that induces educative or developing activities, and where these are found the one thing needful in education is secured" (*Interest* 96, emphasis added). It is one thing to say that we—individual writing teachers—value audio-visual writing, it is another thing to demonstrate that we—programs of study within institutions—do as well. This retuning may be the most important and difficult of the retunings we will encounter as this one gets to the heart of the argument at hand. Values duct taped to our syllabuses are easy for our students to spot as there is likely little to no infrastructural or procedural support for those values.

Here's a scenario: Lee, a student, in section 12 of Writing 101, reports to her roommate, Alex, in section 43 of Writing 101, that moviemaking is encouraged in section 12. Alex reviews her syllabus and finds no mention of moviemaking. They decide to ask around on their dorm floor and soon determine that of the dozen or so sections they have reviewed, only Lee's section encourages moviemaking. What are these college students to make of this evidence? Furthermore, if the computer labs have no video editing software, or worse yet, if they have video editing software and no ports for connecting video cameras, or not enough memory to manage video files—what are these bright college students to determine? Answer: Video is NOT what we do here. Section 12 is not following policy; it is obviously breaking policy.

Dewey adds, "If we can discover a child's urgent needs and powers, and if we can supply an environment of materials, appliances, and resources—physical, social, and intellectual—to direct their adequate operation, we shall not have to think about interest. It will take care of itself. For mind will have met with what it needs in order to *be* mind" (*Interest* 95–96). If we, teachers, are to retune our approach to student-centered writing pedagogy, we must listen for consonance and dissonance beyond the walls of our classrooms and beyond the pages of our syllabuses. Our assignments must be situated not only within the scaffolding of our course goals but also within the institutional scenes of symbolic action, for those scenes shape how our students (and our colleagues) fit their interests and attitudes to our assignments.

Retuning #2: Language is a feature of only some forms of symbolic action. Murray's third Implication, "Students use their own language," is also in direct need of retuning, as it hinges on the word "language." Let's substitute the phrase *forms of symbolic action* for Murray's term *language* and substitute the term *writing* for the term *English* and review the retuned entry for *Implication No. 3*:

> Students use their own *forms of symbolic action*. Too often, [. . .], we teach *writing* to our students as if it were a foreign *form of symbolic action*. Actually, most of our students have learned a great deal of *forms of symbolic action* before they come to us, and they are quite willing to exploit those *forms of symbolic action* if they are allowed to embark on a serious search for their own truth. (5)

For Murray, choice in writing was largely about language. In fact, Murray mentions *language* or *word by word* in each of his first three Implications. Oddly, these terms are absent from the remaining seven Implications—apparently implicit in Murray's use of the term *writing* and *papers*. With our retuning, we open a world of possibilities for both student choice and for how teachers may help students capitalize on their choices—and indeed for how teachers will need to be prepared to respond to a bevy of potential student choices—not only in terms of setting the *scene* appropriately but also in terms of being prepared to react (i.e., re *act*) appropriately. If we are to be writers who teach the process of writing, we are opening ourselves to potentially limitless processes with which to be familiar.

Yet, it is here where we can encounter the greatest opportunity for cooperative learning: not cooperative in the sense that students co-operate by carrying out their assigned tasks; cooperative, rather, in that students reveal writing strengths and goals by being invited to use their own *forms of symbolic action* to embark on a serious search for their own truth. In doing so, they will teach us what they know and what they need to know. Following Murray's lead, Lindemann writes, "Teachers who assume they are teaching 'beginning writers' are mistaken. Most of our students have been writing for many years; [. . .]. To teach them well we must know as much about them as we have time to learn and patience to discover. Otherwise, we can't determine whether our teaching enhances or interferes with their ability to write effectively" (4th ed.11–12).

One way to approach getting to know our students as writers is to lead them to the problems that writers address and look and listen to how they respond. The lesson of such an assignment is not product but process—and not just the process of making a text but the process(es) of solving a writer's problem(s). Assigning a type of text production—for example, a research-based essay (paper)—will likely let you know what your students know about writing research-based essays; however, it may not let you know about the type of writing your students know—the types of writing they have been doing. To learn that, you may assign a problem—one that will demand some form of written response. For example: What are the top five social concerns of students on your dorm floor? To respond to such a problem, students will need to devise a system of inquiry and choose a form of expression that suits them and their subject most comfortably. It removes the exclusive rule of traditional literacy and language expertise and opens all students—native speakers of English and non-native speakers alike—to the opportunity to devise and conduct inquiry in response to a common problem: soliciting, collecting, and reporting on the opinions of their peers. Some or all may write essays. Others may combine articles with photos. Others may create interview-based audio essays or audio-visual documentaries. Others still, may compose blogs, text-messages, or surveys. Some will generate most of the language of the final product. Others will generate very little of the raw linguistic data. Regardless, their choices, made evident in their responses, can help you know them as writers and as intelligent individuals who use writing to solve problems.

Best of all, such an assignment, one that has little to do with crafting or perfecting a particular type of written artifact, will participate in a lesson of collaborative learning, one in which everyone learns, especially you. The students learn about the opinions of their dorm floor peers, about their own methods of inquiry and composition, and about the methods of inquiry and composition of their classmates; you learn all of these things as well, and from this information, you may abduce how to instruct them. You will learn not only what they need to improve but, potentially, what they do well already—or what they default to doing. You will learn about the technologies your students use and the rhetorical possibilities they see in those technologies. From there, you may begin to set learning goals both across the class and for individual students. This kind of an assignment may remain unfinished because its lesson is abductive in nature. Its purpose is not only to teach writers but to learn from them. Its primary goal is to lead to a best guess about what subsequent teaching acts will enhance and not interfere with the development of this particular group of student writers. Burke defines rhetoric as "a symbolic means of *inducing cooperation* in beings that by nature respond to symbols" (*Rhetoric* 43). As such, the work of this lesson is rhetorical in nature; consequently, it may remain unresolved—unfinished. The end of the assignment does not ask you and your students to move on but to take the next step.

Speaking of next steps, let's move on to Murray's second Theme.

THEME II. VARIATION OF PROCESSES AND PRODUCTS

The Implications of Theme II move from *Process* to *process*. Implications 4, 5, and 9 involve the multiplicity of special objects—individual writing processes and written products—that manifest the operation of writing instruction:

> *Implication No. 4.* Students should have the opportunity to write all the drafts necessary for them to discover what they have to say on this particular subject.

> *Implication No. 5.* Students are encouraged to attempt any form of writing which may help them discover and communicate what they have to say.

> *Implication No. 9.* The students are individuals who must explore the writing process in their own way.

Implication No. 5 reads a lot like our retuned version of *Implication No. 3*. However, the focus of *Implication No. 5* is to look toward the writing that students may do in the future, not the writing they've done in the past. As such, *Implication No. 5* remains all about knowing our students and guiding them toward individual development. Here's the full entry from Murray's essay:

> *Implication No. 5.* Students are encouraged to attempt *any form of writing* which may help them *discover and communicate what they have to say.* The process which produces "creative" and "functional" writing is the same. You are not teaching products such as business letters and poetry, narrative and exposition. *You are teaching a process your students can use—now and in the future—to produce whatever product their subjects and their audiences demand.* (6, emphasis added)

Resonance. Implication No. 5 asks us to contextualize each student's writing within a projected, hypothetical writing life. Who better to project that writing life than the student herself? If there is anything my extensive involvement in the LiteracyCorps Michigan project has taught me, it is that we teachers do not know our students very well, nor can we know them very well without dramatic and sustained investigation. However, we can guide our students to reveal likely writing lives by asking them to invest heavily in the first three Implications— self-directed topics and symbolic acts—and applying that investment to forms of writing that are interesting and useful to help students realize both their writing goals and our learning goals. I like to suggest to my first-year students that they imagine my inquiry-based projects as an invitation to take the class they most wanted to take that semester but were not allowed to take yet because they hadn't taken the necessary prerequisite classes. I say, "Grab a subject you are dying to study and start asking questions." This assignment asks students, specifically, to project future selves—not selves in some fantastic future—

though it may indeed be quite fantastic—but rather in a future that is immanently foreseeable: a planned future. Especially in a first-year course, this may give you opportunities to find out what really attracts a student to a specific subject, to find out not only what kinds of *things* they like but what they want to learn and what they want to do. For example, an interest in taking organic chemistry may have more to do with an interest in playing golf than an interest in organic chemistry.

Just saying.

The point is, as Murray suggests, the process (though here I would substitute *Process*) that produces creative and functional writing is the same. While some of your students may be envisioning highly academic futures, the graduation statistics of your institution may suggest otherwise. Following from what we know about the intrinsic relation between intelligent activity, purposeful symbolic action, and abductive logic, asking students to pay attention to their writing processes that are directed at solving virtually any problems of interest is a valuable pedagogical exercise.

That was a difficult thing to do in 1972; however, Murray suggests the process that produces creative and functional writing is the same—especially when all of that writing selects similar means of mediation: linear alphabetic text. However, when we begin to imagine processes for creating a variety of forms of creative and functional writing—e.g., websites, lab reports, audio essays, photo essays, blogs that both publish and solicit opinions, documentary movies, scripted and story-boarded movies—we can see that Murray's assumptions about the writing process may require substantial retuning. This retuning will have a significant effect on how we interpret Murray's Implications about number of drafts (*No. 4*) and time of development (*No. 9*). What seemed a simple conflation in 1972 may now seem simply impossible.

It is not. The value of proclaiming the unity of all of these types of writing as Writing, as Lessig has done, is to be found in the rhetorical power of metaphor. For metaphors to be effective, they need to equate two *obviously different* items. Metaphors do not simply declare things to be the same, they invite an inquiry of *sameness*. They represent a problem to be solved. In short, metaphors do not simply do what they say they do. Movies are essays. Documentaries are poetry. The process of making a movie is the process of writing a recipe for brownies. They are not the same—exactly—yet there seem to be some ways in which they are. The power of metaphor is a rhetorical power, a power of probability, not a power of fact. The power of metaphor is abductive: It leads to the formation of a hypothesis that subsequently leads to the soliciting of evidence to support that hypothesis. Movie are essays. This metaphor is productive if we can first say, "they are not the *same*," and then form a hypothesis that names their *sameness*: They each have introductions and conclusions, they each tell stories, they each are purposeful, they each forward an opinion, they each rely on and respond to genres, they each have audiences, they each use evidence, etc. If we find evidence to support these claims, in spite of the glaring differences, we are likely to accept the metaphor as productive—and by *productive* I mean *instructive*, for metaphors are pedagogical. Metaphors teach, and they teach by asking that we learn by doing the work of testing them ourselves—not by believing in their finishedness but by engaging the process of their unfinishedness. They build knowledge intelligently. Metaphors deal in the cooperative rhetorical act of identification, Burke's master goal of rhetoric. "Identification is compensatory to division" (*Rhetoric* 22), and identification is the act of making things that are substantially different—A and B—*consubstantial* (21). Metaphor makes A consubstantial with B by proclaiming that A is B. Burke says, "A doctrine of *consubstantiality*, either explicit or implicit may be necessary to any way of life" (21).

The better you and your students can *know* the differences that individuate forms of writing, the more intelligently you will be able to proclaim their unity: to identify them as consubstantial. The reason we need to do that is to help students see that the writing they do in our classes is consubstantial with the writing they will do in their future lives, not because you are teaching your first-year students to write research papers that many of them will never again write for several years—if ever, not because you are teaching your students to attend to the conventions of citation and attribution for academic disciplines they will not join, not because you are teaching your first-year students to make electronic media that will be out of date before they graduate from college but because *you are teaching a process your students can use—now and in the future—to produce whatever products their subjects and their audiences demand.* You are teaching them to identify and respond to problems by way of acts of writing.

Retuning #3: Forms of writing are consubstantial. If the first retuning (scene must be a fit 'container' for symbolic action) is the most practically important, this third retuning may be the most conceptually important. *Retuning #3* states flatly that *writing has no immutable, static nature.* Writing is what writers do. Burke writes, "If men [individuals, humans, agents, *writers*] were not apart from one another, there would be no need for the rhetorician to proclaim their unity" (*Rhetoric* 22). Writers are made consubstantial by way of rhetoric. In other words, the only thing that makes Sir Paul McCartney and Professor Donald Murray consubstantially *writers* is an act of identification—that is, the symbolic act of someone saying so. The product of that act of saying will either help us do things (to some extent) or it will stand in our way (to some extent). Peirce writes, "The elements of every concept enter into logical thought at the gate of perception and make their exit at the gate of purposive action; and whatever cannot show its passports at both those two gates is to be arrested as unauthorized by reason" (*Pragmatism* 256). If McCartney and Murray can exit the gates of purposive action together—if they can jam—then we have *reason* to put the band together. If not, then we'll just have to buy their solo records.

I think the metaphor may have just exhausted its use.

Peirce has called abduction a "bolder and more perilous act" than induction precisely because it makes inferences from—i.e., it makes consubstantial—things that are different in kind ("Deduction" 192). Each form of writing is different in kind from all of the other forms of writing. Murray's *Implication No. 5* distinguishes and identifies a simple binary: creative and functional. However, each category of Murray's binary represents a host of forms of writing: plays, shopping lists, novels, book reports, research-based essays, short stories, you name it—and that is before we retune Murray's writing according to Lessig's instrument. Now, we add documentaries, fiction films, remixes of all sorts, music, websites, blogs, PowerPoints and Prezis, you name it. Essentially, whatever you name, provided it can check its passport at the gates of perception and purposeful action, will be deemed a reasonable form of writing.

The important thing about this retuning is to remember that it is in the interplay between stark difference and sameness where the writing lessons come to life. The differences breathe new meaning into the lessons for writers. Learning what our students know—learning how they write already—however it is they write—in whatever form, can open opportunities to lead our students to make the metaphoric as-sociations between what they know and the forms of writing that we are attempting to help them learn. However, this is likely to happen only after they've been convinced that what they know already is of value—that what they know will help them continue to learn. Only then can the lessons of process be portable; only then can their past, present, and future writing be made consubstantial.

Teaching with multiple forms of writing requires two important moves, the first being a commitment to engaging new forms of writing as both a writer and as a student—because a writer teaches writing and because writing is epistemic. Knowing multiple forms of writing helps teachers of writing discover more, and more productive, means of identification between forms. Why is this so important? For example, one of my first-year honor students was head and shoulders beyond her peers in crafting musical soundtracks for the documentary projects she did in our class. However, when it came to her traditional essays, her prose lacked both craft and prosody—it didn't keep a beat. Her talent with audio-visual writing demonstrated an amazing attention to de-tail. She was making fine-grained functional moves that I knew, as an audio-visual writer, took long hours, repeated listening, and multiple drafts. Furthermore, the energy—something I call the pulse—of the music helped move the filmic portions of her work in ways that her classmates and I thought were both impressive and effective. These process moves became the focus of the writing lessons we used to make her traditional writing consubstantial with her audio-visual writing. We listened to her writing as we performed it aloud, hearing where we could increase or decrease the metaphorical volume, where we could establish a consistent or alternate pulse, and where we would need to slow down and listen repeatedly to make sure the overall blend of rhe-torical elements sounded right. Her linear, alphabetic text—through careful attention to listening and by way of consubstantiation with her process for writing multitracked audio-visual texts—consequently became a multilayered text for us to examine and redesign—as a lin-ear, alphabetic text. The form of writing didn't change; however, her process for engaging it did.

This brings us to our second important move for writing teachers, which also happens to be our fourth retuning, a direct quote from Bill Condon:

Retuning #4: No piece of writing is ever finished, it's just due. This retuning remixes Condon's proclamation from *Take 20* (Taylor) and speaks specifically to *Implication No. 9*. I believe this maxim of writing bears repeating because, following from the retuning above, each form of writing will place additional demands on what it means to be "finished" and, consequently, will provide unique opportunities for us to glory in its unfinishedness. Let's review the full entry for Murray's *Implication No. 9*:

> *Implication No. 9.* The students are individuals who must *explore* the writing process in their own way, *some fast, some slow, whatever it takes* for them, within the limits of the *course deadlines*, to find their own way to their own truth. (6, emphasis added)

According to Murray, our students' quest is one of exploration. Now, I believe this is at least partially true for each writing class—regardless of its unique purpose. However, *not all writing classes are designed to yield the same learning outcomes.* Consequently, I can imagine writing classes that are geared toward pushing students toward a mastery of a specific genre or form, for example, an advanced poetry seminar, a professional writing course on web development, or an upper-level writing-for-publication course. Here, exploration may play less of a holistic goal, and genre- or form-specific craft may direct the purpose of the course. These courses may be aimed at finished precision—at honing the fine skills of masters of the form. That said, even for masters, such as Condon, no piece of writing is ever done, it's just due. Writing, at all levels of mastery, is always unfinished.

That said, developing writers who are exploring or being led to explore *a variety of forms of writing,* may need to become less "tidy," to use Bartholomae's term (604), or to become more "messy," to use Lindemann's term (4th ed. 23), in order to develop. Getting messy is different from simply learning the ropes. If by *learning the ropes,* we mean acquiring basic skills or functional literacy, *getting messy* means taking functional literacy and using it to inform critical and rhetorical literacy, and vice versa. Getting messy means taking *a* process and making it *your* process. Getting messy happens most importantly in the middle of development—not in the beginning. Getting messy does not only happen as one learns the rules. Getting messy also follows from saying *you need to know the rules before you can break them.*

How is it that one learns when the rules count and when the rules don't? By testing those boundaries, by experiencing when rules help and when they hinder, by meeting with success and with disappointment, by encountering problems, and by allowing those problems to lead to getting messy.

However, a pedagogy of messiness—of unfinishedness—must still operate in an institution governed by finishedness, that is, by fixed deadlines. Semesters have exact start and end dates. Final grades are due by ___. These are unyielding infrastructural protocols that shape how we must manage our courses and the way we teach the content of those courses. Our third Theme will address content management and assessment directly; however, here I want to conclude our Theme about variation of process and product by asking that we remember to glory in the unfinishedness of student writing *through* the end of the semester, not *until* the end of the semester. That is, if we are truly *teaching a process our students can use—now and in the future—to produce whatever products their subjects and their audiences demand*, one of the most important things our students can take with them as they leave our classes is an unfinished *project*. It is our responsibility, as writers who teach writing, to help prepare that parting gift. Murray's *Implications No. 1* through *No. 5* ask us to lead students to take on writing tasks that ask a lot of them and that mean a lot to them. How can we steal that learning back from our students at semester's end simply because the semester is over—simply because the writing is due? Course deadlines are real barriers that we all need to manage; however, they do not mandate that a piece of writing be finished. What they demand is that learning goals for the semester have been achieved. In other words, what is due, throughout the semester and at semester's end, is a demonstration of progress toward achieving learning goals, not necessarily a finished piece of writing. This requires an approach to course design that resembles setting up an obstacle course more than it resembles setting up a gymnastics meet. The goal is leading students through some well-chosen, learning-goal-directed problems, not judging their mastery of prescribed exercises. If messiness is a goal, obstacle courses help us conceptualize this goal better than gymnastics meets. Gymnastics meets are governed by tidiness—by precision from start to finish. We scrutinize the finished moves of gymnasts in high-definition slow-motion, not to imagine how the gymnast came to create the exercise but to marvel in the precision of its *execution*—a term as apt as *deadline* for declaring the end of a living process. We subject those moves to the scrutiny of *the autopsy*. Obstacle courses, on the other hand, are characterized by participants who are most tidy as they enter the course and who emerge most messy at the course's end. They literally take that messiness away with them—along with the knowledge they have gained by encountering and surpassing (not mastering, necessarily) a series of problems designed to both test and train their developing strengths and endurance.

Now don't get me wrong, there is nothing at all inherently wrong with gymnastics meets—with marveling in finishedness, with exercising the faculties of schooled awe. In fact, there is much right about gymnastics meets; they can be dramatically inspiring. The masterful performances at gymnastics meets inspire millions of people to say, *I want to learn how to do that!* However, most people, especially those with a sense of mortality, do not attempt to learn to *do* gymnastics by simply watching gymnastics meets. Inspiration is a gateway to instruction, and if the point of instruction—of engaging developmental exercise—is to help gymnastics students better understand the process of negotiating problems, then gymnastics meets themselves serve as poor models for the process of teaching and learning gymnastics. Very few gymnastics students go on to become competitive gymnasts. For most students, the goal of instruction is to learn gymnastics—not to master, but to improve. Those students leave one class splattered with messy, caked-on, difficult maneuvers that they are still in the process of learning, and they transport those unfinished products—those ongoing projects—to the next level of development. Along, of course, with the moves that got them that far, the ones they have learned to control and have adopted as fundamental for their continued growth.

The goal that emerges from this fourth retuning is enabling students to finish our courses as purposefully messy, unfinished writers—writers who are in possession of ongoing *projects*. That is not to say that they will not complete texts or tasks: They will. That is not to say that some, possibly many, of those texts or tasks will not be inspiring and bear the scrutiny of schooled awe: They will. It is simply to say that those completed tasks and texts do not need to be pieces of finished writing. This potentially massive shift in the way we perceive the practical outcome(s) of our courses leads us directly to our third Theme.

Theme III. Course Content
Management and Assessment

Murray's remaining four implications deal with the rules of the game—
course content management and assessment in writing instruction:

> *Implication No. 6.* Mechanics come last.

> *Implication No. 7.* There must be time for the writing process
> to take place and time for it to end.

> *Implication No. 8.* Papers are examined to see what other
> choices the writer might make.

> *Implication No. 10.* There are no rules, no absolutes, just al-
> ternatives. What works one time may not another. All writing
> is experimental.

Resonance: Bartholomae defines a *commonplace* as "a culturally or insti-
tutionally authorized concept or statement that carries with it its own
elaboration" (592). Take a look at the mission statements for writing
programs across the country. Pick any five at random and I will bet
you a tall, cool ice water that each will feature a statement in the spirit
of the following: We value content over mechanics. If I'm wrong, the
ice water's on me at the next Cs—well not *on* me, please. We, as a
discipline, have taken Murray's *Implication No. 6* to heart: "Mechanics
come last" has become a *commonplace* of writing instruction, to use
the term championed by Bartholomae—and Aristotle (*topoi*). Of these
final four implications, it may seem as though *No. 6* is the least in need
of retuning. However, the commonplace of *No. 6* hides an elephant
in the classroom: Conventional wisdom serves as "the mist" in Rick
Riordan's *Percy Jackson and the Olympians* series that makes monsters
and magical things have the appearance of common things.

As teachers of writing, you know that mechanics are among the
easiest things for students to identify in each other's papers: sentence-
level grammatical errors, spelling, formatting, etc. In fact, teachers
need to tell students who are about to engage a first-draft workshop,
explicitly, *I do not want you to make comments about mechanics on this
draft.* And still, they will. They can't help themselves. Mechanical errors are low-hanging fruit, and nothing, I'm betting, could be more

common among us. Mechanical errors will be the basis for our fifth retuning.

Implication No. 7 and *No. 8* work together to articulate a commonplace for process-based writing pedagogy. The first part calls attention to drafting, the second part assigns formative, not summative, comments to be made in response to students' drafts, comments that move the work forward by recognizing possibility, comments that keep a piece of writing alive. Yet, as we will see in *Retuning #6*, Murray's controlling metaphor for the completion and submission of student work—publishing—may be a paradigm also in need of shifting:

Retuning #5: A mechanic knows mechanics. Name five common grammatical errors that your students make in their traditional essays. Easy, right? Those were right there in your front pocket. Here are mine: sentence fragments, verb agreement errors, run-on sentences, non-parallel presentation of evidence, and punctuation . . . oh, the punctuation. Sound familiar? Like I said, easy.

How is it that you teach grammar? In other words, how do you teach the lessons demanded by those five tropes of grammatical entropy? If you are like most teachers of college writing, you use what Lindemann describes: an association model of teaching grammar (4th ed. 83–85). That is, you teach grammar as situated in student writing, not as a stand-alone subject, because you do not want to "isolate language study from language use" (85). Plus, "Student writers don't need to 'know' grammar in the same way that linguists and teachers do" (85). Agreed. Consequently, Lindemann supports the use of the association model; however, she adds, "If [. . .] we apply what we know about grammar to helping writers use language, our students will become more proficient in negotiating increasingly complex encounters with language" (85). In other words, a teacher's knowledge of formal, schooled grammar may provide terministic screens for discussing the grammatical features present in student writing. Once they are named, as I've named in my top-five list above, students may be able to consider audience expectations for forms of expression—to move concepts into forms of expression that may best transfer to their audiences.

Wait a minute, this is sounding more like a resonance than a retuning.

OK, let's retune that. Now, name five common grammatical errors that your students make in their audio-visual remixes. Easy, right? No?

OK, well then, take your time. I'm sure they'll come to you. Go ahead. Really, there's no hurry. I'm good. Just five. Really common ones.

Maybe I should order a pizza. Hungry?

In 1982, Maxine Hairston made Thomas Kuhn's discussion of the role of successive commonplaces in scientific study, "paradigm shifts," a commonplace of discussion in composition studies. Well, I have detected a change in the wind that I will introduce, simply, with this question: What is the grammar of twenty-first century writing?

Of course, that question begs the next: How will you apply what you know about audio-visual grammar to help your students become more proficient in negotiating increasingly complex encounters with twenty-first century writing?

Let me begin this discussion by answering my own retuned question from above. Here are five grammatical errors of audio-visual texts that my students commonly make: clip fragments; volume agreement errors; run-on clips; non-parallel, evidentiary editing; and punctuation . . . oh, the punctuation. Sound familiar? Like I said, easy. Or at least it can be once you know what to look and listen for. How does this terministic screen help me filter the way I talk with my students about their audio-visual writing? What do these grammatical terms for audio-visual writing mean? More importantly, what can they help us *do*?

1. *Clip fragments* are chunks of audio or visual data that are unresolved or incomplete. In other words, they do not function as independent statements in places where they are being used independently, for example, a clip in which a speaker's sentence is interrupted, or a clip that suggests a panning movement from one point to another that does not reveal the full range of that motion.

2. *Volume agreement errors* become noticeable as dramatic jumps or distracting disparity in volume levels between clips or between sound sources, for example, between quiet interviews recorded at one location juxtaposed with loud interviews recorded at another location, or background music that is unintentionally louder than the voice-over narration.

3. *Run-on clips* feature superfluous information either preceding or following the "meat" of the clip, for example, a speaker who finishes a sentence and then begins another before the

clip ends, or a piece of music that comes in before or stretches beyond the action of the movie that it is meant to accentuate.

4. *Non-parallel, evidentiary editing* surfaces as problematic when clips, photos, graphics, text, or music being used as supporting evidence for a claim present genres, tempos, or design elements that are inconsistent with that controlling claim, for example, cutting away from an interview to two movie-based clips and one text-based PowerPoint slide that serves as evidence for what is being said in the interview (evidentiary editing), or using both current (present tense) and archival (past tense) photos as evidence of a claim about either current or past events.

5. *Punctuation . . . oh, the punctuation.* Punctuation errors in audio-visual texts are characterized by misuses of timing, silence, blank screen, or stasis that moves the overall audio or visual information along or slows it down in some way, for example, the most common error of punctuation I encounter is when movies simply begin without an exaggerated and definite *start* moment—a moment of anticipation that allows the viewer to know that the actual start is the intended start. Another example is unintentionally inconsistent rests between scenes or clips. These prevent viewers and auditors from establishing the functions of pauses relative to the work being considered.

Now, don't be scared. I do not have a surveillance camera on you. Really. From that glazed look in your eyes, I think we better stop the stand-alone grammar lesson. Reading about grammar will do that for a person, which is exactly why we don't teach it that way. I just reviewed five grammatical rules that are completely unsituated from real examples of the principles they describe. Worse yet, these hypothetical examples are not yours—they have no immediate, practical value. They don't help you solve a particular present-progressive rhetorical problem. Don't worry, I'm done—for now. Even though I'm happy to concede the point, the larger present-progressive rhetorical problem persists: How will you apply what you know about audio-visual grammar to help your students become more proficient in negotiating increasingly complex encounters with twenty-first century writing? I have found that being able to articulate grammatical information like the five above has really helped me make sense of and situate problems and strengths in my students' writing. Yes, strengths too.

When your student asks you, for example: How do you like the music in my movie? You can reply: Not only did you make strong choices in terms of genre and energy, but your clip alignment, and volume agreement throughout was equally strong. In particular, I appreciated how the beats of the bass drum helped you punctuate the end of each evidentiary clip. Summative comments such as these can be formatively instructive—i.e., portable—for your students as they attach grammatical lessons to their own, valued writing. In other words, these grammar lessons follow the association model that Lindemann recommends. These kinds of comments help students see their work as increasingly complex by reducing the all-there-at-onceness of the media they make and remix. That's what grammar does: It provides tools for articulating the relation between big things and their components.

How did I learn about these grammatical features of audio-visual texts? I recognize the decisions that audio-visual writers need to make and control because I make those decisions. I know how these surface errors in students' audio-visual works distract me from hearing and seeing what they are trying to say. I know, or can suspect, what features of their works are open to being tidied up before the final mix, and which may demand more structural or sustained attention, and I know these things, in part, because a writer teaches writing. Murray concludes his piece with the following words:

> None of these implications require a special schedule, exotic training, extensive new materials or gadgetry, new classrooms, or an increase in federal, state, or local funds. They do not even require a reduced teaching load. What they do require is teachers who will respect and respond to their students, not for what they have done, but for what they may do; not for what they have produced, but for what they may produce, if they are given an opportunity to see writing as a process, not a product. (6)

Murray claims here that we need no "exotic training, extensive new materials or gadgetry." I agree; however, that is only because many of the writing technologies I am discussing have, and I predict will continue to, become more and more common. There is nothing exotic about moviemaking. Nothing. The gadgetry involved in making movies is also becoming increasingly common. Which means to say that any training writing teachers may need is most certainly not *exotic*. It, too, is common. It may seem exotic, but it is not. It has simply *been* uncommon—past tense. Bartholomae claims that using the foundational commonplace, "creativity is using old things in new ways," was most likely to be deemed excellent by the reviewers of the college placement essays he studied for "Inventing the University" (604). This book assumes that some training is in order, for if it were not, none of us would need it. One of its foundational commonplaces is the very same one Bartholomae indicates. Another is its inverse: Creativity is using new things in old ways. Both commonplaces share a foundational metaphor: Old is new. As we have claimed throughout the discussion in this chapter, it is metaphor that drives the abductive power of creativity by identifying two things known to be quite distinct. Old is not new. New is not old. And yet . . .

The grammar of traditional writing is not the grammar of new media—of twenty-first century writing; however, it shares much in common with it. Let me, here, repeat something from earlier in our discussion that I believe bears frequent repeating: Teaching with multiple forms of writing requires a commitment to engaging new forms of writing as both a writer and as a student—because a writer teaches writing and because writing is epistemic. New forms are forms that are new to you. If you have not used these forms to write, then they are new. Media theorist Henry T. Jenkins argues that the "new" of "new media" points not so much to the media themselves, but to opportunities for interacting with and participating in the operations of those media (5).

Teachers of writing, the opportunity is upon you. Participate.

Retuning #6: Discovery is a deliverable. This retuning is last, but not least, as it may be the most radical of the bunch, not because it shifts teaching away from product and toward process, but because it shifts assessment away from product as well. Murray's *Implication No. 8* is particularly complex, as it actually contains two implications. He begins *Implication No. 8* by talking about formative assessment: "Papers are examined to see what other choices the writer might make. The primary responsibility for seeing the choices [belongs to] the students. They are learning a process. Their papers are always unfinished, evolving, until the end of the marking period" (6). Murray ends the *Implication*, however, by talking about producing *finished* writers—writers who are done: "A grade finishes a paper, the way publication usually does. Student writers are not graded on drafts any more than concert pianists are judged on their practice sessions rather than on their performances. Student writers are graded on what they have produced at the end of the writing process" (6). I have said some version of these words to my students for many years: *Yes, I am most interested in the process that produces your work—as should you be. That said, I cannot grade your process. I can only grade the work you have written.* I appropriated that approach from Murray; however, I honestly believe that neither the students who heard those words nor the well-intentioned teacher who uttered them ever really bought what they were attempting to sell.

And so, the well-intentioned teacher went to work on that. Murray's *Implication No. 8* articulates a commonplace of composition: Do not grade drafts, grade final copies. The foundational metaphor Murray offers for ending the semester is one that Murray, the journalist, knows well: Grading is publication. The pedagogical perspective or attitude that emerges from this metaphor directs our selection of means for assessment: publishable items—i.e., *finished* texts. Now we see a potential flaw with Murray's foundational publication metaphor. Murray aims his pedagogy at generalizable process and evaluates its success based upon particular products. So have I—for many years. Too many. This is one way that Burke's *A Grammar of Motives* can help us see the relation between big things (motives) and their components (the hexad). Furthermore, its current use follows an associative model that puts Burke's grammatical terms into context to address real, present-progressive problems. The way I see it, this is a real, present-progressive problem for twenty-first century writing instruction.

Before I go any further, let me say that the publication metaphor is not without value. There are perfectly legitimate reasons to engage the publication metaphor, as it eyes the prize of product perfection even as a competitive gymnast approaches the balance beam willing herself to the flawless execution of known maneuvers and exposing herself to the scrutiny of those trained in the critical art of schooled awe. Furthermore, I have been an advocate for the publication of student writing— an attitude that may seem at odds with the attitude I have announced just above. However, the student writing I have helped publish (Blon, Creighton, and Halbritter) has participated in the very thing for which I have argued so passionately above: that students leave the class with a project. The student writing I have looked to publish has not always been the most impressive finished work at semester's end. It has, however, been among the most impressive *works* of writing. That is, these texts represent tremendous intellectual growth—not because of what the students have finished, but because of what they have started. They have started real, present-progressive projects that demand intelligent, symbolic action. The texts have given my students plenty of problems. Consequently, they move students to continue working. They leave students messy at semester's end, not tidy.

Yet semesters *do* end. Students must produce *something*. My attitude selects to follow the trajectory of Murray's first aim: *You are teaching a process your students can use—now and in the future—to produce whatever product his subject and his audience demand.* This attitude emerges from a much different foundational metaphor than the one Murray ultimately selects: Discovery is a deliverable. I don't know how many times I have watched students struggle to find their way into a project only to find it late in the drafting process—too late, in fact, to allow the next round of writing to move the project along far enough to support a product worthy of the title "final." When working in new media—especially audio-visual media—the time frame for drafting and working can compound rapidly. For example, I like to use documentary moviemaking as an introduction to research writing in my writing classes. These projects can be terribly time-consuming, and students often do not know the questions they would most like to ask of people until they have asked a few people questions and have tried to make something of the responses they have solicited. Beyond that, since this is often students' first attempt at using a video camera and/ or microphones, the audio-visual quality of the footage they capture is often mediocre at best. Further, depending upon what hardware and software resources they have available and how much experience they have with those resources, their audio-visual editing can also be quite novice. These factors conspire for making mediocre final products, mediocre final products that are consistently among the most involving and compelling assignments for my students. These assignments usually ask far more of my students than they expect. These projects generate their own audiences, as the people who appear in them become people who want—need—to see and hear the final products, and that creates a pressure far greater than the pressure of a grade for getting these projects as right as possible. Because there are so many variables, and because the final products look even remotely like products they are used to seeing on TV and online, these mundane products deliver big learning opportunities.

Furthermore, my students share these unfinished, drafty, messy products with far more people than they do their traditional finished writing. For example, I received a message from a former student who had taken my first-year writing course. Two years earlier, she and a small group of her classmates had made a documentary about the use of the "study drug," Adderall. They "filmed" the movie in the spring of 2008 on the MSU campus and, after the semester was over, posted the seven-minute movie to YouTube. As of September 2012 the video had more than 27,600 views and had generated 156 comments over the course of three years. In this class, I had students participate in two collaboratively-authored, moviemaking projects. The first was a mockumentary. The second was the documentary project that yielded this Adderall movie. Each documentary received two screenings in class, with class feedback from the first screening used to guide revisions for the second screening. (We will review the details of the assignment sequence in the Chapter 6.) In her final reflection for the documentary project, the student commented about the process of making this movie within the context of the class:

> When we had our "first draft" shown to the class, it helped me to get peer feedback. When people said they couldn't read the text, or hear the interviews, I went back and made sure I did things differently. I still wanted to keep the special effects I had, but I made sure things were crisp and done right. In the last movie we did, the mockumentary, I had a hard time keeping the movie "smooth". It seemed really choppy. I didn't really know the program that well at the time. So when it was time to use it again for the second time, things just came to me easier. I knew the basics, but I was then able to really expand what I knew.

When I first began using moviemaking in my writing classes, I used only one movie project—the documentary. I used this project, specifically, to help students learn inquiry-based writing skills:

• How to select sources (people to interview);

- How to begin research with questions, not facts (questions they had to actually pose to the people they interviewed);
- How to appropriate and make something from things that other people have said;
- And, how to allow a thesis to emerge from questioning.

After running this project for several semesters, I realized that the collaborative groups shared consistent comments in their reflections: specifically, (1) those who had done most of the editing—most of the labor—wanted another chance to make good on what they had learned from the experience (as the student above remarks), and, more surprisingly, (2) those who had not done most of the editing—most of the labor—wanted an opportunity to do it! And so, this well-intentioned teacher went to work on that.

The result was a two-movie, collaborative authoring sequence: a mockumentary and a documentary. The first movie was geared toward the following lessons:

- Teaching group dynamics;
- Functional skills for moviemaking: cameras, mics, scheduling, interviewing, editing;
- Teaching the genre of documentary—the next lesson—by way of parody. To parody something effectively, the author must understand the way the thing being parodied works.
- Fun;
- And bait—for the second project (based on the previous semesters' reflections that asked for more).

My use of the second movie assignment was aimed at the inquiry-based learning goals mentioned above. However, I added a wrinkle to the documentary project: each small group of 4–6 students would propose a subject, shoot footage, and then divide to make two movies from the shared footage. In other words, five groups would make ten movies.

My original learning goals for the documentary assignment were now supplemented with some new learning goals:

- To give more students the editing experience they wanted.

- To demonstrate that the same information—the same interviews and footage—could, and likely would, be put to much different rhetorical use.
- To allow students to expand on what they learned doing the first movie.
- To serve as bait for the single-authored, inquiry-based traditional essays that would follow.

This two-project, three-movie, collaboratively-authored, inquiry-based twenty-first century writing assignment sequence dramatically changed the way I approach teaching writing. That change was largely a grammatical change: It helped me articulate the relation between big things (learning objectives) and their components (assignments). It helped me see that the mediation of assignments was less about giving students experience with specific media, and more about giving writers opportunities to focus on process-oriented grammar lessons, i.e., lessons on the grammar of generalizable writing operations and of their individual, unique, and local writing processes. It also allowed my students to find success in the performance of component activities within a collaborative effort. A process-based pedagogy should be able to reward strong process-based performance, even if that performance does not yield a holistically successful finished product. For example, a student may find that he has an eye for photography or visual transitions, or she may find she has an ear for music mixing or conducting interviews. The Academy of Motion Picture Arts and Sciences recognizes many of these process-based successes with its annual Academy Awards, for example, best cinematography, best sound editing, best soundtrack, etc. These process-based awards recognize not only good artistic decisions, but good rhetorical decisions within compositions that, overall, may come up short of being excellent: for example, Mike Hopkins's and Ethan Van der Ryn's win for excellence in sound editing in the 2006 remake of *King Kong*.

Just sayin'.

The success of the two-movie sequence made me rethink the remix assignments I had been using in my other classes as well. I now assign a two-remix sequence to each student. For example, I taught a writing workshop for English teachers in the spring of 2010 in which a student created a favorable propaganda ("roller-vangelizing") piece for her sport: roller figure skating. Within six months of posting that two-minute remix, the second of her two remixes, it had gained nearly 3,200 views, and more than 6,565 views by October 2012. Here's what she had to say in her reflection about the assignment:

> Though this assignment was incredibly frustrating about 80% of the time, it was a lot of fun and I enjoyed it thoroughly. I think what I liked most about it was that it gave me the opportunity to create something that I not only have always wanted to create and just haven't had the time, but also something that means a lot to me personally.

This author was given a problem—quite a few of them, apparently. However, what made this worth it was her own investment in her subject and her position about it. Furthermore, this was a student who will be going on to teach writing as part of secondary English education—something she addressed directly in her reflection:

> My second remix was the remix where it really hit me that there are so many things I could do with my writing classes as a future teacher. [. . .] Getting students to create in a way where they want their work to be persuasive not only to their teacher but also to the world is a great way to motivate them to work towards becoming intellectual thinkers rather than just robots who work towards a grade.

A writer teaches writing. Writing is epistemic. Discovery is a deliverable. The lesson for this assignment does not lie in my appreciation for the work she produced; it lies in *her* appreciation of that work, it lies in *her* recognition of the rewards earned from fighting her way through the obstacle(s) of the assignment: "The second remix was extremely challenging but incredibly fun and I am extremely proud of it." She did not just write the remix, she thought it through. She overcame its obstacles. The "intellectual" work of it left her "extremely" messy.

Let me say this—with all due respect to these incredibly hardworking, intelligent, and diligent undergraduates: Their works are not finished. They are messy with unfinishedness. However, they are not messy with the failure of not living up to a standard—the shame of taking home a silver medal—they are messy with progress and messy with possibility, they are messy with discovery.

Before we move on, let's take stock of our six retunings of Murray's Ten Implications of teaching process, not product, for the audio-visual writing curriculum:

Retuning #1: Scene must be a fit 'container' for symbolic action.

Retuning #2: Language is a feature of only some forms of symbolic action.

Retuning #3: Forms of writing are consubstantial.

Retuning #4: No piece of writing is ever finished, it's just due.

Retuning #5: A mechanic knows mechanics.

Retuning #6: Discovery is a deliverable.

LEARNING GOALS: THE UNFINISHED WORKS OF TWENTY-FIRST CENTURY WRITING

Let me say this again: Not all writing classes are designed to yield the same learning outcomes. Some writing classes may be geared toward intensive fine-tuning of the writing of particular types of texts for particular purposes, for example, a seminar in Grant Writing. That type of class may not look to build bridges between types of writing, but may concentrate on the uniqueness of the endeavor. Understandable. However, if we are taking on a mission to have students make choices between forms of writing, to develop as writers in general, and, as Murray suggests, to learn an operation they can use—now and in the future—to produce whatever product their subjects and audiences demand, then we need to select means best suited to helping us meet our pedagogical aims. This demands a retuning of our attitudes about our writing assignments. In a process-based general writing course, the texts students create in response to the prompts of our writing assignments are obstacles, not goals. How we choose and sequence those obstacles has less to do with the kinds of media we use than the learning goals we have for our students. What, specifically, are the skills and habits of mind that we are trying to help students develop by way of our assignments? What types of writing tasks may best help them focus on and realize *those* learning goals? How can a moviemaking project help students realize learning goals that are less available in traditional essay assignments and vice versa?

Our assignments are means of symbolic action, in Burke's terms, *agency*. Our students read those means—that agency—and combine it with what they read from the scene and the agent (and her attitude) and the acts that result to abduce the purpose of the class. It is each of our job to be the type of agent who will allow our students to abduce the purposes of our assignments by making our teaching acts consistent with our teaching goals. As Murray has stated, "The teacher of writing, first of all, must be a person for whom the student wants to write" (qtd. in Lindemann, 4th ed. 305). It may be simple enough to translate this advice to mean something like *be a nice person*. That, in and of itself, is good advice, indeed. However, I believe we can also translate Murray's advice to mean, don't be the kind of teacher who claims to value one thing and then rewards another. Because who would want to write for that person? The kind of person students require, as Murray writes, "is a teacher who will *respect and respond to his students*, not for what they have done, but *for what they may do*; not for what they have produced, but *for what they may produce*" ("Teach" 6, emphasis added). If, as Murray states, a grade *finishes* a piece of writing, then that grade responds to what a student has done, "on what he has produced at the end of the writing process" (6). This, clearly, is not respecting and responding to what the student *may produce*. This is *not* giving students an opportunity to see writing as a process, not a product. This is bait and switch.

And our students know it.

Murray describes the process we are to teach. However, as I did above, I will substitute our term, *symbolic action*, for Murray's term *language*. Thus, the remixed Murray tells us that the process we are to teach is not the process of writing, *per se*. Rather, it is the process of *discovery* through *symbolic action*. It is the process of exploration of what we should know and what we feel about what we know through *symbolic action*. It is the process of using *symbolic action* to learn about our world, to evaluate what we learn about our world, to communicate what we learn about our world ("Teach" 4, remixed as indicated, emphasis added). Discovery—the knowledge-making, intelligent product of abductive reasoning—is the deliverable. The symbolic products of those acts of writing-sponsored discovery are the means—the agency—of that discovery. They are the obstacles that students overcome. The lessons they learn in doing so are to be aligned with carefully scaffolded learning goals that are the true products of the process-based writing course.

OK, so how do we grade THAT?

We will get to assessment of twenty-first century writing in our final chapter. Before we do, however, we're going to need to backtrack a bit. More precisely, we're going to return to what we discussed earlier about multitrack audio recording, and expand that into a more comprehensive theory of multidimensional rhetoric, a theory that we will explore, in Chapter Three, by way of exposing and examining the layers of integrated media that make up the multiple audio and visual tracks of movie editing.

3 Reading Like a Writer: Exposing the Layers of Multidimensional Rhetoric

[S]entences (like melodies) are sequential, in contrast with a picture or piece of sculpture (which is "all there at once").

—Kenneth Burke

At the end of the opening scene of Quentin Tarantino's 1994 hit film, *Pulp Fiction*, Pumpkin (Tim Roth) and Honey Bunny (Amanda Plummer) are frozen in mid-action as they begin to holdup a breakfast diner. Dick Dale's guitar rips into the opening riff of "Misirlou" (1961) and the freeze-frame cuts to the opening credits. As the credits continue to roll, "Misirlou" is audibly wiped from the credits as though we had been listening to a radio that someone offscreen is controlling. The radio is dialed until a new song comes in clearly: Kool and the Gang's 1973 hit, "Jungle Boogie." The radio dial sound effect allows us to do two things: Wipe Tarantino's neuvo-spaghetti Western surf music theme out of our ears, and situate the neuvo-blaxploitation funk music theme in a radio. In other words, the audio-wipe calls our attention to a distinct changing of aural scene, even as the visual scene, the credits, remains visually unaffected. In so doing, Tarantino signals a feature of his directorial and authorial voice that we can come to anticipate: he will use music to direct how we are to interpret and determine the scenes of his story. In other words, all we see must be considered along with all we hear. Tarantino's story is told by way of the multidimensional interplay between the multimediated layers of audio-visual rhetoric.

Of course it is. It's a movie. That's what movies do.

"Jungle Boogie" continues to play until the credits end and we open to a new scene that features hit man Vincent Vega (John Travolta) riding in a 1970s Chevy Nova driven by fellow hit man Jules Winnfield (Samuel L. Jackson). Both men are dressed identically in black suits with black ties and crisp white shirts. Jules sports an iconic 1970s short jheri curl hairdo with sideburns. Vincent has shoulder length straight black hair slicked back behind his ears. As they ride and speak, "Jungle Boogie" now plays on their car radio as diegetic music—music that seems to have its source in the action on screen. What had been Tarantino's music—for his offscreen directorial hand must have selected "Jungle Boogie"—now appears to have been lifted from Jules and Vincent because it is clearly playing on *their* car radio. "Jungle Boogie" is their music.

It's not hard to appreciate Tarantino's choice of music in *Pulp Fiction*. It is great music. Unfortunately, because it is so great, it can be difficult to hear it as anything other than . . . well, . . . great music. I love this music. This is precisely the kind of critique that most of us are accustomed to making. We either love a piece of music or we don't. We hear music as consumers; music is something to love, get, and have. From that perspective, we may imagine that Tarantino sat around in his home listening to stacks of old vinyl records—music that he had—and picked the music that he loved the most to supply the musical soundtrack to *Pulp Fiction*. Maybe, just maybe, that is precisely what happened. But I doubt it—or at least I doubt that that is all that happened—because Tarantino's music choices make too much sense when we consider them within the context of their placement within film. To say we like the music or that Tarantino likes it teaches us very little that we don't already know—we are simply reporting on acquired taste, or schooled awe. However, to consider how Tarantino *uses* the songs—to interpret the most relevant rhetorical associations that make these pieces of music work within context—is remarkably instructive because it reveals the kinds of choices available to audiovisual authors, authors who write *with* music, authors who integrate music and other forms of media to tell stories and to make and support claims. To do the former is to write like a reader/consumer. To do the latter is to read like a writer.

We ended Chapter Two by pointing to the importance of a pedagogy for twenty-first century writing instruction based upon learning goals, and not on types of written products. In this chapter we will attempt to expose at least some of the layers of what I call *multidimensional rhetoric*. To do so, we will read like writers, which, in and of itself, is a learning goal for twenty-first century writing instruction. Reading like a writer will expose opportunities for realizing additional learning goals by way of twenty-first century writing projects because it is a lesson in process—even as we saw in Chapter Two as we exposed how the clones of Jimi Hendrix may have stacked up in the multitracks of "Little Wing." In this chapter we will add a dimension, or two, by integrating the multiple tracks of music production into the multiple layers of video production.

Video production involves not only music, but any variety of still and moving images, text, animations, visual transitions and effects, and a soundtrack that may feature audio that is tied to the visual track, sound effects that are "overdubbed," and/or "voice-over" narration. Furthermore, any of these individual "assets" may be *written* specifically for the composition, or may be preexisting or *found* assets. Consequently, these assets may function as dependent clauses—assets that make sense only in the audio-visual text (e.g., transitions or text slides that identify a speaker on screen). However, these assets may also function as independent clauses—stand alone assets that have been created specifically for the audio-visual text or preexisting assets that have been remixed (e.g., songs, short interviews, or news clips). As we will see, each of these assets come to reside in layers of audio-visual writing. Their rhetorical value is to be determined both in their integration (the final mix) and in their separation (the individual tracks or layers). In this way, audio-visual authors are much like bank tellers, who need not only to provide a total tally of their bank drawer ($1000) but also need to account for precisely how many pennies, nickels, dimes, quarters, singles, fives, tens, and twenties combine to make that total. It's all money (a similar type of asset), but not all money is the same—some monetary assets are more or less valuable than others.

In what follows, we will begin by examining multidimensional rhetoric as a means for conceiving the complicated interplay of rhetorical appeals in a piece of writing. We will then begin to chart the movement of those appeals as they participate in the rhetorical dance of multidimensional rhetoric. Next we will co-opt Peter Elbow's advice and embrace the contraries of audio-visual writing, writing that may be both *entitled* as being *all there at once* and *defined* as being composed of multiple *layers* of components that are different in kind. We will then begin to entitle a descriptive grammar for both taking apart and putting back together again the rhetorical elements of audio-visual writing. This work will be aided, in part, by Robin Williams's in-delicate acronym of visual design principles: C.R.A.P. Finally, we will apply what we've collected along the way to the practice of reading like a twenty-first century writer.

What Is Multidimensional Rhetoric?

All rhetoric is multidimensional. Aristotle's discussion of *ethos, pathos,* and *logos* presents a multidimensional approach to understanding rhet-oric. If we think of each of these types of appeals as an axis of a cube, then we may be able to visualize a rhetor's *rhetorical stance* as a point within that cube that accounts for the overall balance of the rhetor's reliance on these three types of appeals (Fig. 3.1). Different types of rhetorical contexts and purposes call for different balance points. For example, a eulogy will often favor appeals to *pathos* and *ethos* above appeals to *logos*. Consequently we may chart an example of a eulogy somewhere in the vicinity of point A (Fig. 3.1). On the other hand, we may chart an academic essay—for example, one on audio-visual pedagogy—that appears in a print journal as a point in a different area of the cube—one that appeals to a much higher degree of *logos* and a much lower degree of *pathos*. Point B may chart the rhetorical stance of such an essay.

However, such a representation is what Burke would call an act of "entitling" (*LSA* 361; "What" 6). As we will see in this chapter, the value of multidimensional rhetoric for teaching twenty-first century writing is found, fittingly, in embracing the contraries of recogniz-ing wholes (entitling) and of recognizing parts (defining). There are times when we need to be able to consider audio-visual texts as being all there at once, and times when we need to break those texts into precisely determined component pieces so that they may be layered in new ways to meet new rhetorical aims. Let's begin with a readerly perspective and examine what most readers encounter first in a text: the title.

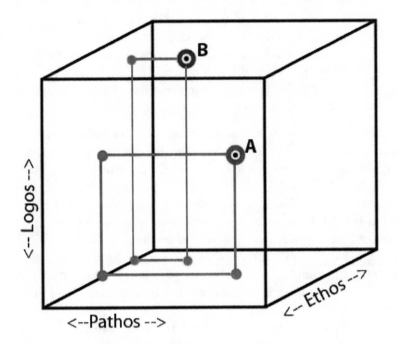

Fig. 3.1 Three Dimensional Chart of Rhetorical Stance

Entitling. As a prolific writer and rhetorical theorist, Burke had an awful lot to say about things that he claims say awfully little in and of themselves: words. Words, as words, are oversimplifications that depend on the things they represent by way of our various experiences with them to fill them out semantically—to fatten them with meaning. Consequently, Burke

> proposes that language be viewed, not directly in terms of a word-thing relationship, but roundabout, by thinking of speech as the "entitling" of complex nonverbal situations (somewhat as the title of a novel does not really name one object, but sums up the vast complexity of elements that compose the novel, giving it its character, essence, or general drift). (*LSA* 361)

Entitling is responsible for helping us sum up all sorts of complex things, actions, and situations. Burke suggests,

> "Entitling" of this sort prepares for the linguistic shortcut whereby we can next get "universals" such as "man," "dog," "tree," with individual men, dogs, and trees serving as particularized instances or manifestations of the "perfect forms" that are present in the words themselves (which so transcend any particular man, dog, or tree that they can be applied universally to all men, dogs, and trees). (*LSA* 361)

Entitling is the synecdochic process by which we make generalizations. Entitling is the kind of determination that creates indefinite articles, not definite articles: it unifies, not divides. The German Shepherd, the Shih Tzu, the Golden Doodle, the mongrel: Each is *a* dog. Or, that dog, that dog, and that dog: Each is *a* Golden Doodle. Entitling identifies by way of oversimplifying, by eschewing details in favor of revealing a general perspective, by summing things up and making claims of shared type or kind. Lessig and I are asking that we *entitle* the complex nonverbal situation of moviemaking as a form and process of writing. Entitling enables us to form, name, and share perspectives.

Entitling also enables us to name a rhetorical stance, that is, to choose a single point as a most representative spot within what is more appropriately conceived as a much more complex rhetorical situation, which takes place not only within the three-dimensional space of our rhetorical cube, but which unfolds along the fourth dimension of time. If we were to track the rhetorical stance of a complex rhetorical situation, we would produce not a single point but a four-dimensional path that could be captured, retrospectively, as a three-dimensional cloud of movement. Or better yet, if a *stance* charts the location of a fixed point on which to *stand*, the collection of such points that unfolds throughout time would chart not a rhetorical *stance* but a rhetorical *dance*: the progression of individual standing points—the tracks left by a rhetorical body in temporal action.

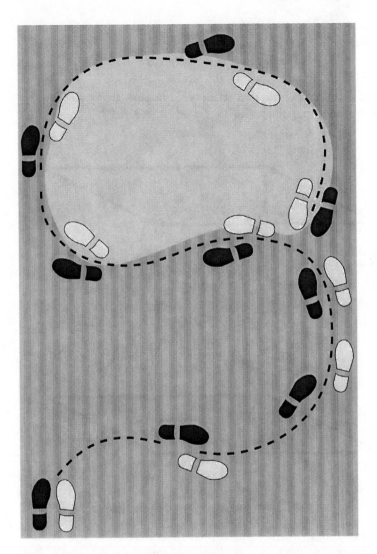

Fig. 3.2 A two-dimensional dance chart.

Rhetorical Dance. This rhetorical dance cloud charts more of an underwater or a mid-air dance—one not obedient to gravity and fixed to a single plane as in Fig. 3.2. Think of a firefly in flight on a dark, mid-summer evening. We can catch a glimpse of the firefly's travel by noting the points at which it illuminates. If we were to know nothing of fireflies other than what we can see, we may assume that the spot at which the firefly illuminated is characteristic of its travel. We saw it there, so that's as good a place as any to characterize its travel since, after all, we "know" it was there. We could say that this flash marks a flight *stance* since it fixes a metaphorical *standing* point. However, if we were to isolate our firefly from its peers and capture its flight through time-lapse photography, we would produce a picture of not a single flash of illumination, but of a series of flashpoints that would present a record of multiple stances during its travel (Fig. 3.3).

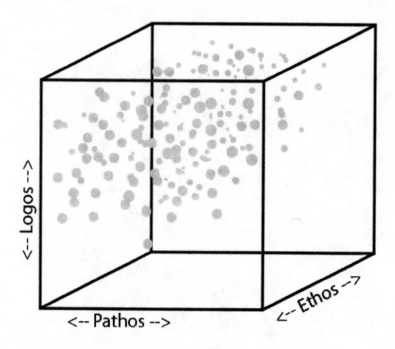

Fig. 3.3: The rhetorical dance and/or the dance of the firefly.

Our two-dimensional photo would chart the firefly's four-dimensional dance of light, and it would appear, most likely, as a two-dimensional cloud of overlapping, intertwining light trails. While it would not record the entire flight of the firefly—only the flashpoints—it would chart a standing area. Our photo would sacrifice details of two dimensions: depth and time. As such, it would present the sequential (chronological, developmental, historical) flight of the firefly in a single snapshot. Its entire history of flight, at least during the period of study, would be able to be captured in the photo: all there at once. Burke has claimed that "sentences (like melodies) are sequential, in contrast with a picture or piece of sculpture (which is 'all there at once')" (*LSA* 416). However, here would be a picture that is both all there at once *and* sequential. If we were to capture the flight of the firefly not as a photograph, but as four-dimensional digital data points, we could create a three-dimensional "sculpture" that could represent/recreate/symbolize the firefly's travel quite precisely. This sculpture would give us many options for regarding this data both sequentially and all there at once. As such, this form of symbolic action would be intrinsically sequential and all there at once. Or rather, the artifact produced by the symbolic action of its creation would be available for either type of consideration: a noun born of a verb—the shape of travel; an artifact that reveals the process of its making in its finished form; a book that may be judged by its cover.

Embracing Contraries. Burke states that a "whole sentence, considered as a title, can be summed up in one word, as were we to sum up the sentence, 'the man walks down the street,' by saying that it had to do with either a 'man-situation', or a 'walk-situation', or a 'street-situation'" (*LSA* 361). Burke claims that how we choose to identify the situation "depend[s] upon the direction or selectivity of [our] interests" (371). If we extend his claim from linguistic to extra-linguistic symbolic action, we could thus entitle our firefly's flight sculpture as a 'sequential-situation' or as an 'all-there-at-once-situation' depending upon the direction or selectivity of our interests. In other words, the way we would choose to consider the data would determine, in part, how we would interpret what we would perceive.

Of course, this is nothing new. The principle of complementarity in physics states that objects may have seemingly contradictory properties. Among the most discussed examples of this principle regards the form/movement of light (that is, not of lightning bugs but of light itself). Depending on the way light is observed, apparently, it may be observed to be particle-like or it may be observed to be wave-like; however, it cannot be observed to be both things at once—*even though it is.* Karl Mannheim contends that

> immediate aesthetic experience takes note of different strata of meaning but fails to keep them apart—at this level, all strata are given in 'psychological simultaneity'. It is because immediate experience can englobe simultaneously different strata which only abstraction can keep apart. (71)

Following from Mannheim, we may understand the "wave-particle duality" of light to be a false duality since "immediate experience" presents a much different, "objective" form of light—one measured not in degrees of particulars or modulations but in degrees of *brightness*—whether or not we squint.

All-There-At-Onceness. Mannheim's "psychological simultaneity" is essentially what I have co-opted from Burke as "all-there-at-onceness." The two contradictory strata we have been considering are sequential (defined) meaning and all-there-at-once (entitled) meaning. When Burke englobes the immediate experience of visual art as "all there at once," he entitles it as a "noun-situation" not a "verb-situation." In other words, our firefly's flight sculpture would be determined to be englobed as a "pattern-situation," not a progressive, "flying-situation." However, Burke keeps his options open regarding sentences, claiming that they are both sequential (and more specifically, modular) and entitlements: They both unfold in time and are all there at once as representations of more complex situations; they are both componential and whole; they are, like granite, aggregates.

It seems that Burke's focus on language (i.e., "logology") stems from his expert knowledge and use of language. In fact, before his theory of entitlement appeared in the *Language as Symbolic Action* collection, it appeared in the journal, *Anthropological Linguistics*, in an essay entitled "What are the Signs of What? A Theory of 'Entitlement'." For example, Burke's theory of terministic screens looks at the semantic possibilities afforded or constrained by terminologies (collections of words). Burke states, "insofar as man is the symbol-using animal, his world is necessarily inspirited with the quality of the Symbol, the Word, the Logos, through which he conceives it" (*LSA* 55). In Burke's *view* of language, words are surveyed not merely as symbols with direct referents in the world but as artifacts that accrue all of the symbolic relevance of something with a high degree of all-there-at-onceness. Burke asks us to consider not just the indexical function of words (i.e., "words are the signs of things") but also the "social content" of words:

> their nature as receptacles of personal attitudes and social ratings due to the fact that language is a social product, and thus builds the tribe's attitudes into its "entitlings" and into their "abbreviations" as words for things. Thereby, the things of

the world become material exemplars of the values which the tribal idiom has placed upon them. (*LSA* 361)

In other words (if you will), Burke asks us to see that words, as they are employed by members of terministic "tribes," have a high degree of all-there-at-onceness. For example, the four-lettered words that we forbid our children to say are words that not only refer most often to naughty, complex nonverbal situations for their direct meanings, they become associated with other complex nonverbal and verbal situations by way of that semantic and rhetorical baggage. Consequently, the words themselves become bad even if they are not being used to mean what they really mean. Which is pretty damned sweet. You know what I mean?

Of course this process of entitling makes social products of all words, not just the dirty ones. For example, the term *movie* may commonly be thought to be symbolic of a motion picture. However, Burke, himself, has expert knowledge that allows him to treat these entitled artifacts with a much lower degree of all-there-at-onceness, articulating component semantic possibilities for a linguistic symbol that arises from its etymology, its varying degrees of social value, and the types of associative semantic values it may carry within a variety of terminologies. So *movie* carries with it not only an indexical relationship with a form of text but with all of its tribal uses, associations, and metaphorical implications. Thus, watching or making a movie makes a person more than just a movie watcher or a moviemaker—it makes that person a couch potato or a connoisseur, it makes a person an auteur or a bartender.

Yet Burke, expert logologist, asks us to regard pictures and sculptures as being "all there at once." He entitles these things from the world knowing full well that, as entitlements, they belie "complex nonverbal situations" (*LSA* 361), and in so doing, Burke both embraces and falls victim to a contrary of symbolic action. In terms of entitlement, all-there-at-onceness makes possible the branding of complex artifacts, e.g., a picture or a sculpture. According to Burke's terministic screen, as announced by his entitlement of "picture or sculpture," Burke is able to discuss all-there-at-onceness as an absolute property, not a quality best measured in degree. Pictures and sculptures, as entitled by Burke, are simply "all there at once," that is, without apparent sequential or component properties—even if pictures and sculptures *have* those properties. Pictures and sculptures are *not* all there at once, unless, of course, we say they are. Pictures and sculptures do not simply exist in the universe, they are made. They are the products of processes of symbolic action that, as finished social artifacts, participate in ongoing processes of symbolic action. For example, a sculpture becomes a sculpture by way of the process of sculpting, a symbolic act that, for example, transforms a piece of marble—chip by chip—into the likeness of a cherub. As a marble cherub, the sculpture goes on to participate in symbolic acts that, for example, reify mythical beings or come to represent events that happened in their presence (that sculpture reminds me of our honeymoon in Paris). However, Burke's description of pictures and sculptures is not meant to *fit* merely pictures and sculptures, Burke's description *fits* his *use* of the terms. In other words, it is defined by verbiness, not nouniness. He is not defining the accurate nature of the items, he is describing his own act(s) of looking. Apparently, when Burke looked at a page of text, he saw more than a page of text. Burke, expert logologist and prolific writer, saw not only the text, he saw the components and the process by which it was crafted. A writer sees writing. To recall Lessig's distinctions from Chapter One, when it came to language, Burke was clearly RW. However, when Burke looked at a picture or a sculpture, he saw a picture or a sculpture—not the composition of the picture, not the block of marble. He, apparently, did not see the components or the processes by which they were crafted. When it came to pictures and sculpture, Burke was RO.

That may seem pretty inconsequential—I mean, who cares, in the long run, if Burke was RO for pictures and sculpture? Well, Burke gave us a theory for seeing language as a species of symbolic action—that is, as only one symbolic process among potentially many for achieving action—and action, as we have seen, involves the exercising of intelligent, ethical choice. Now, let's recall, too, that Burke states that "scene is a fit 'container' for the act, expressing in fixed properties the same quality that the action expresses in terms of development" (*Grammar* 3), and that it is "attitude" that helps an agent 'entitle' the scene, thus "expressing in fixed properties"—i.e., *entitling*—the quality of fitting actions. I suggest, then, that Burke's RO *action* is fitted to an RO scene as determined by his RO attitude, and while Burke's theory of symbolic action is robust enough to accommodate an RW attitude for extra-linguistic symbolic action, his attitude and scene never called for him, apparently, to make good on that theory. In other words, Burke, apparently, never encountered a rhetorical situation he couldn't talk his way out of. When all you have is a hammer, all your troubles start to look like nails. Or rather, all your troubles will present themselves in scenes that your hammer-having interests will direct or select to be entitled as nail-situations. I suggest that had Burke been invited to entitle his scene as a movie-scene, as our students are being asked, Burke just may have selected a movie camera, and consequently, his RW perspective for movies would have helped him see more than the all-there-at-onceness of moving pictures.

My purpose here is not to build the better Burke; my purpose is to demonstrate the importance of RW attitudes because they help us entitle RW scenes that call for RW actions. To return to our previous analogy from physics, an RW scene may be entitled to be wave-like (defined by what it does) or particle-like (defined by the stuff it contains). Descriptions of either view of a scene will be accurate only relative to the selected view of the scene. However, neither view can provide the full complementarity of the scene itself. The way we choose to define scene—as a noun-situation or as a verb-situation—will direct not only what we see but what we will regard as information or data relevant to the study of the scene. In other words, if we say that a conversational scene will be a noun-situation, then we will be most interested in identifying the nouny things: the people, the immediate setting, and things that the people say. These things may all be recorded with a note pad and/or a tape recorder, and a still camera. If, however, we regard the conversational scene as a verb-situation, then we will be most interested in identifying the verby things: movement, articulation, delivery, temporal relationships—in other words, the act of conversing, the telling of stories—not just the transcript of the conversation, not just the stories themselves. That is a thing that is difficult to remediate without taking it over in some potentially important ways. If we are interested in studying these aspects of storytelling, then our acts of retelling may eliminate or transform critical data, for example, those regarding movement, articulation, delivery, and temporality.

My attempt to use language to describe the facial expression of a person I am interviewing, or better yet, the shift from one facial expression to another, depends upon several rhetorical elements not present in the original situation. For one thing, it takes far longer for me to describe and for you to read those changes than to witness them. For another thing, my description relies on my sense(s) of entitlement, not on the actions/motions themselves, e.g., her face moved from signifying a happy-situation to signifying a worried-situation. For yet another thing, my description will likely completely disregard any detail that I do not choose to recognize explicitly as data, including information that may offer interpretive felicity to someone else or at another time. For example, if I interpret the shift in expression to be predicated upon something said to the person being described, then I may have been likely to disregard, say, the sound of a cell phone ringing that may have co-occurred. What I have treated as coincidental and irrelevant, someone else may interpret as a sound that has distracted the subject and may posit another explanation for the events I have described. However, my verbal description of the situation does not provide for further interpretation of this kind; my description tells its own story, and that story tells only its own story. However, if I am interested in studying the scene as a verb-situation, and if I am not looking to have the final word about the scene I am describing, then treating it as a noun-situation will provide little more than snapshots of the events—snapshots, such as those in a family vacation photo album, that demand more interpretive details than they provide; snapshots that ask for stories to be told about them; snapshots that often fit the action of storytelling to the scene in the picture, not that provide a window into the events depicted in the snapshots. You shoulda seen the one that got away.

Because our interests herein direct and select for 'writing-situations,' I will offer that interpreting audio-visual texts is more felicitous for illustrating writing processes when approached as identifying 'component-situations' than 'all-there-at-once-situations'—that to fit RW actions to scenes we have previously entitled as RO, it is important to recognize more of the stuff they contain in order to more fully appreciate the things they do. It is important to see more than just the nails. As I argue above, this predilection selects to look for both verby things and nouny things—for processes and products. Of course, writing theorists have struggled to unify, or as Elbow urged, to "embrace" contrary perspectives throughout our relatively brief history: process versus product, individual versus collaborative/social, gatekeeper versus facilitator, poetic/expressive versus rhetorical/dialogic, writing versus composing. The work of our field (entitled) and its contributing disciplines (defined) has demonstrated that a 'both and' approach is ultimately more felicitous than an 'either or' approach to these distinctions. Lindemann writes in the preface to the third edition of *A*

Rhetoric for Writing Teachers: "This edition regards writing from three complementary perspectives—as product, as individual process, and as a system of social actions" (x). These do seem like three separate, mutually exclusive perspectives, and yet they do seem complementary. Obviously, the perspective that sees them as complementary unifies them in some way. What is the medium for their unification? Entitlement. Entitlement englobes these perspectives as writing-situations by overlooking their various distinctions as nouny and verby components and by selecting and directing our attention according to our interests. Writing is all of these things, and more, not due to its intrinsic nature, but because we *say* it is, and because we say it is, we *see* it is.

I. A. Richards has claimed that, "All thinking from the lowest to the highest—whatever else it may be—is sorting" (30). Burke's theory of "Terministic Screens"—the attention-directing qualities of any and all terminologies—moves Richards's claim about thinking into an examination of the terminologies through which thinkers name their thoughts. Burke says there are two types of terms: those for putting things together (continuity) and those for taking things apart (discontinuity) (*LSA* 49–51). Lindemann refers to processes of continuity as *coordination* and processes of discontinuity as *subordination* (4th ed. 144–45). To this point in this book, we have primarily pursued the work of continuity and coordination by way of an attitude that has allowed us to entitle a variety of symbolic actions as writing-situations. We will now shift our attention to processes of discontinuity and subordination by way of an attitude that will enable us to break apart the all-there-at-onceness of audio-visual texts into the strata—the *layers*—of their RW component processes and products.

LAYERS

If a singularly-mediated piece of rhetoric, e.g., a traditionally-mediated essay, participates in this four-dimensional rhetorical dance, then audio-visual rhetoric creates multiple dance clouds, as each mediation conducts its own dance. We may think of these as the charts of not a single dancer (as in Fig. 3.2 above) but as a chart of dance partners, at times occupying the same space at the same time, at other times occupying disparate spaces, at some times leading its partners, at other times following them. We could imagine that each of these mediations would make a dance cloud of its own—each cloud having its own color. However, visualizing all of this four-dimensional movement would likely bleed into a muddy, multicolored mix. So, while we will return to the dance cloud visualization, for now, at least, we will simplify the visual distinction between these rhetorical strata as two-dimensional layers that may be seen and heard when examined in an audio-visual composition. The horizontal axis will represent temporal sequencing; the vertical axis will represent layered spaces that may contain various types of audio-visual assets. To use Lindemann's terminology, we will notice two primary coordinate strata: visual media and aural media. Each of these coordinate strata is comprised of varying numbers of subordinate strata that are coordinate with each other. Fig. 3.4 shows an example of the visualizations we will employ.

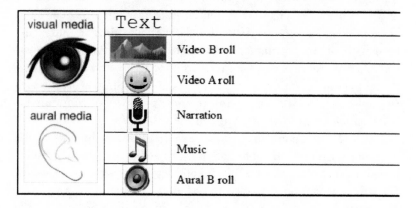

Fig. 3.4 Example of coordinate and subordinate layers of audio-visual assets

Seeing Layers of Sound. The soundtrack of a segment of a movie may be comprised of several layers of sounds, each containing information designed to contribute to the overall rhetorical purpose of that segment and the entire movie. We will discuss these sounds according to two categories: diegetic and non-diegetic (Fig. 3.5).

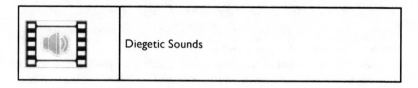

	Non-Diegetic Sounds

Fig. 3.5. Diegetic and nondiegetic sounds

Diegetic Sounds. Filmmakers and film critics refer to the sounds in the immediate scene of onscreen action as diegetic sound. For example, most movies will have a few tracks devoted to the dialogue: the linguistic component of the narrative. This is the portion of a movie that bears the closest resemblance to traditional writing. The audience hears what the author is "saying" by way of what the actors/speakers are actually saying. That, however, is only one aspect or layer of the soundtrack. There may also be a track (or several) for other types of diegetic or *scenic* sounds. For example, if a dialogue is taking place at a baseball game, we may hear the sounds of baseballs being hit, of the umpire yelling "strike" or "safe," of the crowd cheering or booing, of the people in the nearest surrounding seats ordering a hotdog, the theme music for the new batter being played through the public address system of the ballpark, etc. Or we may not. The movie's audience can expect all of these sounds to be present in the scene where the dialogue is taking place. However, it is up to the audio-visual authors of the scene (the director, the sound editor, the foley director, the sound crew, etc.) to determine what the audience actually hears (or doesn't) and when they hear it (or not). Some of the diegetic sounds the audience hears may be *direct sounds*, sounds that were captured during the recording of the scene—the sounds that actually occurred during the capturing of the action onscreen.

Other diegetic sounds may be *foley sounds*, sounds added during the editing process to add, accentuate, or replace direct sounds. Foley sounds almost always sync to some sort of action that is taking place. For example, during the filming of the baseball segment above, the umpire may not have yelled "strike" in a way that the direct recording could capture it or well enough for the audience of the movie to hear it—or possibly the umpire didn't yell it at all during the pitch on film; however, the director(s) may decide that it is important that the audience hear that, and so the director(s) may add the sound of an umpire yelling "strike" (foley sound) as though it were captured during the filming of the onscreen event (direct sound). Or, in the scene being recorded, an actor who cannot play piano is photographed as though she is playing a piano that is obviously in the scene. The sound of a piano being played is added to the soundtrack later during foley editing to give the impression that the actor's onscreen movements are responsible for producing the diegetic sounds of piano playing. This is a very common form of movie magic that, when done well, can be virtually undetectable (see George Clooney's lip-synching of "Man of Constant Sorrow" in *O Brother Where Art Thou?*), but when done poorly sticks out like a proverbial sore thumb, often to comedic effect (see Chevy Chase in Paul Simon's music video for "You Can Call Me Al").

Instead of simply adding, supplementing, or replacing sounds to the direct sound event, the foley editor(s) may also delete sounds. Maybe during the filming of our hypothetical baseball scene an airplane flew overhead, or someone in the stands yelled a foul word, or the crowd cheered at an inopportune moment during the dialogue. The foley editors may decide to eliminate many of these noises or all of them and create a new soundscape all together, one that sounds more like the event *should have* sounded. For example, a documentary may feature a conversation in a restaurant. The sounds of the restaurant during the actual capturing of the conversation may be entirely too distracting to mix behind the conversation. However, removing that noise altogether may make the scene sound artificially quiet—conspicuously un-restaurant-like. So restaurant sounds captured at another time may be mixed behind the conversation to create a faux sonic realism. This type of aural trickery is clearly rhetorical because it makes contributions to and/or deletions from the overall information communicated during the segment of the movie. In general, the sounds carried in these tracks of the soundtrack attempt to direct our *attention* to give us access to the scene in a way that both meets the rhetorical design of the directors even as it attempts to provide audience members with an experience that allows them to feel as though they are present in the scene. Fig. 3.6 shows three layers of typical diegetic sounds.

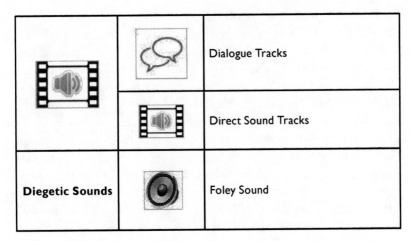

3.6 Typical types of diegetic sounds.

Non-Diegetic Sounds. In addition to these diegetic sounds, the soundtrack may also feature *non-diegetic* sounds, sounds that do not give the impression that they are emanating from the action onscreen or in its implied surrounding scene of action. One of the most common types of non-diegetic sound is the *musical soundtrack* of the scene—the part of a movie most commonly referred to as *the* soundtrack. For example, in countless teen-rebellion movies, characters joyride in cars or on motorcycles nauseatingly often to the accompaniment of Steppenwolf's "Born to Be Wild." At times we may be asked to think that this music is diegetic—that it is being played on, for example, the stereo in the car onscreen—even as "Jungle Boogie" played on Jules's car radio in *Pulp Fiction*. However, most often we regard this music as non-diegetic, as external commentary on the scene, for example, Dick Dale's "Misirlou" clearly did not emanate from the diner being held up by Pumpkin and Honey Bunny. If we ask commentary *by whom*, we would most likely come to the conclusion that this commentary is communicated by the filmmaker(s) or the director(s)—the audio-visual author(s) overseeing the entire work. In this way, non-diegetic music may function as an extension of the voice of the filmmaker(s). Through this vocal extension, the filmmaker(s) can communicate a host of rhetorical appeals—as we will explore later.

Voice-Over Narration. Of course, the filmmaker can also voice her commentary on the scene by way of spoken voice-over narration. In fiction films, or films of "wish fulfillment," as documentary scholar Bill Nichols calls them in the first edition of his *Introduction to Documentary* (1), this commentary is most often voiced by an actor reading from a prepared script. For example, protagonist H. I. McDunnough (Nicholas Cage) supplies the voice-over narration that sets the scene for the action of the Coen Brothers' film *Raising Arizona*. During the opening montage, H.I.'s narration does not emanate from within the procession of clips in the sequence but rather talks over these clips from somewhere outside of the action we see in the clips. In the case of documentary films, what Nichols calls films of "social representation," the documentary maker may read this commentary himself, as Michael Moore does in his films (e.g., *Roger & Me*, *Bowling for Columbine*, or *Fahrenheit 9/11*), or may have the script read by an actor as Academy Award-winning actor Morgan Freeman did for director Luc Jacquet in *March of the Penguins*.

Foley. Filmmakers may also comment on the action onscreen by way of non-diegetic foley sounds, most often called *sound effects*. Sounds such as breaking glass, screeching tires, and cracking whips are often used for comic effect to comment on a character or her situation. These sounds do not sync to onscreen action—at least not directly. These sorts of sound effects are clearly not intended to be interpreted as part of the onscreen action but as commentary directed at the onscreen action by someone outside of that action. Laugh tracks that accompany televised sitcoms are also examples of non-diegetic foley sounds. While they may suggest a kind of diegesis (if we imagine the show is a stage performance), they may just as easily be regarded as rhetorical commentary made by the audio-visual authors of the episode (you should think this is funny too!). Other audio-visual compositions use non-diegetic foley sounds as well to different rhetorical ends. Science fiction and horror productions use a variety of creepy sounds to evoke tension or fear. Television news programs used to employ a ticking/typing sound, presumably to conjure the impression of a continuously operating newsroom constantly being fed the latest news feeds from around the world. In Barack Obama's infomercial "American Stories, American Solutions," we can detect the ever so faint sound of wind chimes at various times throughout the thirty-minute production—chimes that are moved to music, presumably, by the winds of *change*. Fig. 3.7 shows three layers of typical non-diegetic sounds.

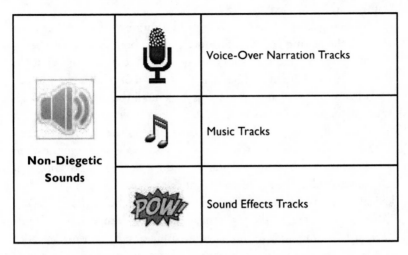

Fig. 3.7 Typical types of non-diegetic sounds.

What is important for our immediate purposes is to recognize that what may seem to be a singularly entitled thing—the soundtrack—is comprised of many component layers of independently defined (and authored) artifacts. Learning to hear these layers of composition helps move an auditor (a listener) from critique of consumption to critique of production—or from reading like a reader to reading like a writer. Access to the artifacts manipulated by the audio-visual authors can give the auditor information not only about the types of information used but also to postulating the types of decisions that were made about how to employ that information. Knowing that, for instance, the documentary filmmaker has access to a multitude of options for controlling what we do and don't hear may allow us to hear the voice of the filmmaker in places where we may not have anticipated. For example, in *Fahrenheit 9/11*, during a sequence about George Bush's original inauguration, filmmaker Michael Moore mentions in his voiceover narration that Bush's limousine was "pelted with eggs" during its procession through throngs of protesters. As Moore mentions the pelting, we see a single egg hit the door of a limousine. As the egg hits the door, we also hear a noise that sounds as though it were produced by the egg we see hitting the door we see. That door happens to be on a limousine that we are likely to interpret as the very limousine transporting Bush and traveling in the very same procession described in the voice-over narration.

But is it?

Moore is asking us to believe him in a number of ways. Let's just attend to the pelting portion of Moore's claim about Bush's limo being "pelted by eggs." Moore's visual evidence seems to be obvious enough: we see an actual egg hit and burst against the door of an actual limousine. Plus we hear it happen, making it seem all the more compelling, especially if we assume, as we are often asked to do in a documentary, that the sound was recorded at the same time as the visual action. In other words, if we assume that the pelting sound is direct sound then we are likely to regard the event as an audio-visual record of the event being described in the narration—that the action onscreen has an "indexical relationship" with historical reality, as Nichols calls it (35-36). If, however, we regard the segment of film as a composition of multidimensional rhetoric, we may begin to look and listen for layers of rhetorical elements in the audio-visual composition.

Knowing something about the sounds made by an egg hitting a limousine door, especially when recorded from the distance implied by the camera shot, and knowing something about the noise generated by a crowd of protesters may give us cause to ask, "How is it we can hear that one egg hit the door of that limousine above the throng of noise we may assume would come from that crowd of protesters?" That question may then lead us to reason that we most likely could not hear that sound above the throng of the crowd, which, in turn could occasion our asking, "Well then, did *this* particular egg hit the limousine somewhere other than in the midst of the throng described, or was it added as foley sound?" Either of those questions will alert us to the fact that Moore has chosen to use the clip as a piece of evidence for his claim about pelting, a claim supported by the sight and sound of one egg hitting a limousine. We may now ask just how compelling this evidence is with reference to Moore's claim, and why he has constructed the argument as he has. If, as illustrated in Fig. 3.8, the pelting noise was indeed recorded as direct sound, then that suggests the pelting event may have taken place somewhere other than in the throng of protesters Moore has asked us to imagine to be present.

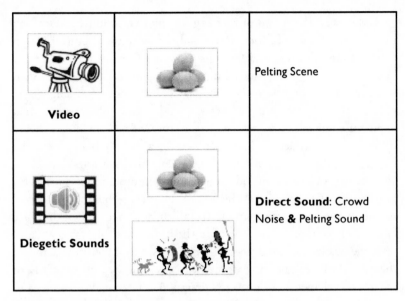

Fig. 3.8 Scenario pelting sound as direct sound.

If, however, Moore has doctored the pelting event with foley sound, as illustrated in Fig. 3.9, that suggests Moore has boosted the rhetorical impact of the footage he is using as evidence to his claim.

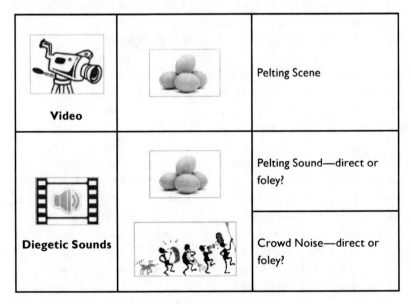

Fig. 3.9. Pelting event doctored with foley sound.

Either way, the sound of that egg hitting that limousine door asks us to hear the voice of Moore in not only his narrative, but in that egg-pelting sound. That sound helps us hear that the movie is not simply "all there at once." That sound didn't just happen, it was recorded. It was composed. It was written. The sound resides not in *the* single layer of soundtrack, but in *a* single layer of soundtrack. In other words, what is presented as all-there-at-once—*the* soundtrack—may also be heard to be not only sequential like a sentence or a melody but sequentially stratified in the way that an orchestra is sequentially stratified: each instrument plays its own melody concurrently in order to produce a rich progression of harmonic all-there-at-oncenesses, a rhetorical dance of harmony. We can either attend to the all-there-at-onceness of the voice of the orchestra, or we can attend to the individual voicings that comprise the whole. The former would be to attend to readerly concerns: to the textual whole. The latter would be to attend to writerly concerns: to the discrete elements of the overall design. At that level, we may start to recognize that the composition calls not only for woodwinds, but that the woodwinds are to be flutes, clarinets, and bassoons, and that the composition is stratified for not just one, but three bassoons, etc.

Once we begin to question the layering of the soundtrack, we can begin to question *how* the sights and sounds came to be presented in the way we see and hear them. For example, where would the microphone(s) need to be in order to "hear" the pelting sound present in the film? What kind of microphone is good for that sort of thing? Where is the camera? Is this a staged event? If not, why would a filmmaker have a microphone trained on the door of a limousine? Now, you may be saying, "How should I know? I'm not a filmmaker. Isn't there a microphone on the camera? There's a mic on *my* video recorder." How *should* you know? *Why* should you know? Well, if you are making or teaching moviemaking—i.e., if you are teaching twenty-first century writing—you will need to confront questions such as these. Suddenly, as if being pelted by an egg anonymously thrown from a crowd, you'll realize that knowing something about microphones, for instance, is not simply convenient, it's as necessary for moviemaking—for twenty-first century writing—as knowing how to change the font in your word processing program. Consequently, in Chapter Four, we will shift our attention to assessing and recording listening situations—from hearing layers to filling them.

For now, however, let's stay in the multidimensional rhetorical layers of twenty-first century writing. So far, we've exposed layers of audio-visual multidimensional rhetoric by making them both audible and visible: we've shown how they separate and how they stack up. However, we have not yet discussed how they interact, that is, how they integrate to form an all-there-at-onceness. Integrating these layers into a whole, entitled text—one greater than the sum of its parts—requires an act of writing. Discussing that act of writing requires a grammatical terminology—one that writers can use to reveal relationships between components and to predict how they may be arranged to accomplish desired rhetorical effects for specific audiences. In Chapter Two, we discussed Burke's dramatistic grammar of motives as a means for engaging the rhetoric of audio-visual texts, and I offered five grammatical errors of audio-visual writing that I see most often in the audio-visual texts my students have written. However, those "errors" may be equated with surface-level distractions of grammar and usage in traditional text. What about the more structural grammar? What about the arrangement of subject and predicate? What about the integration of dependent clauses? The point of breaking up the all-there-at-onceness of twenty-first century texts is not simply to expose layers of components but to study how those layers interact with and against each other, to establish not only how the layers separate, but, critically, how they contrast.

Entitling a Grammar for Multidimensional Rhetoric

[W]hen you can recognize and name the contrasts, you have power over them—you can then get to the root of the conflicting problem faster and find more interesting solutions.

—Robin Williams

Contrast—a term that both takes things apart by way of separation and puts things together by way of relation—is the capital C leading the charge of Robin Williams's four-lettered grammar of visual design. Williams does not call her grammar a grammar; however, she is not talking to *us*, specifically, even though she is addressing us, specifically. Let me explain. Williams's book, *The Non-Designers Design*

Book: Design and Typographic Principles for the Visual Novice, addresses non-designers. I will acknowledge that writing teachers and professionals are not steeped in the language and practices of design, *per se*. In that regard, we are non-designers. Yet the five canons of classical rhetoric (invention, arrangement, delivery, memory, and style) seem to be infused with a spirit of design—most notably, perhaps, in the canon of arrangement. Furthermore, our expanding definitions of writing are compelling us to do the work of—you guessed it—design, namely, audio-visual design. Williams recognizes this and talks to us—sort of. Even as we have not been directing our disciplinary attention through a terminology of design, *per se*, Williams has not been directing the attentions of "non-designers" through the terminology of rhetoric and composition, *per se*. Consequently, what Williams announces as principles of visual design, we may recognize as grammatical principles of audio-visual writing.

At the heart of Williams's discussion are her "four basic principles" of visual design: Contrast, Repetition, Alignment, and Proximity. C.R.A.P. (13). Let's briefly explore each of these four sorting terms to both see and hear how they may direct the attentions of audio-visual writers and readers.

Contrast. "Contrast," says Williams, "is often the most important visual attraction on a page" (13). Williams urges non-designers to avoid the muddiness of similarity among the elements of a visual composition. She says, "If the elements (type, color, size, line thickness, shape, space, etc.) are not the *same*, then make them *very different*" (13). Extending Burke's claim that there are two types of terms into a terminology more suited to a discussion of symbolic action, we can begin to see how contrast can direct our attention to a variety of audio-visual symbols. Contrast, because it both separates and joins, allows us not only to determine characteristics of contrast for either audio *or* visual information but critically allows us to name relational characteristics of contrast *between* audio and visual information, especially in terms of characteristics of social use. For example, let's say we are discussing a student's remix assignment in which she has integrated clips of product advertisements from the 1950s set to the music of David Bowie's 1983 hit, "Modern Love" and/or to the music of Lady Gaga's 2009 hit, "Bad Romance." Here we can establish and discuss degrees of contrast between characteristics such as genre, historical time period, technol-

ogy of access/broadcast, popular culture, fashion, social mores, generational values, and even the variety of social positions associated with
the musical artists and the products being advertised. Contrast is a
distinction of both grammar and usage that can help direct our attentions to readerly and writerly concerns.

Repetition. If contrast helps us articulate characteristics by which we
may reduce similarity between rhetorical elements, repetition helps us
articulate ways to exploit similarity. Williams claims that visual designers can "repeat color, shapes, textures, spatial relationships, line
thicknesses, fonts, sizes, graphic concepts, etc." in order to develop
organization and to strengthen unity (13). Music, especially popular
forms of music in American cultures, utilizes repetition as a regular
part of its composition. Songs have verses and choruses. Verses are
most often identified by way of their shared melodic structure, but
distinguished by their unique lyrics. Choruses are most often identified by way of their shared melodies and lyrics. Verses and choruses
are almost always distinguished by way of clearly differentiated—i.e.,
clearly contrasting—melodies, for example, the verses and choruses of
hits such as "Beat It," "Billie Jean," and the title track from Michael
Jackson's *Thriller* album (1982), the best-selling album of all time (as
of 2010).

Repetition in music may help audio-visual writers identify and coordinate or contrast repetition in the visual elements of their works.
For example, in an audio-visual remix, each repeated chorus in a piece
of music may be associated with contrasting visual information. The
similarity and repetition of the musical information could function,
essentially, as a metaphorical vehicle that unifies otherwise contrasting
content in the visual track, or vice versa—that is, visual images may
be repeated over contrasting pieces of music. It becomes clear that in
audio-visual writing, contrasts apparent in any one layer of information may participate in repetitions with other layers of information—
and vice versa. However, the layers of audio-visual writing do not only
stack up, they unfold in fixed ways through time. It is this temporal
quality of audio-visual texts that directs our attention to the third of
Williams's principles.

Alignment. Williams says, "Nothing should be placed on the page arbitrarily. Every element should have some visual connection with anoth-

er element on the page" (13). If we substitute the term *text* for page and the term *rhetorical* for *visual*, we get a mantra for audio-visual writing:

> Nothing should be placed in the text arbitrarily. Every element should have some rhetorical connection with another element in the text.

This principle asks us to recognize the moments when things start and stop. Consequently, audio-visual alignment is often expressed in terms of synchronization (information that is presented at the same time) and sequencing (information that is presented at different times). Elements that are misaligned often show, for example, explosive visual action that does not co-occur—i.e., that is not aligned or synchronic—with explosive information on the audio track. Misaligned elements also happen sequentially, for example, when a piece of music is introduced arbitrarily. This can be a common error for novice audio-visual writers, especially if that piece of music is being used simply because the author likes it or because she knows that a piece of music should probably go in there somewhere—because, well, that's what movies do. Alignment helps audio-visual writers name the whens and wheres of rhetorical elements and opens opportunities to discuss the rhetorical relationships of those elements.

Proximity. Williams claims that "Items relating to each other should be grouped close together. When several items are in close proximity to each other, they become one visual unit rather than several separate units" (13). Williams's discussion of this fourth and final principle is applied to static images that are presented, in Burke's terms, as all there at once. Consequently, Williams's use of proximity most often seems to apply to visual documents with distinct visual boundaries, for example, flyers, menus, and a variety of web- and traditionally-mediated pages. Consequently, proximity, for Williams, may be measured in terms of two-dimensional inches or pixels. These are very important distinctions to make, as many web-based multimedia texts arrange both static and active media on a single page. However, *within* the audio-visual portions of those pages, proximity may also be measured temporally. How closely, in terms of time, are rhetorical elements grouped together—or separated? And if we are to extend Williams's spatial proximity into a temporal proximity, we need to consider what may serve as audio-visual analogs to the page—to audio-visual space with distinct temporal boundaries.

When attempting to contain time in this way, I most often look to the dramatic boundaries of *scene* and listen to the temporal boundaries of non-diegetic music. Scenes have beginnings and ends. They can be long or short in duration. They can take place in one or several visual locations. However, in order to be identifiable *as* scenes, they need to have some form of entitling action—action that unfolds in time. For example, an introductory scene of a documentary may span many locations and involve several characters; however, the *scene* may be identified if each of the elements participates in the action of introduction. This is little different, conceptually, from what defines the introduction of a personal essay or of a research paper. Consequently, two-dimensional and temporal space may be unified in terms of proximity relative to conceptual, scenic, or entitled boundaries; in short, the proximity of audio-visual elements are determined relative to placement within rhetorical boundaries.

Music often marks distinct boundaries of time for grouping related items together. For example, just prior to the 2008 U.S. presidential election, Barack Obama released the half-hour political infomercial, "American Stories, American Solutions." The roughly ninety-second introduction to this piece sets up the tour-de-force of political rhetoric that follows. In twenty-seven minutes, the film moves us from introduction through four vignettes with American families, through dozens of endorsements from public officials, through biographical segments about Obama's life and family, and through the presentation of Obama's positions and bullet-pointed plans to address the pressing issues of the 2008 presidential election. Since we were just talking about a hypothetical introduction in the previous paragraph, let's see how Williams's grammar may empower our analysis of the opening ninety seconds.

First: Taking Inventory. What Do We Notice—What Is in the Layers?

The first note of a slow four-note melody sounds as the visual field fades from black to a field of amber waves of grain swaying in slow motion. After the first two ascending notes played by a single French horn (I believe—though it may be a flugelhorn or baritone), the visual field cross-fades to a second, closer shot of the swaying wheat field as the third and fourth notes of the melody descend. The four-note melody is repeated with two slight alterations: (1) the single horn is joined by a second horn playing a lower sequence of notes in harmony, and (2) the final note of the four-note sequence ascends in this second iteration. Also, the horns are joined by the sound of Obama's voice slowly and steadily narrating these opening words: "With each passing month our country has faced increasingly difficult times." This narration is overlayed by three shots that roughly follow the movement of the melody—though slightly more slowly. The first is of amber fields now filmed from what appears to be a moving bus window, then a field of outstretched hands, apparently at a political rally—some waving small American flags, and finally a shot of people at a political rally—more small flags in the foreground. The middle-aged man in the middle of the frame wears a cowboy hat. The camera is behind this man to his right, so we don't see much of his face; however, we do see him lean forward to match the posture of those around him as they appear to strain to see something offscreen to the right.

The melody begins its third iteration joined now by a harp and what sounds to be the soprano voice of a clarinet and the deep tones of a bass violin and possibly of a timpani drum. As this chorus of classical instruments repeats the first melodic movement, Obama narrates, "But everywhere I go, despite the economic crisis, and war, and uncertainty about tomorrow, I still see optimism." As Obama narrates, a sequence of four shots, still in slow motion, plays. The subject of these shots is of anonymous, but obviously American people. These are people who appear to be at political rallies. Obama appears in the first of the four shots, however, the shot is filmed from behind Obama, showing him shaking the outstretched hands of people in a crowd—his shirtsleeve rolled up on his own outstretched arm. The second shot of the sequence shows a close-up profile of an African-American woman. She is filmed from an angle lower than her face—the camera clearly looks up to her—even as she looks up toward something offscreen to the right. She is not tall, or at least the young man to her immediate left is taller than she is. Yet our camera angle is below her eye line. As Obama narrates, "and war," we notice her lower lip quiver. Over "uncertainty about tomorrow," a blonde mother holds her strawberry blonde children in her arms, as her profile looks offscreen to the left— even as her children look toward us—toward the camera. As Obama states, "I still see optimism," the shot cross-fades to a close-up of a

young girl smiling brightly amid a tangle of adult arms and bodies—
several hands waving small American flags. The young girl looks up
toward the person standing before her—a person with what appears to
be the same gingham shirt and rolled-up sleeve and darkly tanned arm
that we saw three shots ago.

The fourth melodic movement differs slightly in pattern from the
other three and is now joined by a group of singers following the new
melody with a chorus of "ooh." Obama's narration completes the list
he started with optimism by adding, "and hope, and strength" as the
video track cross-fades from the smiling young girl to an elderly war
veteran waving from what appears to be a parade float—the sleeves
of his crisp white shirt rolled up on his outstretched arms. This shot
fades to black, which immediately fades to a close-up of Obama as he
speaks from what appears to be a formal office. He wears a navy suit,
a crisp white shirt, and a deep red tie. Each visual transition since the
initial opening has been carried with a cross-fade—one shot fades directly into another. However, the visual transition from the opening
sequence to the shot of Obama sitting in the oval-ish office is decidedly different. It opens to a new scene, even as it keeps the basic fading
transition. The fade to and from black is accentuated, ever so slightly,
by the introduction of another orchestral instrument: wind chimes.
As the fourth melodic movement concludes, Obama says, "We've seen
over the last eight years how the decisions of a President can have a
profound effect on the course of history and on American lives."

That concludes the first forty-seven seconds of the introduction.
We're only halfway through—but we'll stop the detailed inventory
here. Throughout the rest of the scene, there is only one additional
shot, one that lasts nearly a full minute, in which Obama describes
what will happen throughout the rest of the film. The music we have
been hearing continues throughout this scene and fades completely as
the final visual of the scene fades to black. Scene over.

Second: What Does It DO—How Do the Layers Interact?

Notice I have created an inventory of rhetorical elements that are present in the first forty-seven seconds of the text we are considering. Notice, too, that this inventory stretches over the linear space of several
pages and amassed more than eight hundred words. That may seem a
bit excessive for forty-seven seconds. However, when we actually begin
working with this material, we may determine we need more.

Before we proceed with using the C.R.A.P. principles to guide our analysis, let's quickly review the statement we took from Williams and remixed above:

> Nothing should be placed in the text arbitrarily. Every element should have some rhetorical connection with another element in the text.

That said, we can now assume that all of what we noticed—all of the items in our inventory—*should* participate in the overall rhetorical mission. In other words, we should expect the layers to overlap and connect. Of course, that does not mean they actually do. However, one thing we do know about the film we are studying is that the stakes were extremely high and that the purpose of the film is tightly focused. This film was meant to move Americans to cast their votes for Barack Obama. Its message and the rhetorical purpose it was attempting to fulfill were completely kairotic. With those things in mind, let's see what kind of C.R.A.P. this thing is made of.

Contrast and *Repetition* guide our analysis in several important ways, especially with regard to the music, which, in the first forty-seven seconds, seems to control the action. There is little contrast in the melodic structure between the first, second, and third lines. Each four-note sequence is nearly identical melodically—meaning there is a lot of repetition within this musical composition. However, each four-note sequence features a building, harmonic contrast: each line adding more and more instrumental voices. To some extent, the visual accompaniment matches the harmonic development: more and more people are present in the shots as more and more instruments are added to the musical arrangement. There is also repetition in visual transitions between video clips: they are exclusively cross-faded, with one contrasting variation at forty seconds in when the video clip fades to black, then fades from black to the first close-up of Obama in the oval-ish office. This difference signals a visual change that is accentuated by the sound of wind chimes, symbolic of the winds of change. Also, a form of aural repetition comes in the timbre of Obama's voice: There is no noticeable difference in the timbre of his voice during the first forty seconds of voice-over (non-diegetic) narration and the timbre of his voice as we watch him narrate the remainder of the introduction (diegetic).

While there is no contrast in timbre, there is considerable contrast in the tempo or pulse of Obama's narration. In the first forty seconds, Obama recites thirty-three words. In the ensuing seven seconds, he recites twenty-seven words. This contrast in pulse corresponds to the relationship the narration has with the music. In the first forty seconds, the narration is loosely aligned with the melody, and this *alignment* makes the narration obedient to the music. In the first sequence, each image gets two notes. In the second sequence, three images correspond to the four notes of the melody. In the third, an image appears for each of the four notes of the melody. Obama's voice-over (non-diegetic) narration does not begin until halfway through the second melodic sequence—after six notes have sounded. The first forty seconds behaves much like a music video, and Obama's narration synchronizes with the melody. However, after the transition to Obama's on camera (diegetic) narration, his vocal delivery no longer synchronizes in the same way. The shift now is to a conversational pace, to match Obama's new role as an on-camera speaker. Importantly, the music is no longer leading the narration. The music now assumes a support role—as it should—because this text is designed to get the speaker elected to the office of President of the United States of America. That guy in that oval-ish office should be in charge—not the French horns.

Not only is Obama's role different, there is no longer competing visual information. A clear contrast between the first forty seconds and the remainder of the introduction is that the first forty seconds employs ten visual clips. The remainder employs two. In the first forty seconds, the clips provide a loose form of evidence for the things mentioned in the narrative. In the remainder of the introduction, Obama himself is the evidence. In fact, the nearly one-minute long final shot of the introduction is an *ethos*-building shot: it shows Obama speaking without cuts—in one take. This shot aims to ameliorate the sense of construction in the text, even though this introduction, like the rest of the film, is painstakingly constructed. Even though Obama himself did not direct this work, we get the impression that this is his work of twenty-first century writing as his steady and present voice moves seamlessly between its on camera and off camera roles.

Proximity, according to Williams, allows separate things to be considered as similar due to close grouping. The first forty seconds clearly behave differently from the remainder of the introduction, and while the music contains the entire introduction, Obama's interaction with the music and his shifting role as voice-over narrator and on camera narrator distinguishes two distinct sections of the introduction.

Now, let me cheat a bit and make a claim about the introduction based upon my observations from the entire text. The musical theme of the introduction sets the tenor for associations that we will make about Obama throughout the text. His, especially when he is in a formal speaking role, is a classical music soundtrack. This clearly contrasts with the music of the Americans who appear in the vignettes, who most often are associated with guitars. When I show this work in class, I ask my students, once they have identified the French horns of the opening moments, "Who plays French horns? Anyone in class? Does anyone in class have a French horn in her dorm room? Does anyone you know?" Most often, no one in class plays the French horn or knows anyone who does. I have yet to meet a college student who owns a French horn. I ask, "Do people teach themselves to play the French horn, or does playing the French horn usually entail some type of formal training? What associations do we have for horn music such as this?" My students usually associate French horns with formal musical education and often cite "Taps" as a military application for horn music. These associations are all rhetorically consistent and valuable for the overall rhetorical mission of this introduction.

I then ask my students if any of them or any of their roommates play the guitar. "How many of you actually own a guitar?" Usually a handful of my students own a guitar and nearly everyone in class has a close friend who plays guitar. Next I ask questions such as "How many of you guitar players are formally trained?" and "How many are self-taught?" and "What associations do we have for guitar music such as this?" My students normally identify guitars, guitar players, and guitar music with informal contexts. They tell me that unlike French horn players, guitar players are likely to *jam*—that is get together with other guitar players and improvise or play music without reading it from sheet music. No one ever makes these claims about classical musicians.

The point here is that the filmmakers have organized this film, in part, around clearly *contrasting* musical sections. Within these sections, the story sequences and all of the dramatic elements they employ share close *proximity* to the style of music—they are grouped to support the rhetorical aims of the subsections and to support the organization of the full text. Obama, as a formal politician, appears in the film to the tune of classical music. Everyday Americans—even when they are speaking with Obama (with his shirtsleeves rolled up)—appear to the tune of guitars. In fact, the elderly gentleman who is one of the main characters of the second vignette actually plays the guitar onscreen. These themes are *repeated* consistently through the text. Of the many things we may associate with French horns and guitars, two seem to surface as most relevant within this composition: French horns are formal and uncommon; guitars are informal and common. Both are critically important in this piece of multidimensional rhetoric because they *align* both temporally and rhetorically with other audio-visual information.

Contrast, Repetition, Alignment, and Proximity: These principles of visual design can help us see and hear how the rhetorical elements of an audio-visual composition participate in the choreography of the overall rhetorical dance of the work. The C.R.A.P. principles can help us not only take apart a work of audio-visual writing but they can help us put it back together again. That is what I mean by reading like a writer. Writerly reading is a form of reading that arrives at an all-there-at-once understanding of audio-visual writing by way of exposing layers of multidimensional rhetoric and establishing how they meld together to make an audio-visual alloy. Learning to read like a writer takes practice; it benefits from making exhaustive inventories of texts because no audio-visual information is placed arbitrarily in an audio-visual work. Learning to read like a writer also benefits from experience with editing, for once you or your students have some practice creating layers and moving bits of information around, you will better be able to identify and inventory the bits of information used by other audio-visual authors.

Because a writer sees and hears writing.

This, in and of itself, is a wonderful skill to develop. However, with this skill, you and your students will enter into a writing dialogue with the audio-visual writers of the audio-visual texts you read. You and your students can then learn directly from those authors, not only about the content of their writing and their ideas but about the craft of their writing—the types of writerly choices they have made and the qualities of the assets they have used. From this dialogue, you may begin to model your own writing moves, ones that benefit from the all-there-at-onceness of the texts (I want to make a movie like *Roger & Me*), and from exposing the layers of multidimensional rhetoric (I want to maintain a non-diegetic presence in my movie—unlike Moore's diegetic and non-diegetic presence in *Roger & Me*).

Because a writer teaches writing.

Why do writing teachers teach grammar? Let's recall, from Chapter Two, Lindemann's recommendations about the association model: "If [. . .] we apply what we know about grammar to helping writers use language, our students will become more proficient in negotiating increasingly complex encounters with language" (4th ed. 85). Now, let's recall Williams's epigraph to this section: "[W]hen you can recognize and *name the contrasts*, you have power over them—you can then get to the root of the conflicting problem faster and find more interesting solutions" (145). Williams tells us that by breaking apart the all-there-at-onceness of complex texts, and by naming those components and determining their relation to one another, we may direct our attention in productive, writerly ways. This fits perfectly with what we have considered so far—not only from Lindemann, but from Murray, Dewey, and Burke as well. To teach audio-visual writing, we not only need to make audio-visual writing (because a writer teaches writing), we need to have power over the all-there-at-onceness of complex acts and instances of audio-visual writing. That power emerges by way of our ability to break apart the components—to direct our writerly attentions by way of a terminology that identifies and names the relationships within and between the rhetorical elements of a complex piece of audio-visual writing. While it is true that a writer teaches writing, being a writer is only one of the multidimensional layers required of twenty-first century writing teachers. Twenty-first century writing teachers also need to recognize and name the grammatical features of twenty-first century writing in order to have power over those features so that they may help their students set developmental goals, identify and get to the root of grammatical problems, and find more interesting solutions for their works of twenty-first century writing.

Putting This C.R.A.P. to Work: *Pulp Fiction* in Black and White

We began this chapter by looking at and listening to the opening sequences of *Pulp Fiction*, an audio-visual text with a much different rhetorical mission from the Obama infomercial we just reviewed. Let's return to *Pulp Fiction* with our new critical tools to see what we notice in Tarantino's work of fiction—or, to use Nichols's term, his work of *wish fulfillment* (1). Unlike "American Stories, American Solutions," *Pulp Fiction* has no original score, no music written specifically for the soundtrack. All of the music can be loosely categorized as popular music that is both genre- and era-specific to the actions and characters of *Pulp Fiction*. Tarantino has admitted, "One of the things I do when I'm thinking about starting a movie, is, I'll go through my record collection and just start playing songs" (qtd. in Garner 188). I will argue, in my critical analysis, that Tarantino uses the songs in the soundtrack to reflect the power relations among characters along racial lines in various scenes of the film. In essence, Tarantino uses the songs as an aural filter for how we are to interpret each scene featuring music. These songs also signal when we are seeing 1990s neuvo- blaxploitation and when we are seeing 1990s neuvo-spaghetti Western in Tarantino's hybrid film. However, the point in discussing this critical analysis, here, is to expose how grammatical analysis—that is, analysis that considers the layers of multidimensional audio-visual rhetoric and the principles of design that integrate them—helps us interpret not only what the text is about but how it may have been made.

Inventory and Analysis. Let's pick up the action in *Pulp Fiction* where we left off at the beginning of this chapter. As Vincent Vega and fellow hit man Jules Winnfield begin to speak, "Jungle Boogie" audibly shifts from non-diegetic music that had been playing during the opening credits to diegetic music that now plays on the radio of the 1970s Chevy Nova in which they are traveling. Jules is the driver in every sense: He controls the car, he controls the action that plays out during the preamble to the hit they are going to make, and he controls the action during the hit itself. Even though the scene opens with Vincent doing most of the talking as he describes some of the little differences he has observed between America and Europe, Jules is clearly in charge of the action. Jules decides when they will enter the room where the hit will occur, Jules initiates all of the gunfire, and Jules ultimately decides when they will leave the scene after the hit. Also, Jules is clearly the local veteran; he's from Inglewood whereas Vincent has been working, albeit for the same boss, in Amsterdam for the past three years. He tells Vincent some insider gossip about a fellow thug who was reportedly thrown from a fourth-floor balcony for giving their boss's wife a foot massage.

Tarantino's choice of music prepares us for this power structure. The music plays only until they leave the car. There is no music until the action changes venues. Tarantino uses "Jungle Boogie" to set the scene. Both visually and aurally, Tarantino creates an allusion to the blaxploitation films of the early 1970s with a powerful, smooth, and handsome black male character in control of the crime scene. Once the scene is set, Tarantino seemingly has no further use for a musical layer of the soundtrack until the next power relationship is encountered. He certainly does not use music, as film critic Ken Garner suggests, simply to amplify the mood of the scene, "a musical equivalent of visual action" (198), because as the tension of the sequence mounts and Jules recites his biblical prelude to assassination, Tarantino chooses to use no musical accompaniment. Tarantino's musical choices do correspond to the visual action, but visual action is obviously not the only criteria driving Tarantino to employ music in his scenes; he is appealing to more than *pathos* with his musical choices, as we hear in the audio-wipe during the credits. "Jungle Boogie" is not used primarily as a mood enhancer; it is used primarily as a scene setter. Tarantino's use of "Jungle Boogie" does not appeal primarily to *pathos*, it appeals primarily to *ethos*. It is theme music for the primary rhetorical agent of the scene. In other words, Tarantino's music choice provides the Burkean *attitude* through which we are to interpret the scene, its actions, and the means and purposes of its agents. All things considered, "Jungle Boogie" is Jules's music.

As we fade to black from the hit, we open to a new sequence with a new power relationship between an aging white boxer, Butch Coolidge (Bruce Willis), and black mob boss Marsellus Wallace (Ving Rhames). Wallace, boss of Jules and Vincent, is paying Butch to take a dive in the fifth round of an upcoming fight. Wallace is clearly in charge. The scene opens with a relatively fixed camera position, roughly from Wallace's point-of-view, focused on Butch's face. They sit in an empty barroom with red décor and dim lighting. For this scene, Tarantino selects Al Green's 1971 hit "Let's Stay Together" as the attitude filter for the scene—more blaxploitation. In fact, the song plays during the title screen for the new scene, before the scene actually opens, then it continues to play throughout all of the action at this location—though the music does not always appear to be diegetic, i.e., emanating from a jukebox or stereo in the bar. Throughout the action in the barroom, the music sounds like non-diegetic soundtrack—an aural signal that this is Tarantino's musical commentary on the scene. However, when Vincent and Jules arrive at the bar to see Wallace, we don't hear the music for a few moments while they are obviously outside of the bar. Only when the door is opened and they begin to enter the bar do we hear the song continue to play, as though the music is emanating from the barroom. However, once we all are inside of the bar, the music, again, seems to come from outside of the film world. With this bit of aural trickery/acoustic filtering, Tarantino alerts us to the scenic nature of the music and also to his own presence as musical mix master. Surely, Tarantino, as director and audio-visual author, must be the wizard behind this aural curtain; he apparently wants us to associate the music with the location and the scene, but lets us hear that he, not the characters in the scene, has chosen the music. Having said that, the music does fit the scene as well. In other words, we're not surprised when the music seems to be diegetic—coming from the club. Al Green's voice fits the scene; however, the ways that we are asked to hear Al Green's voice—shifting from diegetic to non-diegetic—signal Tarantino's voice. Consequently, we can hear the music not only as a characteristic of scene setting but also as authorial commentary on the scene, and in this instance, the music appears to identify the power relations within the scene. This is Marsellus Wallace's territory and he is clearly in control. Wallace conducts the meetings. Here is where he holds court. Because the music lasts throughout the entire scene, we can infer that Tarantino uses the song to color both the location and the action, even as the focus of the action moves away from Wallace to an altercation between Butch and Vincent, the two white characters of the scene who are clearly *owned* by Wallace. In fact, at different points in this scene Wallace refers both to Butch and to Vincent as "*my* nigger."

The next scene opens in the home of Lance (Eric Stoltz). Vincent has come here to buy some heroin from Lance. All of the characters in this scene are white. Suddenly, Tarantino shifts back to surf music: first "Bustin' Surfboards" (1962) by The Tornadoes, then "Bullwinkle Part II" (1963) by The Centurians. We have not heard surf music since the segue between the opening heist by Pumpkin and Honey Bunny (both white) and the opening credits. Now surf music returns at the scene of more crime committed by white people with no direct ties to—in other words, not owned by—Marsellus Wallace. Pumpkin and Honey Bunny are *not* Wallace's *niggers*. Tarantino has drawn a color line that extends from the visual world to the aural world. 1970s soul and funk is his music for black crime with Marsellus Wallace at its epicenter; 1960s surf music is his choice for unaffiliated white crime. In each of the situations, the music matches the key power players in the scenes. In this scene featuring the heroin deal, the key power players are Lance and Vincent. Lance makes the black/white distinction all too clear in the dialogue. When Vincent questions the quality of Lance's heroin, Lance responds, "Am I a nigger? Are we in Inglewood? No. You're in my home. Now, white people who know the difference between good shit and bad shit—this is the house they come to." Vincent is no longer with Jules, a resident of Inglewood, in the home of black crime; he is now with Lance in the home of suburban white crime. Tarantino's choice of music appropriately signals this distinct *contrast* as well. "Bustin' Surfboards" lasts only throughout the drug deal; Vincent and Lance continue to converse without background music until Vincent prepares to shoot up. As Vincent shoots up and subsequently drives to meet Wallace's wife Mia (Uma Thurman), we hear The Centurians's song. While Vincent is officially working for Wallace as he drives to pick up Mia, his heroin experience is apparently off the clock since Vincent goes through Lance for his heroin and does not get it through Wallace's organization. Tarantino's choice of music signals his bifurcated, biracial criminal allegiances appropriately.

When Vincent arrives at the home of Mrs. Mia Wallace he enters to Dusty Springfield's "Son of a Preacher Man" (1969). Springfield, a soul singer from England, had been referred to variously as the White Negress or the White Queen of Soul. This song, in fact, had been recorded by the famous production team of Tom Dowd, Jerry Wexler, and Arif Mardin (three white men) who had produced the otherwise unqualified Queen of Soul, Aretha Franklin's, breakthrough efforts in soul music at Atlantic Records a few years earlier. Springfield had moved from England to America to become a white woman making black music (VH-1). While audience members may not know all of this information, it is not trivial. The music sounds like music that thus far would signal a scene determined by Wallace's power—it takes place in his home and the action transpires between two white characters he *owns*: Vincent and his wife (the recipient of the foot massage in the pre-hit dialogue of Jules and Vincent). However, this black-sounding music is made, at least in part, by white people. As such, it performs an aural slight of hand: a deception. Tarantino's music choice makes perfect sense in this scene. Mia is a white woman living in a powerful

black man's world; she is a white negress, or in terms more appropriate
to the twenty-first century, a white African-American. Vincent is paying this visit to escort Mia to dinner at the request of Wallace while
he is away on business. Vincent is now back on the clock. Mia is in
control for the evening by virtue of her relation to Vincent's boss. Vincent's job is to entertain Mia, do her bidding, and keep her out of trouble—whatever that may mean in the complicated *ethos* of organized
crime. The music, according to my argument thus far, should reflect
her position of *relative* power in the scene, and it does. Also, this music
is diegetic; the scene ends with Mia lifting the needle from the record
and announcing, "Let's go." Mia has obviously selected and played this
music, and as Garner reminds us, this constitutes "a performative act
of display of identity" (190). Tarantino allows Mia to tell Vincent and
us exactly who we should think she is: Wallace's nigger.

1. Synthesis: The C.R.A.P. that Puts it Back Together

Tarantino uses his soundtrack to promote an *ethos* for making meaning in his film. Tarantino uses music to comment on the action of
the film, to spotlight his attitude toward the scene, and to help his
audience track the development of this story told out of sequence. As
such, it is an indicator of *his ethos* as much as an indicator of *the ethos*
of characters within the scenes. Music is a road map for Tarantino's
audience to track who is in charge, and by what authority, in the scenes
of his film. The analysis I have forwarded is possible only when we attend to the entire framework of interpretation by which we may judge
the musical soundtrack. For instance, my analysis of Tarantino's use
of "Son of a Preacher Man" makes use of attributive categories beyond
the piece of music itself to the performing artist, the music genre, the
production team, and at least one other artist associated with that production team: Aretha Franklin. It is here that I am able to establish a
consistent use of music throughout the film. That consistency emerges
through the grammar of the C.R.A.P. principles. *Contrast* allows us
to determine the distinct differences between the musical genres (and
their associative social properties) we have identified above—funk/
soul and surf music—and the contexts in which those contrasting
genres surface. *Repetition* enables us to establish patterns of consistency that emerge from not only the repetitions of the two genres we
are discussing but also the scene-setting power that the musical genres
have when we recognize how the music directs the audience's attitude

toward the scenes that feature music. *Alignment* groups those scenes as similar types of scenes with similar types of actions and primary agents. In a text that unfolds in the temporal space of film, not the two-dimensional space of a page, scenes are aligned, in part, by way of the qualitative filter of musical genre. Finally, *Proximity* helps us filter the associative properties to determine the most relevant characteristics of the specific agents and actions grouped in individual scenes. Furthermore, we can differentiate agents and actions that are arranged with a low degree of proximity.

Possibly even more importantly, Contrast, Repetition, Alignment, and Proximity can help us recognize an important characteristic of popular genres of music and, especially, popular pieces of music: its audience-gathering powers. Music, as used in both of the movies we've discussed above, helps draw stark contrasts between people—both persons and groups of people. Repetition of music—of genres, of specific songs and artists, of types of instrumentation and arrangement—inscribes the collective memories of those who encounter music, forming much of the mnemonic glue that makes music so associatively sticky. Music aligns people according to the scenes of their lives—of our lives—that have been defined in part by the music we encounter and choose to play. Music brings us into proximity with each other, uniting us according to musical genre; identifying us by way of racial, socioeconomic, and generational affiliation; and synchronizing our central nervous systems—making us tap our toes and bob our heads to a common beat.

Music is powerfully associative. Consequently, music, especially popular music, provides many vehicles for metaphoric reasoning: psychologically interactive nonsequential reasoning. Because popular music facilitates so many possibilities for attributive properties, an author may use it to enable the audience to look to the topic of the scene to find the most appropriate vehicles to use to make metaphoric meaning from the music. Tarantino uses a sequential text, a film, to promote nonsequential meaning making. He does so by way of metaphor and by way of his impious narrative structure; his sequential text is temporally structured nonsequentially. This narrative structure asks the audience to get involved with making sense of the action, much as the metaphoric use of music throughout the film asks the audience to get involved with assigning associative categories fitted to the containing scene. Tarantino's musical selections act as a theatrical spotlight that identifies the main character of each scene.

Tarantino also plays upon piety and impiety with the musical soundtrack he has compiled. On the whole, Tarantino's soundtrack is impious in terms of the popular music of 1994, the year his film was released. Tarantino made use of several genres of music that were truly alternatives to the popular music genres in vogue in America in 1994; one of the most popular of those, ironically, was a genre called "alternative" music. Tarantino's alternative-to-alternative (and rap/hip-hop) soundtrack was able to exploit the then-current popular music genre's title, *alternative*, without licensing many of the associative properties of the then-current popular music. Consequently, Tarantino is able to ask us to apply attributive categories that we *remember* to then-current topics. Those audience members not old enough to remember the eras evoked will attribute categories they have been told about those eras, i.e., what others remember of those eras. In this way, Tarantino sidesteps racism in 1994 by licensing racial stereotypes from more (or differently) overtly racist eras. Tarantino asks us to consider African-American criminals in 1994 by way of black music, and much of what we may associate with it, from the 1970s. Tarantino also asks us to consider white, American, suburban criminals by way of popular music made before Americans began openly to embrace black musical artists—back when black music was whitewashed into musical subgenres like rockabilly and surf music, back when black musical artists could headline a marquee but had to enter the venue through the service doors.

Ultimately, Tarantino's point about black and white crime is not important to our discussion. That is, it is unimportant if we agree that his use of music is effective or if his sorting of crime along racial lines is appropriate or even tolerable. What is important for our concerns is to begin to hear his writerly choices—to begin to see and hear the regular patterns of his musical choices so that we may learn from them. However, we do need to consider his point in order to determine how he goes about making it. That *is* our business: determining authorial moves and revealing authorial choices. It is our business to read like a writer. Tarantino uses his musical soundtrack, both the presence and absence of popular music, to focus the ways his audience may make meaning from his film, to filter for the attitudes they need to assume to regard each scene appropriately.

Again, I have no idea if Tarantino, or anyone else for that matter, actually made the choices I have identified. As with my writerly analysis of "Little Wing" in Chapter Two, my aim here is not to establish historical record but to abduce some of the audio-visual writerly choices made by Tarantino. However, his choices are regular and systematic. Because they help us make meaning, they help us identify with the action in specific ways. These choices are rhetorical and help illustrate the many rhetorical possibilities that music can lend to an act of communication. Audio-visual composers can exploit the many attributive properties of music, both original and found musical items, to provide vehicles for focusing the metaphorical meanings of their topics.

Analyzing such audio-visual multidimensional rhetoric is arduous work. There are so many associations to explore. However, I hope this discussion suggests that writers—and writing teachers—do not have to look too far outside of rhetorical theory to be able to discuss the rhetorical properties of music in audio-visual compositions. In my discussions of *American Stories, American Solutions* and *Pulp Fiction* I used no music-specific language apart from attempting to identify some of the instruments we hear in the former movie. My point is that we don't have to be musicians to analyze critically and employ music in our rhetorical works—that is, to write *with* music. We just have to be rhetoricians—and designers. We just need to listen to the grammar of multidimensional audio-visual design.

We need to be writers, and we need to name the choices available to writers in order to have power over them. Otherwise, we will be stuck seeing and hearing the multidimensional rhetoric of twenty-first century writing as being all there at once—not as layers of discrete rhetorical elements.

We need to ask our students to question the many ways that music speaks to them, or fails to do so. Asking them to apply critical examination to the rhetorical appeals being made by music in a variety of contexts can help them see and hear music and other art forms as pieces of rhetoric—not simply as pieces of art that are all there at once. When they begin to see and hear the layers of rhetorical possibilities in music and other art forms, they can make informed decisions about how and when to employ them in their own symbolic acts of audio-visual writing.

4 Mics: What Do Writing Teachers Need to Know about Audio?

It is to the invisible that listening may attend.

—Don Ihde

As we move into a pedagogy for audio-visual writing, the information that will likely *sound* most familiar is that of spoken language. Teachers of academic and inquiry-based writing will recognize the interview situation as the kind of scene of inquiry that mediates both to traditional writing and to audio-visual writing, and since language in these types of situations is among the most valuable data, we will start with the audio portion of audio-visual writing. In fact, I'll go so far as to say that you can make a good movie with bad video; however, bad audio is a project killer. Let me explain.

Of all the anecdotes I employ regularly, I remember none more vividly than this incident. I was teaching in the Program in Writing and Rhetoric (PWR) at Stanford University. Andrea Lunsford was the director of PWR, and she continues to be one of the most impressive people I have ever had the honor to be around. Todd Taylor and I were, at the time, finishing the editing phases of *Remembering Composition* and realized that we really wanted to add a discussion with Andrea, especially since we now had access to interviewing her. So I asked, and she graciously agreed to the interview. I scouted the location, prepared my questions, and set up the shoot. The outdoor location I had chosen looked great; however, it was near an occasionally noisy, high-foot-traffic area. I needed to be able to hear what Andrea would say, but did not want to hear what those passersby would say. The video camera I had access to that day had built-in microphones (mics); however, those mics are the type that pick up sound from all around the camera. In other words, they would hear both Andrea and the passersby. Fortunately, that video camera had a jack for an external microphone. I chose to use a lavalier microphone, one that I could get as close to Andrea as possible (by pinning it to her lapel) and as far away from the foot-traffic noise as possible. Unfortunately, the video camera did not have a jack for headphones, so I had no access to hear what the microphone was hearing. I simply had to trust that it was doing what it was supposed to be doing. Unfortunately, that's exactly what it did for the duration of Andrea's brilliant performance during the interview session.

I took my tape filled with rhet-comp cinematic gold to the editing station. The footage looked great. The location was stunning, as was Andrea, of course. She wore a dark patterned dress and a long necklace of light-colored beads—beads that moved slightly in response to movements of her embodied, rhetorical delivery. She was great, and so was the microphone; it resisted the noise of passersby and reproduced the sound to which it was closest. Unfortunately, that was the sound of those lovely beads striking the head of the microphone—continually—throughout the entire interview. The result sounded like I had asked Andrea to sit in the back of a pickup truck and speak while someone shoveled gravel onto her. The videotaped session was useless—killed by bad audio. What's worse is I knew better. I wanted someone to shovel gravel onto me.

What I did was swallow my pride and ask Andrea if I could interview her a second time, this time *sans* necklace. She agreed, thus saving my life, and delivering the best lesson of my moviemaking life. I say "best" because this lesson had a happy ending: we got some great footage for our movie. Here is the lesson: bad audio is a project killer—especially in projects that value audio-based data. Emerging from this lesson is the following rule:

Lesson #1: Always use headphones when videotaping interviews.

The camera's view screen will allow you to see, more or less, what the camera is capturing. You'll see if the shot is out of frame, if the lighting is bad, or if there are other distracting actions or items in the shot. However, without headphones—and a video camera that has a jack for plugging in headphones—you cannot know what audio is going onto the tape. So we can articulate a second lesson emerging from the one above:

Lesson #2: Always choose a video camera with a headphone jack when videotaping interviews.

You can think of lessons 1 and 2 as the chicken and the egg from the proverbial sequential question: you can choose to focus first on the headphones and then on the camera, or the camera first and then the headphones, but either perspective will yield a listening-first perspective, and either perspective prioritizes the audio in audio-visual writing and audio-visual rhetoric.

In this chapter we will think carefully about the rhetorical information of listening situations. We will then pay careful attention to means for listening in listening situations: (1) the ears of the listening system: the microphones; (2) the memory or destination of the listening system—the video camera, audio recording device, computer, or mixing console—and the points of connection in between; and (3) the mind of the listening system—how to choose listening systems that will help you hear what you need to in a variety of listening situations.

PART ONE: MICROPHONES

Microphones are the ears of a listening system, and like ears, microphones don't pay attention, they simply hear according to the way they were made. Since microphones and ears don't pay attention to what they hear (or will hear), you must. Words are no more precious to a microphone than the noise of a fan. That said, some mics are designed to hear the sounds made by human voices better than they hear sounds made by mechanical fans, and vice versa. We will begin this section by asking, What does your audio-visual text need to do? Answering that question will lead to the assessment of what kinds of information (data) your project will value. From there we can get to the two questions that will control our discussion here: (1) What do you want/need to hear? and (2) What do you NOT want/need to hear?

1) Microphones for What?

Listening Situation #1—Outdoor Interviews. Let's return for a moment to my interview with Andrea Lunsford. I knew going in that I needed to hear Andrea's voice. I also knew, because Todd and I had already edited the rest of the footage, that I did not need to hear the voice of the interviewer. I knew, too, that I did not want the tape to hear the sounds of nearby passersby: their voices and footsteps as they traveled along the polished stone walkway under a stone archway. I also knew that minor, incidental sounds from the immediate environment—the sounds of birds or light wind, or the swishing of leaves in the light wind—would be OK and possibly even desirable. That knowledge was gained by paying careful attention to the listening situation, by listening carefully to the variety of desirable and undesirable sound sources in the sound scene. With this knowledge I was able to make the determination of what kind of microphones to use. In the following section, we will pay attention to the microphones themselves, but first, let's imagine a few more listening situations.

Listening Situation #2—Classroom Presentations. Imagine that we are charged with making an audio-visual text that reproduces a student presentation in a classroom. The purpose of the text will be to facilitate a draft workshop of the presentation for the presenters. Knowing what the text needs to do, we can now make some decisions about what kind of audio data we will value: the sound of the speakers' voices (so we can hear the content of the talk), the sound of the room (so we can hear what it may sound like from an audience member's point of audition), the sound of any audio-visual presentation media, and the sounds of audience questions and feedback. Primarily, we will value the sounds of speaking voices. Knowing this, we can now ask what we do and don't need to hear, specifically. When listening for content, we need to hear the speakers' voices carefully, i.e., the sound of the speakers' voices to the exclusion of other sounds. When listening for performance, we may also need to hear the sounds of the room that compete for the listening attention of the audience. Regardless, we probably do *not* want to hear the sounds of shuffling feet or the cooling fans of computers in the classroom as these sounds will probably not contribute to improving the draft workshop; rather, they will most likely simply add noise to the mix. This suggests that we may want to hear a varying balance of the speakers' voices and the audience's voices to the exclusion of the other types of sounds present in the room.

Listening Situation #3—Crowded-Room Interviews. Let's say we are now charged with collecting audio-video footage at a party following an award presentation. The purpose of the text we produce will be to recreate the energy and events of the party and to share the impromptu comments of a few of the partygoers interviewed during the party. Consequently, at any given point in time, we will value any or all of the sounds of the party: the clanking of dishes and glasses, the sounds of people milling around, the sound of the music played during the party, the sounds of clapping and cheering, and the sounds of voices that may pop up or call out from anywhere at any time. However, in the moments when we are getting the interview comments of party-goers, we will want to feature the sounds of the speakers' voices over the sounds of the party, which could likely be louder overall than the sound of the speakers' voices.

Listening Situation #4—Voice-Over Narration. OK, this could go on forever, but let's choose one final listening situation for now. In this one, our purpose is to produce the scripted voice-over narration for a documentary about biofuels. Let's also say that the movie, at this point, is edited. All that remains is for us to produce the narrative voice. This suggests that the sound data we will value will be the sound of the narrator's voice to the complete exclusion of all other sounds. In other words, because the narrator's voice is disembodied in the movie, we do not want any aural evidence of the narrator's embodied experience of narrating. Hers should be the voice from nowhere: no room noises, no squeaking chairs, no other incidental speaking noises. We will value only the vocal content and performance of the narrator. Also, since the purpose of the movie is to offer a sober presentation of information about a relatively sober subject, we will value a vocal performance that is, well, sober: steady, present, and easy to understand. Since we will hear a lot of this voice, it should also accentuate the attractive qualities of the speaker's voice. The performance will need to be relatively quiet, yet dynamic. We will want to give listeners the impression that the narrator's voice is the appropriate container for the information that it conveys.

2) What Microphones?

Before we start matching microphones to the four listening situations above, let's first review some of our general choices for types of microphones. Let me say here that I will not discuss the use of specific microphones, for example a Shure SM58 or an AKG C414B. Microphones, like all other technological products, come and go far more quickly than books such as this one. (That said, the two I just mentioned are still going strong since the middle of the twentieth century!) The basic variety of microphones is just that: basic. Consequently, the types of microphones have been relatively stable. Our conversation will deal with those basic types and their primary functions.

Types of Mics: Dynamic and Condenser

There are two basic types of microphones: dynamic and condenser. For our purposes, we will limit our discussion to just a few of the qualities that distinguish these two types: Power, Sensitivity and Clarity, and Quality of Reproduction.

Power. Dynamic microphones generate their own electrical current by virtue of their design and, consequently, do not need external power from a battery or other power source to operate. Condenser microphones do not generate their own electrical current and consequently do need to be powered by a battery or some other external power supply.

Sensitivity and Clarity. While dynamic microphones are relatively rugged, they are also less sensitive than condenser microphones. This should not be translated as a blanket endorsement of condenser mics. As we will see in our discussion of Fair Use in Chapter Six, it's not the texts themselves that are deemed to be Fair or not, it's the *use* of the texts that is judged. The same text that was created and used fairly in a college class may be used unfairly when posted to YouTube. Similarly, it's not the microphones that are superior or inferior relative to one another, it's the uses to which they are put that helps us make these decisions. Consequently, we will discuss the need for access to both types of microphones. The sensitivity and clarity associated with condenser microphones will make them good choices for many of the applications we will discuss. However, their sensitivity can become a liability in a situation where they are being handled frequently or roughly. Thus dynamic mics can offer superior performance for hand-held applications.

Quality of Reproduction. While dynamic microphones reproduce sounds less faithfully or accurately than condenser microphones, they are often thought to reproduce sounds, especially vocal sounds, more flatteringly than condenser microphones. Consequently, a special type of condenser microphone exists to retain the sensitivity of the condenser while boosting the flattering qualities of the vocal sounds they reproduce. These large-diaphragm condenser mics are wonderful for capturing voices in highly controlled listening situations; ergo, they are used most often in recording studios, where they can be isolated from other sounds and movements that can otherwise make their sensitivity a liability. As of 2010 or so, large-diaphragm condenser mics have begun to get serious competition from a new breed of vocal mics that plug directly into computers via the USB port. These microphones are vast improvements over the microphones built into most computers, and many do a fine job of approximating the sound of large-diaphragm condenser microphones.

Types of Attention

Let me repeat something I think is really important: Microphones can't pay attention, so you have to. Of course, like most maxims, this is only partially true. The second half of the expression—so you have to—is spot on. The first half is more of a half-truth, since microphones *can* pay attention. In fact, they are engineered to pay attention in very specific ways; however, they cannot *shift* attention, at least not on their own—and that's where you come in. For the most part, microphones pay attention to two important variables: *pickup pattern* and *frequency response.*

Patterns of Attention: Pickup Patterns

Pickup Patterns focus the listening attention of microphones. In essence, they focus attention in the way that other types of filters focus attention: by removing unwanted information. In a crowded restaurant, if the person across the table is speaking, you may turn your head and cup your hand to your ear to help hear what your companion is saying and to help eliminate unwanted noise. This act points your ear more directly at the speaker and your hand further directs the wanted sounds to your ear canal, but the v-shape of your hand and your head also blocks unwanted sounds from competing with the desired sounds. Microphones have similar filters, or not. Those without listening source filters are called *omnidirectional* microphones (they accept sound from all directions); those with source filters are called *directional.* Both dynamic and condenser microphones come in these varieties. While it may seem as though omnidirectional microphones are unfiltered, I'll ask that we think of them as microphones that listen for something specific as opposed to microphones that simply listen to everything. In texts that feature sound, silence is a sound; silence is chosen, consequently it marks a presence (of silence) as much as it marks an absence (of sound). Similarly, omnidirectional microphones are marked by a presence (of sound from all directions) as much as they are marked by an absence (of source filter).

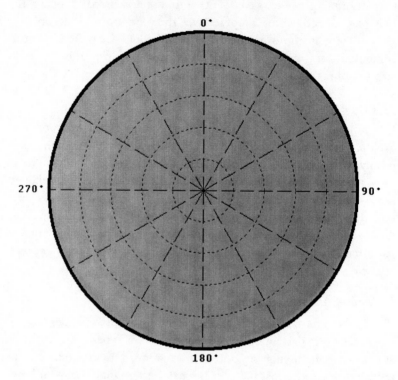

Fig. 4.1: The Omnidirectional Pattern accepts sound from all directions around the perimeter of the microphone.

Our third and fourth lessons are these:

Lesson #3: Microphones can't pay (shift) attention, so you have to.

Lesson #4: Always choose the pickup pattern of your microphones.

If you don't make these choices intentionally, you may unintentionally filter away the sound information you want or lose the information you want in a clutter of unwanted sounds. Sometimes you will want to collect sounds from all directions. Most consumer video cameras feature omnidirectional microphones because they are most often used in situations where wanted sounds may come from any direction, especially from behind the camera (the voice of the camera operator, e.g., Mom or Dad) and directly in front of the camera (the subject being filmed, e.g., the five-year-old birthday girl), but also from the sides of the camera (e.g., other, off camera partygoers in the room). In this instance, we probably *want* all of these sounds. Using the camera's built-in omnidirectional microphones would be a good *choice* in this instance.

However, sometimes you will *not* want all of that sound, because some of it will be *noise* that prevents you from hearing the *sounds* you want. Choosing the proper directional microphone will help you focus the listening attention of your audio-visual text. Directional microphones focus attention along a spectrum of one or two directions. In Fig. 4.2, the *cardioid* pattern is a type of unidirectional listening attention pattern because it accepts sound from only one side of the microphone: the front. The cardioid pattern, however, accepts sound not only from the spot directly in front of the microphone but also from a wide angle in front of the microphone.

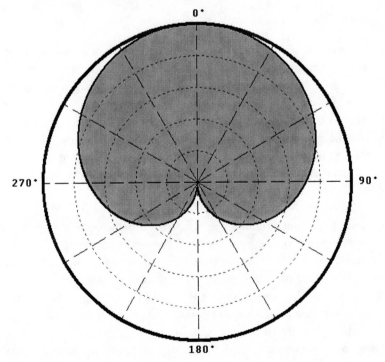

Fig. 4.2: The Cardioid Pattern: Heart-shaped, uni-directional, rejects sound from directly behind the microphone.

The cardioid pattern can allow two people, very close together, like Paul and George in Fig. 4.3, to share a microphone.

Fig. 4.3: Paul McCartney and George Harrison share a mic in *A Hard Days Night* (1964). © 1964 by Proscenium Films.

However, as you can see, the cardioid pattern of Paul's mic will not accept noise from The Beatles's audience—well, in theory, at least—which is good because all of those people are an awful lot louder than Paul and George. The cardioid pattern is perfect for a situation where the desired sound source is in front of the microphone, where sounds behind the microphone are undesirable, and where the desired sound source is in motion. Paul and George are likely to be dancing around a bit. When it's time to be on mic, they really only have to be in the area of the mic, not at a precise point.

Hypercardioid patterns (Fig. 4.4) are similar to the cardioid; however, they select a much tighter area in front of the microphone (Fig. 4.5). A special version of the hypercardioid pattern is the shotgun microphone, which selects a very tight pattern in front of the mic. Shotgun microphones are often mounted to video cameras for interviews, as they "point" at the same thing as the camera's lens (Fig. 4.6). Shotgun mics are also used on boom poles when the speaker is moving (Fig. 4.7). The tight pattern of a shotgun microphone performs well when trying to isolate wanted sound in a noisy environment and when put-

ting a microphone on or very near the sound source is either undesirable or impossible.

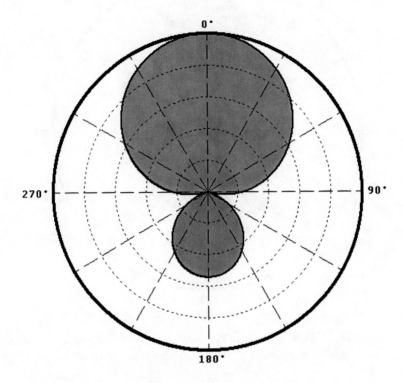

Fig 4.4: The Hypercardioid Pattern focuses on a tight spot in front of the
microphone and often accepts a little signal from behind.

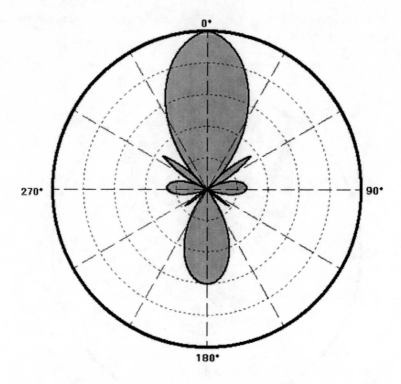

Fig 4.5: The Shotgun Pattern is an exaggerated hypercardiod pattern that accepts sound from an extremely tight spot in front of the microphone.

Fig. 4.6: The author filming an outdoor scene for LiteracyCorps Michigan. The camera has both a wireless microphone receiver and a camera-mounted shotgun mic (with a "muff" style mic cover to reduce wind noise).

Fig. 4.7: In this scene from *The Social Network* the dialogue is being captured by a shotgun mic on a boom pole that is held above the action just out of the camera shot. *The Social Network Behind The Scenes Documentary* © 2010 by Columbia Pictures.

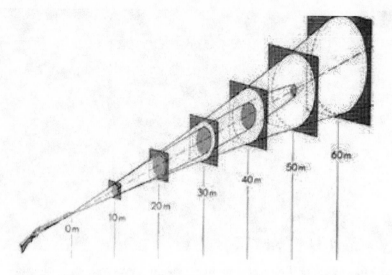

Fig. 4.8: The spray pattern of a shotgun.

For example, if we want to be in motion as we videotape an interview, we may value having as much freedom of movement as possible, so we would likely select a shotgun microphone that allows us to be not only remote from the source but literally unattached (by a microphone cord) to the source as well. The shotgun mic mounted to the camera would allow us to both focus on the sound of the speaker's voice and move with relative freedom.

The shotgun microphone works precisely in the inverse from its namesake, but its overall pattern of performance is similar. A shotgun sprays lead shot from the small opening of the shotgun barrel. As the lead shot is projected toward its target, it spreads out increasingly throughout most of its range of travel. The shotgun microphone doesn't project anything; it accepts sound as though from a funnel. The farther the "target" sound is away from the microphone, the larger the funnel's opening. The closer the "target" sound, the smaller the funnel opening. Actually, it's the generators of the sound, not the microphone, that are most analogous to the shotgun. The sound of a person speaking leaves the relatively narrow opening of the speaker's mouth and progressively spreads out in the form of sound waves as it travels through space. The further away from the receiver, the wider the movement of the sound wave; the closer, the narrower. If there are several sound producers, their sound waves will overlap increasingly through space; consequently, the farther from the receiver—the microphone—the more the overlap. So even though the shotgun mic may be selecting for a narrow area in front of the mic, the closer the mic is to the sound source, the better it will be able to isolate the wanted sounds from the unwanted sounds.

The *bidirectional* microphone (Fig. 4.9) accepts signals from both the front and the back of the microphone. These can be preferable in situations where speakers are facing each other, for example, when they are sitting across from one another at a table. The bidirectional microphone will reject sounds from the sides.

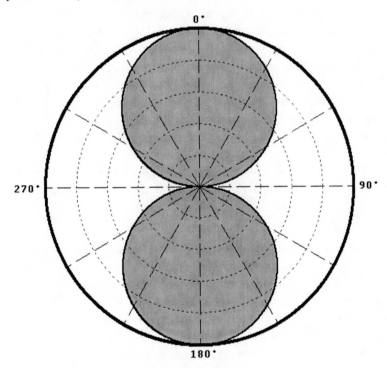

Fig 4.9: The Bidirectional Pattern

Qualities of Attention: Frequency Response and Volume

Microphones also listen for two specific measurements of sound wave movement: *frequency* and *volume*. The measurement of frequency is expressed in terms of Hertz (Hz). The measurement of one Hertz corresponds to a sound wave that travels one cycle per second. The lowest fundamental frequencies from human speaking voices are usually measured from about 80 Hz to 500 Hz (Alten 182). However, the highest harmonic frequencies of human singing voices are usually measured at nearly 16,000 Hz (16 kHz), which just so happens to coincide with the upper limits of hearing for most of us (Alten 5). If the microphone you are using does not reproduce these frequencies, it will not be preferable for capturing the sounds of human speakers. If you intend to capture the sounds of a musical performance, you will likely need to expand that frequency range quite a bit. A common range for musical frequencies is around 20 Hz to about 20 kHz—roughly the full frequency range of people with excellent hearing (Alten; Sonnenschein).

Some microphones are made for special uses. For example, some are designed to detect very low frequencies at very high volume. Volume is measured in terms of *decibels* (dB). The higher the dB number, the louder the signal, and vice versa. Microphones for recording the sounds of bass drums and bass guitars, for example, need to be sensitive down to 20 Hz but durable enough to endure volume levels of 160 dB or so—well above the human threshold of pain (between 120 and 140 dB). The human voice generally produces dB levels between 50 and 110 dB, with normal conversation usually registering around 60 dB when measured at the distance of one meter (Alten; Sonnenschein).

Types of Placement

Above we mentioned placement of the microphone when discussing the large-diaphragm condenser microphone, the shotgun microphone, and the bidirectional microphone. However, placement is a big consideration when selecting a microphone, and some microphones are designed to be placed in specific ways that correspond to specific types of uses. In this section we will discuss five types of mics that are classified according to their placement: shotgun mics, lavalier or lapel mics, handheld mics, studio mics, and wireless mics. Before we do, however, I want to remind us of how we got here in the first place. The point of all of this is not to draw your attention to what microphones are and do, *per se*. The point is to draw your attention to what your audio-visual texts need to do. Depending upon how you answer that, this section is intended to help you select felicitous means for gathering the data you will value most and to minimize the noise of your data—quite literally. With that in mind, let's now return briefly to shotgun mics.

Shotgun Mics. The shotgun microphone is designed to put you in close aural proximity with sound sources to which you are not in close spatial proximity. They attempt to draw a line of audio connection that allows you to listen closely without being located close to the source, and they do so by ignoring as much of the intervening sound information as possible. These generally long, tube-like microphones usually have a series of slits along most of their lengths.

Fig. 4.10: A shotgun microphone.

These *venting* slits are not intended to allow sound to pass *into* the mic's condenser; they are intended to allow sound to pass *through* the mic. The farther the shotgun mic is from the source, the greater the opportunity for other, potentially unwanted sounds to intervene with the signal. Shotgun microphones are most useful for spanning short distances in noisy settings and longer distances in quieter settings. Shotgun mics are often mounted on video cameras to sync the direction of listening with the direction of visual attention. However, shotgun mics may also be attached to a boom pole and placed closer to the sound source than the camera itself. Consequently, the boom pole is designed to be held above or below the speaker, close to her voice, but just out of the camera's view (Fig. 4.7).

Lavalier or Lapel Mics (Fig. 4.11). These condenser mics are intended to be clipped or otherwise fastened to a speaker's shirt or lapel. They generally feature a small microphone head attached to a very slender cable that leads to a larger tube or box designed to hold a battery for powering the condenser and a balanced (three-pin) plug for connecting to a regular microphone cable.

Fig. 4.11: A lavalier microphone.

Both wired and wireless versions of these mics are useful for placing a relatively inconspicuous microphone very close to a speaker's mouth without obstructing the view of the speaker's face. We will discuss wireless mics in more detail shortly. The wired lavaliers physically connect the speaker/wearer to the camera or recorder. When they are secured properly, the microphone moves with the speaker and remains at a relatively constant distance from the speaker's mouth, thereby delivering relatively consistent and strong performance. However, being so close to the source has some drawbacks, as we learned in listening situation #1 above. Because these mics are literally attached to the speakers, the speakers can do lots of things to interfere with the performance of the mics. For example, they can fidget with the wires, creating noise that the sensitive condenser mics detect and amplify. Because they are often so close to the speaker's esophagus, lavalier mics can also pick up gurgling noises produced in the speaker's body—an indelicate but not unlikely occurrence in nervous speakers. A speaker's long hair or loose clothing can brush against the microphone, making a loud scratching noise. Finally, for now, pinning a microphone to someone's chest and/or running a wire through that person's shirt can be invasive, time-consuming, and often incredibly embarrassing. You can probably imagine how uncomfortable you may be staring at someone's chest as you try to decide the best way to pin a microphone to his or her shirt—and then actually pinning the thing on. That said, once placed, the effect can be well worth the effort—but not always.

Handheld Mics (Fig. 4.12). Another way of getting a microphone close to a speaker's mouth is to give that person a handheld microphone.

Fig. 4.12: Handheld microphones.

Because handling is a relatively rough bit of business, handheld microphones are generally the more rugged dynamic mics, not the more sensitive condensers. We are used to seeing news reporters using handheld microphones. They require far less setup than lavalier mics. They may be directional or omnidirectional, so they may be useful for individual speakers or groups of speakers. They are also easy to point or to hand to speakers. However, a drawback of handheld mics is that we are used to *seeing* them. They are conspicuous, and, if you do hand them to speakers, they may do many undesirable things with them: for example, people may handle them so roughly that they produce noise, or tap them, or hold them too far from or too close to their mouths. The latter is more common; people have a tendency to "eat" the mic, and eating the mic can often produce distortion of the signal. Distortion negatively affects the clarity of the voice being recorded. Even without distortion, if several people hold the mic at varying distances from their mouths, you're bound to get varying levels of sound on the tape. This can be avoided by having the interviewer hold the mic at a relatively constant distance from those being interviewed. You may decide to heed a common trope of television journalists: "Never give up the mic."

Studio Mics. Many condenser mics, and especially the highly sensitive large-diaphragm condenser mics, are designed to stay stationary. The slightest movement of these mics will produce audible noise because they are intended to be placed on a stand that is isolated from contact. They often feature a shock mount, a holder that allows the microphone to "float" between two rings separated by elastic bands (Fig. 4.13).

Fig. 4.13: This is a large-diaphragm condenser microphone mounted to a mic stand by way of a suspension mount. Elastic bands allow the mic to "float" in the stand, isolating the mic from minor motion that may otherwise produce audible noise. A symbol of the cardioid pattern is marked on the microphone housing just above the suspension mount.

I refer to these mics as "studio mics" because they are most often used in home or professional recording studios: environments that are quiet, isolated, and stable; environments where the lack of intervening sound can contribute to a clean and uncluttered record of the sounds being captured. Large-diaphragm condenser mics are well adapted to close miking (putting the mic very close to the speaker's mouth) and thus are especially good for capturing richly textured voice-over narration (Fig. 4.14). Consequently, they are often used in conjunction with a windscreen that prevents "plosive" sounds (especially the heavily aspirated plosive "p") from making a popping sound due to the closeness of the strong puff of air that characterizes the sounds.

Fig. 4.14: Eric Bogosian as "Barry" in Talk Radio (1988) shown being close miked by a shock-mounted large-diaphragm mic—this model, made specifically for radio broadcast applications, features an internal "popper stopper."

Wireless Mics. If you are like most Americans, you probably use at least one wireless microphone every day of your life (Fig. 4.15). Cell phones are, in part, wireless mics. However, the wireless phones you use in your home or office are more like the wireless microphones available for recording or "live" sound reinforcement. These microphones are most often from the first three categories mentioned above and are connected to a transmitter and receiver. So just like your home phone, there is a handset (the mic) and a base unit (the receiver), which is then wired into the recording deck, video camera, or mixing board. Wireless microphones allow the person who is miked to move around, in the words of Nigel Tufnel from *Spinal Tap*, "without all the mucky-muck" of intervening cords and cables. Sounds too good to be true, doesn't it? Well, as you know from your use of your wireless telephones, quite often it is.

Fig. 4.15: When using a wireless mic, such as this wireless lavalier setup, always have a wired backup.

I like to think of wireless microphones as convertible sports cars for people who live in Anchorage, Alaska. On a few days each year, man, they sure are sweet. However, on most days, they're way more trouble than they're worth—unless they're second cars. As second cars, man, they sure can be sweet. Here's my rule about wireless microphones:

Lesson #5: When using a wireless microphone, Always have a wired backup.

If you use a wireless microphone as your only microphone (or back it up with another wireless mic), you very well could find yourself in a location that "drops your call," so to speak. In such a "dead zone" you are essentially without a mic if all you have is a wireless mic. Sometimes, even if you do have a few bars of signal, that signal could very well have static noise that renders the signal as useless as the signal I recorded in listening situation #1 above, even without the necklace! Also, wireless mics often operate on specific transmitting "channels"—you can think of these as different programs running simultaneously on the different channels of your television. Imagine the horror if your cable provider suddenly started broadcasting Fox News and MSNBC News on the same channel at the same time! Your cable provider is too smart for that. So let's follow their wisdom and keep our competing simultaneous transmissions on their own channels as well:

Lesson #6: When using more than one wireless mic, be certain each mic transmits and receives on its own unique channel.

Part Two: Destinations and Connections

Now that we know a bit about the ears of our listening system—the microphones themselves—we need to pay attention to what they will plug into—the memory or destination of the listening system and the points of connection in between. Once a microphone converts sound energy into an electrical signal, that signal is no longer audible. Therefore, it needs to travel to a destination where one of two things will usually happen to that signal: (1) it will be turned into a form of data that may be stored and/or edited (either analog or digital data recorded on magnetic tape or some other storage format); or (2) it will be turned back into sound energy by an amplified loudspeaker. Because we are interested in writing with audio, we will concentrate our attention on the former of these possibilities. We need to be able to hear sounds (aural energy), store those sounds (as aural symbols), and manipulate those sounds to express an edited version of the record (in an act of symbolic action). As such, this process of symbolic action is much like the basic moves of traditional writing in which we encounter a thought (mental energy), realize and record that thought by way of words (linguistic symbols), and manipulate those words to express an edited version of the record (in an act of symbolic action). The information from the ears (the microphones) is the aural data in its most raw form, and, like a thought, it is portable—that is, it can be moved from our personal experience of it to someone else—only if we can store it and convert it into something that someone else can recognize as a representation of the original impulse. Thoughts are realized through language, crafted into language products (spoken or written), and shared. Sounds are realized through recording, edited into sound products, and shared. When this process works smoothly, the end product stands a good chance of being successful. When the process breaks down, the end product often bears the scars of botched transformation.

We've looked at ways to pay attention to sounds in the first part of the process—listening—now, let's pay attention to how we store and manipulate what we've heard.

A. Destinations

In audio-visual rhetoric, the destination for the things we hear is almost always one of three kinds of recording device: a video camera, an audio recorder, or a computer. As in the microphone section above, we're not going to discuss specific brands or models of recording equipment here. Instead, we will think about the general similarities and differences of these types of devices. Again, our mission is not to train recording engineers, it is to provide writers with a basic functional literacy of audio recording. Consequently, we will attend to only three concerns of recording destinations for audio-visual writers: tracks, recording levels, and editing.

A1: Tracks. In Chapter Three, we saw how audio tracks participate in the multidimensional rhetoric of audio-visual writing. We will talk about layers of audio tracks again in the "editing" portion of this section, where we will have many more tracks at our disposal; however, we need to attend to the tracks available to us in the first stages of the process as well. Video cameras and basic audio recorders, most often, record two tracks of audio. The tracks are often recorded simultaneously as stereo sound. Stereo sound is controlled on most audio devices by way of the "balance" control, a knob or slider of some sort that allows you to pan between Left and Right (frequently labeled L and R). What the balance control allows us to do is to turn the volume up or down on two audio tracks, the Left and the Right. In true stereo mixes, these two tracks contain different information. Put on a pair of headphones and listen to the title track of The Beatles's *Sergeant Pepper's Lonely Hearts Club Band* album. If you don't have headphones, play the song and move the balance knob from extreme left to extreme right and back again as the music plays. As the music begins, you'll notice that the bass, drums, and rhythm guitar are present in both ears (or on both sides); however, the lead guitar (the melody line) and then Paul's singing are entirely in your right ear. This is an example of stereo separation in audio, and its function is to create the impression of aural space. It does so by playing two separate audio tracks simultaneously. We may easily mistake audio settings marked "left" and "right" as simply controlling the volume to one or the other speaker or earpiece of the stereo system's output. The mistake would be assuming that the underlying information being supplied to each side was the same; however, as we heard in "Sgt. Pepper's," it's not. True stereo sound is comprised of two separate audio tracks. I say "true" here because sometimes the underlying tracks are the same. This confusing distinction will actually give us power when we learn to use it to our advantage, something that is actually common when recording audio with more professional quality video cameras. Furthermore, why am I talking about stereo *output* at a time when I said I'd be talking about audio *input*? Let me explain.

A device that records stereo information will have two independent audio tracks. These audio tracks will usually be synchronized in a way that together they may either record or play; however, one track may not play while the other records. A multitrack recorder is distinguished from a stereo recorder by its ability to do the latter. While the two independent audio tracks of a video camera or audio recorder are usually linked, it is best to remember that they are still independent. That means that each can contain different information, or each can contain the same (or similar) information. Depending on how the recording device allows you to plug microphones or other sources into the device, you may be able to assign what sounds go on what track. Some video cameras, for example, have one mini-stereo jack for audio. That may seem as though you are only able to plug in one microphone (i.e., one plug, one mic), but it actually means you *can* plug in at least two. A mini-stereo plug uses one plug divided into two sections—the tip and the collar—to make two distinct connections (Fig. 4.16).

Fig. 4.16: This is a mini-stereo plug with two individual inputs. Notice the two black insulating bands on the plug. The metal between the two bands carries one signal and the tip carries another signal.

Sometimes a single microphone splits its signal into both of these inputs. Remember my comments above about "true" stereo? A split signal is not true stereo, but it does fill both tracks of the stereo recorder. However, true stereo may be recorded if instead of one mic, we use two mics (or a stereo mic: one with two separate elements), each leading to its own corresponding input. On a video camera, or audio recorder, or computer with a mini-stereo microphone jack, you will need a splitter, similar to the one pictured in Fig. 4.16, to plug two mics into the one jack. However, on a video camera or audio recorder with professional audio inputs, you will likely have two independent input jacks. These inputs are most often three-pin balanced inputs (Fig. 4.17), and they will usually be linked to a switch that gives you some flexibility about how to use them (Fig. 4.18). For example, you can use one mic and have its signal sent to both audio tracks, or you can use two mics and have each sent to its own audio track.

Fig. 4.17: This photo shows one shotgun mic plugged into one of the two professional audio inputs on this video camera.

Fig. 4.18: This photo shows the controls that correspond to the audio inputs. Depending on how these controls are set, the one mic may be sent to one or both audio tracks. These audio controls also allow manual input volume levels to be set and includes a phantom power (+48 volts) switch for each input, as well, for powering condenser mics.

When would the second option be desirable? Imagine you are videotaping two people, Kim and Antawn, having a conversation and you decide to use a lavalier microphone for each speaker. While Antawn speaks, Kim does the kinds of things people often do during conversations: she grunts agreement, coughs occasionally, shifts in her chair, etc. By using separate audio tracks, we can mute the mic of the non-speaker when we are editing, thus cleaning up the overall audio. If we record both mics on the same track, we won't have that option because muting one mic while editing would mute them both. Imagine you are making cookies. If you decide that the recipe calls for too much sugar, you can reduce the amount of sugar without affecting the rest of the ingredients—as long as it's not already in the batter. The best way to keep your options open is to isolate the ingredients as long as possible because once they're mixed, they're mixed. So, if we keep Kim and Antawn on separate tracks, we keep our options open. We will know we're doing this correctly if we can hear each speaker in only one ear of our headphones (e.g., Kim [L] and Antawn [R]).

Here's another, potentially less obvious scenario with equally desirable outcomes. You may remember that I concluded the opening paragraph of this chapter by claiming that bad audio is a project killer. With this in mind, you may imagine that I go out of my way to always have a backup. Consequently, when I interview someone, I most often use two microphones: a lavalier or a close shotgun mic on a boom pole, and a camera-mounted shotgun mic. Why? Well, this gives me both audio backup and audio variety. If the lavalier (my main mic) fails, I have the shotgun to capture the sound as well. I also have two signals of the same event that sound slightly different that I may be able to mix during editing. I also have one mic that resists room noise that I don't want (e.g., my footsteps as I move around with a handheld video camera), and another that will pick up room sounds that I may want (e.g., the questions that I ask or sounds that help me set the scene of the interview, such as traffic noise, birds singing, or machine noises). Having two separate audio inputs allows me to hear the scene in two different ways, to value more than just one audio source without necessarily devaluing either. By paying attention to the options available at the destination—the memory of your listening system—you will be able to make informed decisions about how best to listen. Know your choices.

A Little Bit of Perspective

I think I can hear what you're saying. "So many choices. Too many choices. Please, can't we just keep it simple?" I don't know, can we? Should we? Imagine a word processor that allowed you to type only words that are six letters or less in length. You could do a lot of work and write a lot of texts with such a tool, such as this senten ce, for exampl e (☺). In fact, it'd prbly b gr8 4 txting, IMHO. Of course, this tool for writing would most likely cause you to swear an awful lot more than you would if you had a more robust word processor, which would actually be OK, since most of those words have only four letters. Most basic audio and/or audio-video recorders similarly restrict possibilities about *how* and, consequently, *what* audio or video information you can record. They are designed to make most of the multidimensional rhetorical decisions for you. Sometimes that's pretty sweet. Other times, however, it's really not. What we need to pay attention to at the moment is identifying the kinds of choices that the audio-visual writing tools that we use (1) make for us, (2) allow us to make, and/or (3) demand that we make.

Some video cameras allow us to record audio only with their built-in microphone(s). Others, as we've seen, have jacks that allow us to plug in external mics. Others, like most professional-grade video cameras, don't have mics built in at all. Why? Because the camera manufacturers know that professional or frequent audio-video writers will encounter many different types of listening situations and will want to select microphones appropriate to each situation and purpose. In the following chapter, we will see that professional-grade cameras similarly allow the photographer to choose lenses that best suit the visual situations they encounter. However, this is a good place to assert that I am *not* suggesting that inexpensive consumer-grade video cameras with internal mics are always bad choices any more than I am suggesting that expensive professional-grade video cameras without internal mics are always good choices. What I am suggesting is that we see both of these types of video cameras as choices. That is, it's not that one type of camera is better than the other type, it's that one type of camera is better *for* some things than the other type, and vice versa. In still other words, it's not what these cameras *are* that determines their value, it's what they enable you to *do*, or not.

Just as I prefer to have audio backup, I also prefer to have video backup. The nice thing about video is that it comes with audio—most often, two independent audio tracks. One really great way to get back-up or "b-roll" room sound and backup or "b-roll" video footage is to use a second video camera with internal omnidirectional microphones. This gives me a chance to use both a fixed camera (tripod mounted) and a variety of other visual and audio perspectives that I can work with when I'm editing the footage. An inexpensive consumer-grade camera may, by design, greatly limit my audio-visual rhetorical choices when I use that camera simply by default. However, that same camera can increase my choices when I use it in conjunction with another camera or when I select it as the right camera to do what I need it to do, that is, when I use it by *choice*—not because of what it is but because of what it does.

We will return to this thread of logic and discussion in the final chapter of this book when we discuss designing and expanding institutional infrastructures for teaching audio-visual writing. For now, though, let's move on to the second concern of memory: recording levels.

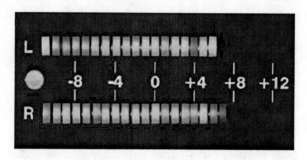

Fig. 4.19: Sound levels at about 75%. These levels are most often indicated with the color green. Red levels indicate "hot" levels that may result in clipping. Notice, too, that the two tracks are registering different levels, indicating "true" stereo.

A2: Recording Levels. Sometimes, too much of a good thing is worse than not enough. When recording digital audio signal, this is most certainly the case. However, too little can be just as bad. The rule for recording levels is analogous to prudent decisions at your favorite buffet: *enough is as good as a feast.* Compared to the other three destinations, managing recording levels is relatively simple. A good average to shoot for will be about 75% of the input-level signal bar (Fig. 4.19). Why? Let's follow Goldilocks's lead and see what happens when recording levels are too hot, too cold, and just right.

Too Hot. Don't panic if your signals occasionally bounce up into the red; however, if they stay there pretty regularly, pull back the levels. Levels in the red are called "hot," and you can think of heat coming not only from the color red but also from the sound that may emerge (Fig. 4.20). When the levels are too high—too hot—the sound becomes distorted and begins to sizzle. When this frying sound happens, there is virtually no way to get rid of it. Recording engineers refer to this type of distortion as "clipping." Clipping, much like the sound of those beads against the microphone in listening situation #1, can be a real scene killer.

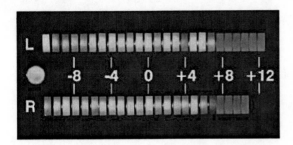

Fig. 4.20: Sound levels at approximately 100%. These levels are most often indicated with the color red, indicating "hot" levels that may result in clipping.

Too Cold. Earlier in this chapter, we discussed the relative nature of silence. Silence is always contextual, it is a marker of contrast, and it is practically never truly silent. Think of some of the silences you have heard: the inside of your car before you start it on a snowy night, your house in the morning before anyone else is awake, your classroom when you ask for a volunteer to turn in the research essay a week early. These scenes all have their own kinds of silence because none of them are truly silent. They are characterized by absences of certain sounds even if other sounds are present. Recording levels that are too cold show poor contrast between the sounds you want to hear and those you don't want to hear. I claimed earlier in this chapter that silence marks a presence (of silence) as much as it marks an absence (of sound). When your levels are really cold, the presence of the sounds of "silence" may even drown out the sounds you want to hear (Fig. 4.21).

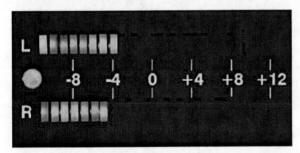

Fig. 4.21: Sound levels at less than 50%. Low recording levels almost always produce noisy audio tracks.

In such cases, silence may sound like a hissing noise, or it may sound like a fan, or a wall clock, or the TV from the apartment next door.

For the most part, you may not even notice these sounds of silence until you try to contextualize your cold-level content with other "just-right" sounds, because, to balance these mismatched signals, you will need to boost the volume of the cold-level content. Thus, with those good sounds come the "bad"—the sounds of silence can become all too present with the general volume boost. If your recording levels are consistently registering below 50%, you will want to raise your input levels.

Lesson #7: Set your recording levels in the green—at around 75%. The levels of the sounds you want should drown out the sounds of silence.

Fig. 4.22: Goldilocks has determined that this porridge is "just right." "Goldilocks and the Three Bears" by Debbie and Friends. YouTube. 2009. http://www.youtube.com/watch?v=UaulRHrJGeU

While too-cold levels are as undesirable as too-hot levels, they are not always as irreparable. The presence of silence often can be, well, silenced, with noise reduction and EQ (equalization—tone control).

The aural presence of clipping is much harder to eliminate than the aural presence of unwanted silence.

Just Right. When recording levels are "just right," Goldilocks can hear all she is supposed to and little to nothing of what she is not. Levels should bounce between 50% and the beginning of the red levels, with levels falling around 75% most of the time. These levels will allow wanted sounds to (1) drown out competing background noise, (2) avoid creating clipping noise, and (3) send Goldilocks on her way to find a comfy chair.

A3: Editing. OK, so let's remember back to our discussion of "tracks" above. I suggested that you think of those stereo tracks on your video camera, possibly labeled L and R, as separate, simultaneously recorded and played tracks. I also asked you to notice that in your headphones the information on the L track (Kim's voice) plays only in the left speaker of your headphones and the signal of the R track (Antawn's voice) plays only in your right ear. You may be saying, however, "I don't want to hear their voices in different ears. I want to hear each of them in both ears." Understandable. That's why your editing software will most likely allow you to assign the stereo balance of that information and all of your other audio tracks during the editing process. What other audio tracks are we talking about? Well, as we saw in Chapter Three, there could be quite a few: among them voice-over narration, music, and audio from other video tracks. To extend our baking metaphor, in order to preserve our aural options, we will want to keep these items as separate as possible, for as long as possible, to give us as much control over the items as possible as we continue to mix them. By keeping them separate, we will be able to mix how we hear them *and* retain the power to unmix or remix them if we don't like what we hear. The moment we start mixing our audio batter, the harder it will become to alter the recipe. Keeping our aural ingredients separate is the power of multitracking.

Let's end this part of the discussion not with a baking metaphor but with a writing analogy. Imagine that during the act of revision your word processor only allowed you to move around entire sentences. You could cut and paste the words only as they were currently mixed. How helpful would that be when trying to work with poorly worded, excessively long, or excessively short sentences? How would you be able to change the wording of a claim to that of a question? How could you take back a point you no longer believed because of what you learned while writing the rest of the work? How could you take risks during drafting that you may not be able to take back during editing?

The variety of audio destinations should participate in a dialogue that informs the audio-visual writer at each stage of the writing process. Any single audio source will proceed through a process of audio-visual writing that may layer it with any number of other audio tracks and ultimately mix that aural potpourri into two stereo tracks or into the multiple channels of surround sound. Knowing these possibilities, these dimensions of audio-visual functional literacy, will inform all of the writer's decisions from collection of data through the completion of final products.

B. Connections

So far we have talked about microphones (the ears of our listening systems) and we have talked about multitrack recording (the memory of our listening systems). Now we need to consider the points in between. How is information carried from the ears to the mind? Tow trucks. Let me explain.

Imagine you live in Michigan where four months of the year (that seem more like eight months of the year while they are in progress) the landscape is covered in ice and snow. Because the roadways are part of said landscape, driving can be especially treacherous during this part of the year. Let's imagine that it's simply your turn to land your car in a ditch after a slide across the terra gelato. Thankfully, your wireless microphone—your cell phone—has good reception and your call for a tow truck goes through successfully. In a matter of moments, a brand new, heavy, powerful tow truck with massive snow tires pulls up alongside your entrenched minivan. Saved! Wait a minute, with all of its potentially productive power, this towing situation lacks a critical component: a chain. If you can't connect the solution to the problem, you have no solution at all. In fact, you have yet another problem. What you need is not a tow truck. What you need is a tow truck capable of connecting to your car. Be careful what you wish for.

Lesson #8: Pay careful attention to your connections! Remember, without the right chains, even the best tow truck will leave you stuck in the ditch.

I have mentioned a few types of connectors in this chapter, for example, three-pin balanced microphone connectors and mini-stereo plugs. These are among the most stable types of connectors; they have been in use for well over fifty years. However, I have no intention of going through a comprehensive list of connections or connectors. Connectors are always specific to the connections being made: *this* microphone and *that* camera; *this* camera and *those* microphones; *this* microphone and *that* computer. You will need to know, at any given moment, that you not only have, for example, a shotgun microphone, a lavalier microphone, and a video camera but that you have a shotgun microphone and a lavalier microphone that will plug into this particular video camera—or that you have the proper adapters to allow them to connect. The point is, without the proper connections, your microphones and your camera or computer will not be able to communicate. They will be fully charged cell phones with no signal. They will be speakers of different languages without a translator. They will be word processors without keyboards. They will be tow trucks without chains, and you will be stuck in an icy ditch on a country road in Michigan in February.

PART THREE: MATCHING LISTENING SYSTEMS TO LISTENING SITUATIONS

But hey, enough of the gloom and doom! Let's move out of Chapter Four by discussing some happier situations. In these, we will make sure that our tow trucks have the proper chains to do the work we need. First, let's assert another global lesson that will govern our discussion in this chapter:

Lesson #9: Your rhetorical purposes should guide your choice of listening systems, not the "quality" of the equipment itself. Pay more attention to what the equipment does than what it is.

Let's return to our four listening situations from the beginning of this chapter: Outdoor Interviews, Classroom Presentations, Crowded-Room Interviews, and Voice-Over Narration.

Listening Situation #1—Outdoor Interviews. Let's recall the parameters of this situation: We are interviewing a single person in an outdoor public setting that is near a relatively busy and noisy walkway with lots of hard surfaces (stone and concrete) and consequently quite a bit of natural reverberation (echo). In this listening situation we will want to reduce all of the unwanted foot-traffic noise and reverberation, so we will want to mic the interviewee as closely as possible with a mic that takes its signal from a tight pattern: either a unidirectional lavalier mic or a shotgun mic. If you remember, I used a single lavalier mic for both interviews because my questions were not going to be present in the final edit. In the first interview, the interviewee's necklace rattled against the lavalier microphone, rendering the audio tracks of the footage useless. In the second interview I asked the interviewee to remove her necklace, which she did, and the audio worked quite well. How could I have avoided having to do the second interview? Well, I could have had the prescience to ask her to remove the necklace in the first interview, or I could have used a second microphone. In other words, I could have used the lavalier plugged into Track One and a shotgun mic plugged into Track Two. Even with the necklace debacle, this option would have allowed me to use the shotgun track, and I would not have had to schedule a second interview. The lesson here is to always have a backup. I didn't have one built into the first interview, so my backup became a second interview. I was lucky to have access to my interviewee; however, this can be a rare luxury. There is an old carpenters' adage that my dad used to say whenever we would build something: measure twice, cut once. Remixed for our purposes, the adage becomes our tenth lesson:

Lesson #10: Mic twice, record once.

Listening Situation #2—Classroom Presentations. This is a hard one. In this situation, we imagine that we are charged with making an audio-visual text that reproduces a student presentation in a classroom. The purpose of the text will be to facilitate a draft workshop of the presentation for the presenters. There will be a Q&A session immediately following the presentation, which means we will need to be able to pay attention to the questions coming from the audience as well as the responses coming from the presenters. We may also want to pay attention to periodic responses throughout the presentation in order to judge audience involvement. Of course, we will also need to pay careful attention to all of the presentation: the presenters' voices and all sounds associated with the audio-visual materials used in support of the presentation. In other words, we'll need to pay attention to a lot. However, if we simply *hear* everything, we'll have a hard time paying attention to any of it. So, how do we do it? Well, we have a few choices, but let's narrow those choices down to a few primary types of options: (1) multiple live mics controlled through an audio mixer, (2) multiple mics associated with multiple video cameras, and (3) some combination of these two configurations.

For the first option, we will use multiple microphones attached to a mixer. A mixer allows us to vary the volume levels and often the tone settings for each mic we use (Fig. 4.23).

Fig. 4.23: This audio mixer allows at least eight microphones to be connected. The white buttons at the bottom of the mixer are attached to sliders that allow for individual volume levels to be set for each microphone. The dark buttons are attached to sliders that control the overall stereo levels coming out of the mixer and leading to the audio recording device.

To return to our baking metaphor, an audio mixer allows us to not only mix the overall audio "batter" but also allows us to change the consistency of the batter as we mix. Imagine being able to taste the batter as it is mixing and deciding it needs less eggs, and then simply dialing back the eggs; or adding more vanilla, then less vanilla; or taking out the salt entirely. While these options are not available to baking mixers, they are available to audio mixers, which is good since we'll want to turn off, or down, some of the mics (e.g., mics on the audience) during different portions of the presentation. The audio mixer allows us to make these kinds of decisions during the event. However, even though we can control the mix during the event, once the mix is recorded, we will lose independent control of the mics. In other words, as long as we're still mixing the batter, we have control of what and how much goes in or stays out, but once the batter becomes cake, we're stuck with our mix. If we want to keep our options open, we need to keep the ingredients separate as long as possible, something we will better be able to do in option two below.

Using an audio mixer, we can position microphones in several locations around the room. We could use a microphone on a stand at the podium if the speakers will deliver the presentation from a fixed position. A strength of this choice is that it allows for multiple speakers to use the same mic as they rotate speaking duties. If there are differences in the volume levels of speakers, the person doing the sound mixing can adjust these on the fly, or they may be leveled during the editing process. However, if the speakers will be moving or speaking from multiple positions, this option probably will not work. So we may want to use a wireless lavalier microphone for each of the speakers. That would allow the speakers to move around and take the mics with them as they move. However, as we've noted above, wireless mics are not the most reliable. Therefore, we would back them up with a shotgun microphone attached to the camera assigned to follow the speakers.

That takes care of the speakers—the presenters and the participants in the audience. What about the audio-visual presentation materials (e.g., the PowerPoint or movie presentation)? How can we selectively pay attention to those? We may be able to run the audio for the presentation materials through the mixer as well. That would give us high-quality sound and the ability to control it. However, because our ultimate purpose in this exercise is to facilitate a draft workshop for the presentation, we may want to approximate more of what an audience member will hear. Consequently, we may want to place a microphone in the audience and direct it to pay attention to the audio system of the room. If we use an omnidirectional mic, or two, to do so, we may be able to use it/them to pay attention to the Q&A session as well; and, by running it through the mixer, we can adjust the sound levels—that is, we can shift attention—as necessary.

All in all, this is a pretty efficient way to shift our attention among the variety of sources of this listening situation. However, it's also pretty intrusive; in this scenario we have between three and six microphones connected to a mixing board, which entails microphone cables and stands being placed in the room as well as the presence of a person operating the mixer—shifting attention between microphones and balancing what s/he hears on our behalf. This setup will also demand a lot of preparation: We'll need to go into the room and run the mic cables (and then tape them down with—yup, you guessed it—duct tape so no one trips on them), set up the mic stands, and test all of the mics and connections. Ah, but some of you may be pointing out that we could be using wireless microphones—thus eliminating those microphone cables. Nice try. Wireless systems only eliminate the cable from the microphone's transmitter to the receiver. We still need to run a cable from the receiver (wherever it is in the room) to the mixer. Finally, there will be two cables connecting the mixer to the audio recorder or the main video camera. That's a whole lot of audio cables—and a whole lot of duct tape!

If we have the opportunity to do all of this set up, we may indeed elect to go this route—especially if we'll get a high return on the investment of all of this labor. For example, if we will be capturing data from four or five presentations, all of the set up may be well worth the effort. However, if we can't set up the room first, we'll need to come up with another plan. Fortunately, we have such options.

So far, we haven't talked much about cameras. In Chapter Five, we will talk at length about paying attention to what we see. However, we'll need to think about it here a bit as well because where there is video, there is audio—two tracks of it in fact. So, depending on how we want to see the situation, we may be able to use the audio tracks of several video cameras to pay attention to a variety of things we want to hear as well. This situation (Layout I, Fig. 4.24) seems to me to call for at least three cameras, and therefore up to six audio tracks in all. For example, if we plan to have a camera (camera 1) pay attention to the speakers, we may be able to attach a shotgun mic that will direct our listening attention to follow our visual attention from speaker to speaker. We may also place a fixed camera (camera 2) in the back of the room to survey the whole panel—the full visual presentation and possibly some of the audience as well. We may want to use the camera's internal omnidirectional mics to capture the sounds of the room, including general audience reactions. Finally, we would then want to have a camera (camera 3) to capture whatever seems to be most relevant at any point in time. This camera could provide alternative shots of the speakers, capture the visual data onscreen, study the audience from the front of the room, and/or focus on individual audience members who participate in the discussion. This camera would also likely use a fixed shotgun mic in order to listen carefully to the things it pays attention to visually. The benefit of this setup (Layout II, Fig. 4.25) is that we have multiple points of interface in the room, and aside from our one fixed camera (which may not need someone operating it), we will have two mobile cameras that can move about without all the mucky-muck of microphone cables. This multi-camera setup will allow us to edit a final product that will be more like the experience of an actual audience member—one that shifts attention to the most compelling or relevant information at any moment.

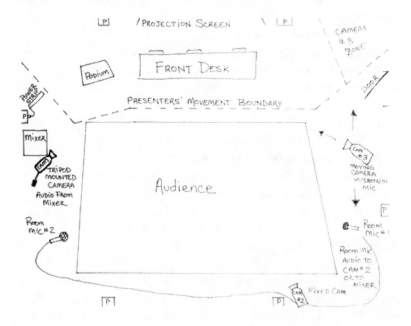

Fig. 4.24: Layout I of the presentation room showing where mics would be positioned and where the mixer and the camera(s) would be. Boxes marked [P] indicate power outlets in the room.

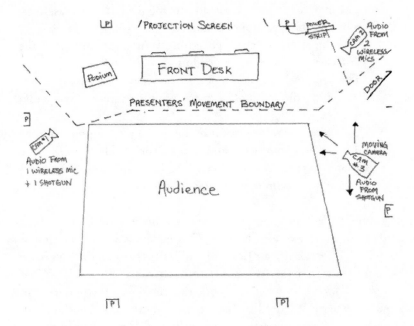

Fig. 4.25: Layout II of the presentation room showing where the cameras would be positioned. Boxes marked [P] indicate power outlets in the room.

Of course, where there is editing, there is writing, and where there is writing, there are decisions to be made. That all takes time. A single fixed camera with a single pair of audio tracks will certainly be able to capture a perspective on the presentation. However, as the camera operator shifts her attention in the moment, other material that may be equally compelling or relevant may go unnoticed, unrecorded, and consequently, may remain off the record. This three camera setup gives us a great number of options. It allows one camera to stay steady on the presentation and empowers two people to pay selective attention to the two dynamic elements of the listening scene: the speakers and the audience.

The third option would simply empower us to utilize some combination of elements from the two listening options discussed above. These combinations, like all rhetorical acts, will be highly situated. They will depend upon some combination of all of these considerations:

- The material resources available to you (i.e., the cameras, mics, mixers, cables, and/or operators to which you have access).
- The rhetorical purposes governing your documenting of the situation (i.e., what you intend to *do* with the footage).
- The time and attention required to review and possibly to upload and edit the footage from multiple cameras and audio sources.
- Your access to setting the listening scene (i.e., to preparing the room to suit your needs and to rehearsing in that space).
- Your access to "tearing down" the listening scene (i.e., to returning the room to its original condition).

As I said at the beginning of this section, this is a hard one—much harder than it may originally seem. Consequently, when planning to "film" a presentation, your first order of business should always be to focus on your purpose(s) for doing so in the first place. Ask, "What will we *do* with this footage?" With the answer to this question in mind, now ask, "What (all) must we pay attention to? And how will we facilitate shifting our attention accordingly?" Remember, mics cannot shift attention, so we need to. The more we plan to do so, the better prepared we'll be to do so as it happens. I highly encourage drawing listening maps such as those I have offered in Fig. 4.24 and Fig. 4.25. Visualize the scene of the listening situation and its sound sources, both those you want to hear and those you don't. This will help you make the best decisions about how to pay attention to the listening situation and, consequently, how to design the most effective listening system to help you meet your needs.

Listening Situation #3—Crowded-Room Interviews. OK, so it's your turn. We're now filming at a party, attempting to document the energy and actions of the event—or, at least, a PG-13 version thereof. We will want to pay attention to a variety of sounds: music from the band, announcements being made to the crowd, and individual speakers in the teeming flow of the party. You will need to be mobile, moving around the room with relative ease to accommodate the dynamic action of the party and the partygoers. How will you pay attention to this listening situation? What will allow you to hear the room best? What will allow you to put a microphone as close as possible to the speakers you interview at the noisy party? What will allow you to have the greatest mobility? How can we be sure that we will be able to hear the questions that you and/or the camera operator ask—questions that we may not be able to plan in advance or remember well afterward?

My Response to Listening Situation #3—Crowded-Room Interviews. Since we want to be as mobile as possible, we'll want to eliminate as many tethers as possible, and while lavalier mics would put mics close to the mouths of the folks we interview at the party, we would need to attach those mics to those folks. A directional (cardioid) dynamic handheld mic would be much easier to put into their hands—if, at times, all the harder to get back from some folks! It will be durable and reliable. However, when they are not holding it, we will be. Furthermore, since its strength in this noisy listening situation (its directionality) will prevent it from hearing the questions we ask, we will also need to mic ourselves. Here, a lavalier mic would be great because it would free our hands to operate the camera and handle that handheld mic. The lavalier could be an omnidirectional mic that would capture room sounds and our questions. When we are not doing interviews, we could either use the lavalier mic or simply use the camera's built-in omnidirectional mics to capture the sounds of the party—allowing us the greatest freedom of movement. Remember, just because you have external mics doesn't mean they are your only choices. Use built-in mics when they work best for the situation. They can be great when chosen to do what they do well, but a real liability when used as a default.

Listening Situation #4—Voice-Over Narration. This last situation may seem a bit like a setup; after all, there is only one type of microphone that we've not yet discussed and that you probably found little use for in the exercise immediately above. Hint, hint. However, before you simply answer with the obvious let me throw in a wrinkle or two: You may or may not have access to a microphone stand. If you do have a microphone stand, what will you choose? If you do not, what will you choose? And what if you do not have access to a quiet room for recording? What then?

My Response to Listening Situation #4—Voice-Over Narration. Let's first imagine that you do have a mic stand and a quiet room in which to record. The clear choice for this assignment is a large-diaphragm condenser microphone. This choice will allow us to accentuate both clarity and aesthetically pleasing characteristics of the narrator's voice. It will also demand, beyond the stability of the mic stand, a relatively quiet and stable recording environment. Furthermore, it will demand that we actually have access to one of these sorts of mics. If we meet all of these criteria, the large-diaphragm condenser mic is the clear winner. If we do not meet all of these criteria, and certainly if we do not have a mic stand, then we'll need another choice. What would I do? My first choice would be to use a directional lavalier condenser mic. That will put the mic at a constant distance from my mouth and leave my hands free to work the controls of the recorder or computer. In essence, I would become my own microphone stand. While I may lose some of the aesthetic qualities of the large-diaphragm condenser mic, I would retain the clarity associated with condensers, and I may be able to "warm up" the sound during the final editing by adjusting the tonal qualities of the track. If I don't have a lavalier mic, then either a shotgun mic (also a condenser) attached to my video camera may work in lieu of a mic stand (I can separate the audio from the video—break apart its all-there-at-onceness—when I'm editing). Or, finally, a handheld dynamic mic may work pretty well. It will likely boost the aesthetic quality of the vocal sound, even if it does sacrifice a bit of clarity. If this is my method, I will want to keep handling noise to a minimum and try to keep the mic at a relatively even distance from my mouth as I narrate, which may be difficult if I'm also trying to operate the recording controls at the same time.

CONCLUSIONS

We have considered quite a few dimensions of audio recording in this chapter. Maybe too many, but not nearly as many as will become relevant to you as you participate in audio-visual writing. The ten global lessons to take from this lengthy discussion are these:

Lesson #1: Always use headphones when videotaping interviews.
Lesson #2: Always choose a video camera with a headphone jack when videotaping interviews.
Lesson #3: Microphones can't pay (shift) attention, so you have to.
Lesson #4: Always choose the pickup pattern of your microphones.

Lesson #5: When using a wireless microphone, always have a wired back-up.

Lesson #6: When using more than one wireless mic, be certain each mic transmits and receives on its own unique channel.

Lesson #7: Set your recording levels in the green—at around 75%. The levels of the sounds you want should drown out the sounds of silence.

Lesson #8: Pay careful attention to your connections! Remember, without the right chains, even the best tow truck will leave you stuck in the ditch.

Lesson #9: Your rhetorical purposes should guide your choice of listening systems, not the "quality" of the equipment itself. Pay more attention to what the equipment does than what it is.

Lesson #10: Mic twice, record once.

Plan well. Know your options. Map out your listening situations. Pay attention. The audio you record for audio-visual writing is the equivalent of the research you do for traditionally-mediated, inquiry-based writing. Without access to authoritative data, the best writers will write bad research papers—not because they are bad writers but because they cannot adequately fulfill their purposes as writers, at least in this instance. Without authoritative sound—sound that demonstrates that the author(s) have paid attention carefully enough to enable their audience to pay attention to the relevant aural data, the best audio-visual writers will not fulfill their purposes as writers, at least in this instance. Bad audio can be a project killer, but that doesn't mean that it is our only concern. As we can predict in a theory of multidimensional rhetoric, sound is only one facet of our concerns in audio-visual rhetoric. In the next chapter, we will now open our eyes and see what we can learn by paying careful attention to what our video cameras see.

5 Cameras: What Do Writing Teachers Need to Know about Video?

> *One can, and perhaps should, always ask, 'Who could see this scene in this way?', 'Where would one have to be to see this scene in this way, and what sort of person would one have to be to occupy that space?'*

—Gunther Kress and Theo van Leeuwen

If microphones, relatively simple technologies, demanded so much attention in the previous chapter, then this chapter's discussion of cameras will have to be a tome! Right? Wrong. Remember, microphones can't pay/shift attention, so you need to. Well, video cameras can and do, so you don't have to if you don't want to. At least, that is, with regard to what they *see*. Consequently, much more of the work is done for us with cameras. While *experienced* photographers will want to disable many automated features of cameras to suit their highly-informed, expert sensibilities, it is the attention-paying/-shifting abilities of consumer and prosumer cameras that enable novices to make movies that look pretty good—often, even better than pretty good. In other words, advancements in video camera technologies are resulting in video cameras that invite people to gain video/photography *experience*—they ask people to play. If someone hands you a consumer video camera, you won't need lessons to get started. That, however, doesn't mean that getting started won't lead to lessons. Finding our way into those lessons will be the focus of Chapters Five and Six.

If the viral popularity of YouTube culture is any indication, a whole lot of folks appear to be accepting the invitation to play made by new video technologies. Cameras, however, are only the first part of the operation of video writing. Video cameras allow us to collect information, but they don't, in and of themselves, often allow us to manipulate or share that information very efficiently. It is the operation of *capture* —> *upload/edit* —> *share* that has transformed video cameras—things we've had for several decades—into instruments of writing (Fig. 5.1). The cameras have changed, yes; but the most critical development for our purposes is the way they fit, literally and figuratively, into the operation of video *writing*. Chapter Five will discuss some of the rhetorical and functional concerns that present themselves to audio-visual writers who use video cameras to pursue their work. Along the way, we will amass a code of conduct, much as we did in Chapter Four: ten rules for both doing and teaching the operation of audio-visual writing.

Fig. 5.1 The operation of video writing: *capture (via cameras)* --> *upload/edit (via computers)*--> *share (via social media)*.

First, let me give you an example:

In the fall of 2010, two undergraduate students in my multimedia writing class, Nina Elias and Bethany Tomaszewski, proposed to do a video mashup: a music video using the song "Lisztomania" by the group Phoenix. There was an immediate problem with their doing so: The song was fully protected under copyright law and they had not sought permission from the copyright holders to make their video. However, there had already been several other high-profile mashups made with this song. The first, apparently, featured "Brat Pack" actors from John Hughes's 1985 hit film, *The Breakfast Club.* In Hughes's film, the characters were dancing to the song "We are Not Alone," by Karla Devito. In the remix, they were reedited to be dancing to "Lisztomania." This "Brat Pack" remix spawned a series of tribute mashups that featured new footage of young people performing their own dances derived from the Brat Pack's iconic dance moves from the 1980s. Many of these mashups had been posted to YouTube, and most had received tens of thousands of views. The "Brooklyn Brat Pack Mashup" had, at that time, been viewed close to a quarter million times. Furthermore, YouTube had placed links to resources for buying the music—a sign that the artist was considering the mashups to be in their interest, not compromising them. So Nina's and Bethany's classmates and I all said, yes, do it. Make that video.

And they did. Most of their classmates had chosen to pursue short, interview-based, documentary projects; consequently, the "Michigan State Brat Pack Mashup" looked and sounded quite different from its peer projects. For one thing, although it was a project controlled by sound—much like the interview-based projects—it had only one audio source: the song. This allowed their project to be collected without much attention to audio, as they would only use audio in their footage as a reference for synching specific moves to specific parts of the song. They would actually eliminate all of that sound during editing. The other projects demanded careful attention to recording sound on-site, as that sound would carry much of the primary information of their documentaries. The major visual difference actually follows from that audio distinction. Interview-based works use spoken phrases of varying length to tell their stories. Those spoken phrases are communicated not only in words, they are delivered in *time*. The visual information that accompanies spoken content must dance to its groove, so to speak, and it does so, most often, with one of two purposes: (1) to provide evidence of the spoken *performance* (i.e., a photographic record of the person saying what he or she is saying), or (2) to provide evidence of the spoken *content* (i.e., visual support for the claims being delivered).

The visual footage in the "Lisztomania" mashups behaves differently in both kind and degree. It dances to the groove of the song with, essentially, no reference whatsoever to the lyric. As a result, that visual information is generated, captured, selected, and edited according to three primary aims: (1) it accentuates movement and timing within the song, (2) it replicates moves from *The Breakfast Club* and from the other mashup videos, and (3) it obeys self-referential energy. Wait a minute. It obeys what? The *self-referential energy* is the part of the video footage that behaves most like eye candy. Sometimes, a person who dances to a song may be brilliant, and long cuts of that person may make us sit forward in our chairs, watching in amazement. Other times, a person who dances to a song may be more like me and deliver essentially no useful footage. Yet that footage of awful dancing will likely be only largely, not completely, useless. The editor will recognize that thirty minutes of terrible dancing may yield a few instances of useful movement—even if it is out of synch with the beat when performed, even if the move was completely disconnected from other moves, even if the dancer falls down immediately after performing the move. The editor doesn't need the dancer, necessarily, to be a good dancer. The editor needs useful footage. Sometimes that footage is hard-won, but what makes it useful is what I call its *self-referential energy*: its *itness*. Its magic. To be fair, this is true for good dancers too. In the "Lisztomania" mashups, even though many of the dancers deliver skillful and beautiful performances, the clips of that dancing are as long as the energy of the clips themselves will allow. In many ways, these clips represent the *entitlement* of the energy of each performance. They sum up the symbolic action of the dancers. The editing both reveals and entitles the dancers' essential moves.

This self-referential energy is not only useful to the talent (or the talent impaired, in my case), it is also an asset to the photographer(s)—especially novice photographers. Let's imagine that I am not the one dancing—that we have a truly competent dancer doing magnificent stuff. We burn sixty minutes of video and every move is magical—and we feel pretty good about this since we have sixty minutes of magic to edit down to a four-minute music video. Sweet. The trouble is, for thirty of those sixty minutes we have aimed the camera not only at the dancer but also at a window directly behind the dancer, one exposed to full sunlight—an effect of photography called *backlighting* (Fig. 5.2a) that surfaces as a common grammatical error in novice photography (Fig. 5.2b).

Fig. 5.2a: Backlighting as intentional aesthetic effect in the "Lisztomania Michigan State Brat Pack Mashup."	Fig. 5.2b: Backlighting as unintentional grammatical error.

The result: Our dancer is in silhouette for half of our footage. Not sweet. The remaining thirty minutes of videotape was not backlit; however, the camera was handheld and was zoomed in for many of the shots, yielding extremely shaky footage. Really not sweet. However, we do have about five minutes of pretty decent shots that may yield two minutes of useful footage when edited. Great, sixty minutes of footage for a four-minute music video and we're only halfway done— at best. Looks like we have to reshoot the whole thing.

Not so fast. We have two minutes of solid stuff, and fifty-eight minutes of junk. We only need to mine two minutes from all of that fifty-eight minutes: a few seconds here, a dozen seconds there. The moments are all that matter. The dancing is all good, we only need to select and collect the moments where the camera is getting it right— or at least, not getting it wrong. We only need the *essential* moments. Plus, a silver lining in this cloud emerges when we begin editing, because our backlit footage allows us to create contrast in the final work—shots that are clearly different. We may be able to use the editing software to reframe some of the shots. We can use the self-referential energy of the clips that we select to build our video, second by second—brick by brick, if you will.

That sounds like hard work. It is. But along the way, the photographers learn what they did well and what they did poorly—not because they obeyed or broke prescriptive grammatical rules of photography but because their actions yielded footage that was more or less rhetorically useful. The editors learn what they need and what they can transform—what they can use and what they cannot—and the writers can walk away from the project with a product that was made by way of imagination, determination, planning, and a whole lot of triage. One of my graduate students entitled the act of videotaping interviews by exclaiming, "What a fun exercise in damage control!" The writers will learn that sixty minutes of unedited footage was pushed to yield four minutes of edited footage that took twenty hours to select and put together. The writers will learn their limitations and their strengths. They will make many mistakes and they will seize victory from the jaws of defeat—and they will share their finished works with their friends, their peers, their family, and potentially thousands of complete strangers. They will get feedback. One four-minute music video will deliver all of this opportunity for learning, and some of these folks, through luck, hard work, and careful craft and revision, will make something really wonderful, just as Nina and Bethany did.

In her final reflection of the semester, Bethany said about their "Lisztomania" video, "Indeed, it was a lot of work—by the end of the project, we did three five-hour shoots and spent between 50 and 75 hours editing. It really seems worth it, though, because it's really rewarding to be able to create something that is both enjoyable to make and fun to share with others." What made the hard work worth it? The operation of writing: many hours of planning, followed by fifteen hours of collection, followed by up to five times as many hours editing, followed by publishing the work to YouTube—a work that received more than 1,500 views within one week of its posting and more than 4,700 views by October 2012.

My wife, upon watching the "Michigan State Brat Pack Mashup," asked me a familiar question:

> OK, so how is this writing? How is sending a couple of students out with cameras to film their friends jumping around to a cool song the work of writers? Sure, it's art. But is it writing?

Yes. It is writing because it participates in the operation of writing—even if it yields a product that is one we would qualify as a work of art. Songs are works of art that are written. Poems are works of art that are written. They are written, but not because they feature words. Instrumental songs are written as well: they are composed; they are composed of symbols put to rhetorical ends by way of the operation of writing. The operation of writing allows people to capture, mediate, manipulate, revise, and share ideas across time and space. Cameras, throughout most of the twentieth century, allowed most of us to collect, mediate, and share ideas by way of consumer photography. However, most of us were unable to manipulate or revise the images we created, and our range of sharing those images was limited to our immediate face-to-face contacts. We made photo albums and *home* movies—movies not only shot at home but only ever played—shared—at home. Because we could not edit those movies, we needed to perform the movies for others—to fast-forward through the irrelevant bits; to explain what was being captured; to apologize for the shaky camera work, bad lighting, fast zooming, and foul language of the camera operator. Well, at least that's how it always seemed to go in my home.

The "Lisztomania" videos are not home movies. They speak for themselves. They were composed by audio-visual writers who were guided by rhetorical aims. My students were motivated to join a conversation in the Burkean audio-visual editing parlor. To pull off this mission, they needed to perform a critical analysis of the genre. They had to *listen*, carefully, to what was being said and how it was being said. They needed to plan what they would say in response. They needed to find talent—dancers—and arrange schedules for videotaping. They needed to find and secure locations where they would videotape the dancers—locations that would help them tell *their* story, help them make *their* contribution to the conversation. They would need to be both recognizable and unique. They would need to storyboard— i.e., plan—the shots they knew they would need. They would need to schedule and secure the cameras and tripods and other equipment they would require to collect their footage.

All of that planning would facilitate their response(s) to the local demands and opportunities of the actual scenes of video collection. They would inevitably enter a location that they scouted to find something better around the corner, or lighting that made the location look very different than expected, or a group of people having class in an improbable location on campus. This work demands planning and revising. It requires the abductive work of hypothesis. Let's remember something we considered from Dewey back in Chapter Two: "The more adequately the functional relation can be apprehended *in the abstract*, the better can the engineer detect defects in an existent machine and project improvements in it. Thus *the thought of it* operates as a model" (*Quest* 163, emphasis added). The plans of the music video makers function as a working thesis, a claim that sets the audio-visual writers into directed action—much as our abstract listening situations did in Chapter Four. Yet along the way, the audio-visual writer will learn. The act of collecting will direct her to make new decisions, to hatch new plans, to compose new theories based upon the experience of being in the new scene—in the kairotic moment. In other words, the operation of audio-visual writing will be realized through a series of *ad hoc* adjustments that will yield the local process of carrying out the operation. As one of Nina's and Bethany's classmates put it: "Planning is essential. Plan as much as possible ahead of time and expect it to go wrong. When it does, don't stress; be flexible. That sums up everything that has to do with the technical side of things."

The experience of audio-visual research and writing shares much in common with traditional research and writing, and it is here that writing teachers may find many analogues—many decisions and moves that define the operation of writing—even if they do not define each and every process of writing. Remember, "Processes are local and temporal, particular. But the relation of means and consequence which defines an operation remains one and the same in spite of these variations. It is a universal" (Dewey, *Quest* 162). When people carrying cameras are doing so with the intention of editing and sharing that material—of placing that material into the operation of writing—they carry the cameras not only as photographers but as editors as well. In other words, they will respond not only to the immediate variations in the photographic scene but also will be motivated by the eventual constraints and possibilities of the editing scene. With that knowledge— that attitude—they will photograph not merely as photographers but as writers.

Photography is not writing. Capturing is not writing. Collecting is not writing. Unless, of course, it is. And so, the first big lesson of Chapter Five is this:

Rule #1: Remember where you are going.

Because we teach writing, the features and the specs of the cameras mean nothing to us if those cameras cannot communicate with the equipment we will use to edit the content collected by way of those cameras. Editing is writing. Editing allows photographers to revise, reconsider, recontextualize, rearticulate, and redistribute the information they capture on "film." Consequently, a cell phone capable of capturing, storing, editing, and sharing video is a writing tool that your students can use to engage the operation of video writing. A professional video camera that will not connect to the computers your students will use to edit and share their work is *not* a writing tool because it will not allow them to engage the operation of video writing— regardless of how good the camera itself may be. As with all writing tools, the capability of the camera—what *it* can do—is irrelevant if it does not engage the capabilities of the writer—what *s/he* can do. The camera must be able to participate in the writer's individual and local process of the operation of writing, and the operation of writing is an operation of symbolic action, which is, of course, an operation of rhetoric. The operation of rhetoric is always about connecting more than cameras and computers—it is always, first and foremost, about connecting (identifying) people. It employs symbolic means for "inducing cooperation in beings that by nature respond to symbols" (Burke, *Rhetoric* 43). It is always compensatory to division.

This, of course, brings us right back to the epigraph from Gunther Kress and Theo van Leeuwen that opens this chapter on video cameras: "One can, and perhaps should, always ask, 'Who could see this scene in this way?', 'Where would one have to be to see this scene in this way, and what sort of person would one have to be to occupy that space?'" (143). If microphones are the ears of the audio-visual writer's listening system, cameras are the eyes. Those eyes draw the most direct visual line of identification between the audio-visual writer and the audio-visual reader because they serve as the rhetorical eyes of the audience. If, as Burke claims, the "scene is a fit 'container' for the act, expressing in fixed properties the same quality that the action expresses in terms of development" (*Grammar* 3), then the position of the camera(s)—the *point of view*—will suggest "what sort of person" one would "have to be in order to occupy that space" (Kress and van Leeuwen 143). The perspective with which we regard not only the scene but the *acts* that it will or will not license will depend upon who we think that *sort of person* may be—what sort of person the scene is asking *us* to be by agreeing to consider this point of view, potentially, as our own. All of that information—all of that authorial, rhetorical, symbolic action—so long as it participates in the operation of writing—is tied up, in part, by where the audio-visual author has chosen to place the camera(s).

So, there's quite a lot riding on these cameras. That's not all, however; cameras are not just means of collecting. Cameras are vehicles for taking agents to actions. If I ask a student to engage an inquiry-based project on an annual local event, that student may use her laptop to access more information than she could possibly use and never have to leave her dorm room. However, if I hand her a video camera and say, "Use this as your primary tool for data collection," then she will have to leave her room because the only way to get data into that video camera is to take it to the scene of the action. The only way to get quotes from people is to take the camera to those people (or invite them to come to the camera). The only way to get b-roll footage (footage that will be used to support the primary footage: the a-roll) into that camera is to take the camera to the scenes of action and to snoop around—study the scene, see it, be there. Cameras are more than devices for collecting data, they are vehicles for connecting people. They are instruments of *scene-seeking*.

Consequently, Kress and van Leeuwen's questions about the hypothetical audience who *would* or *could* see the scene as it has been photographed must also be rearticulated to ask who *will* or *is likely to* actually see the scene at all. With this revision, we revisit Lisa Ede and Andrea Lunsford's classic discussion of "Audience Addressed/Audience Invoked: The Role of Audience in Composition Theory and Pedagogy." The audience invoked is the fictional audience written by way of analysis: the generic or entitled audience. The audience addressed is the actual audience who is able to access and consider the work. The operation of writing demands both, and, when the writer and the reader are not the same person, the operation of writing also demands a form of mediation that can span both space and time. If video cameras are *scene-seeking*, then the products they yield by way of the operation of writing are *scene-speaking*. In other words, they speak for the writer(s) about the scenes they represent—most often, to real people in the writer(s)'s absence—and, most importantly, what they *say* is something other than what the cameras were *told*. The products have been filtered by way of a symbolic screen—one managed by a writer/editor.

Studying Nina and Bethany's "Lisztomania" mashup allows us to invoke an audience who could and would see the references in their work, both the camera angles and the homage elements within the genres. In other words, the invoked audience is placed both physically, within the scene by way of point of view, and socially, within the genres by way of point of reference. However, Nina and Bethany's "Lisztomania" mashup allows us to study the audience addressed by way of the comments and views counter that accompany their movie on YouTube. That information is not about hypothetical audience members but about actual and specific audience members. Part of *Remembering Where You Are Going* is paying rhetorical and critical attention to these two types of audiences. Another part of *Remembering Where You Are Going* is paying functional attention to the physical connections that allow the cameras to communicate with the editing software and hardware and the publishing media. We will turn our attention, now, toward the functional concerns of cameras, remembering that we are not merely photographers but writers. Remembering, that is, that the eyes are only the windows of the looking/seeing system. As we encountered in Chapter Four, within the operation of writing we need not only to see but to capture and process what we see, to make sense of what we've seen, to edit and revise what we've seen, and to share what we've learned by making what we've seen available to be shown to others.

Does This Purse Go with My Video Camera?

"Keep people first." My mentor, Todd Taylor, insists that commandment number one for computers and composition is that we "keep people first" ("Ten Commandments" 234). If we do, we will remember that the capabilities *of* the technologies that we use are only as good as the uses we have *for* them. The operation of writing—a people-oriented operation—may help us recognize stability in an otherwise fluid world of technological change. By the time I finish writing this sentence, a new means for recording or storing digital visual information is likely to have been introduced—possibly one that makes current technologies for doing these things completely irrelevant. At the moment I write this sentence, in fact, we are in what appears to be the final days of the very technology that introduced Baby Boomers to consumer photography: photographic film. The coming of 2011 brought the passing of Kodachrome, the Kleenex of color photography (Axelrod).

Consequently, our functional concerns about video cameras will be filtered by the following questions:

- What do you need your students to do with video cameras? In other words, what is the lesson?
- What acts of writing will the video cameras need to facilitate?

For most applications in writing classes, we will want to choose cameras that are as easy to operate as possible, as we are concerned with the operation of writing, not the technology of photography. Students such as Nina and Bethany need a camera that can record nice images. Most of my other students need cameras that can also record sound worthy of being heard. Those cameras need to be able to record nice images *and* good sound, which means, as we learned in Chapter Four, they must be able to accept external microphones. If our lessons are designed to yield finished—that is, polished—final products, we will want to make camera decisions based upon ease, quality, and connectivity. If, however, the lesson glories in the unfinishedness of audiovisual writing, our camera choices will be based primarily on ease of use and connectivity. Each of these legitimate aims in writing classes will look to different means. Consequently, we should expect that no one kind of video camera will fit all of our needs or uses.

OK, so let me ask you a question that I bet you are not expecting: How many pairs of shoes do you need to do the work of your life? Could you possibly get by with just one pair of shoes? Well, that is going to depend on what you *do* in your life, but I will venture to say that most of us could not—or would not—be able to get by with just one pair of shoes. We need slippers for around the house, sandals for the beach, running shoes for the gym, dress shoes for work, boots for snow, blue suede shoes for party time. We choose our shoes for function—what they help us do—for ease of use—comfort—and for rhetorical effect. Video cameras are like shoes: We wear them. Sometimes, a little discomfort is worth the function or the effect. Sometimes, comfort rules. Sometimes, we need all three. The next big lesson of Chapter Five is this:

Rule #2: Video cameras are the shoes of your audio-visual wardrobe.

Because we keep people first, we will think first about what kind of audio-visual shoes *they* should wear, and not about what audio-visual shoes, in and of themselves, are best.

At the moment, *we* happen to be the specific people who we are keeping first. We are writing teachers, and we are handling video cameras as means for pursuing audio-visual writing projects. Our purpose is to help our students develop their writing abilities. While the cameras they are likely to use will make many of the "decisions" that will allow them to capture viewable images, those "decisions" that seem right to the cameras—or rather to those who programmed the functions of the cameras—may not meet the rhetorical needs of the audio-visual writers using them. In other words, our automated video collaborators may know seeing in general (the operation of seeing), but they don't know what *we* are seeing or why we are seeing it (our situated processes of seeing). They know the grammar, but not the rhetoric that facilitates, contains, solicits, and shapes it. *That* is our job. Where their grammatical choices don't match our rhetorical choices, we will need to develop workarounds that enable us either to change the automated functions of the cameras or to alter our expectations about what we may or may not accomplish with the cameras we have. As in our discussion in Chapter Four, I will take the position here that no technology is superior or inferior to another, it is simply more or less suited to some rhetorical purposes than others. There are no bad cameras, *per se*—so long as they do what they are supposed to do. However, there are many cameras that are very bad choices for meeting some rhetorical purposes—and sometimes, it may be the "best" cameras that are the worst choices. Let me explain.

Two of my students proposed a documentary movie project that would take them into an underground music club and art gallery in Lansing, Michigan. Much of the footage they would shoot would be collected at night and/or in rooms with very little light. Their intention was to document the "scene" of this venue and the colorful folks who frequent it. From a technical standpoint—informed by functional literacy or a grammatical perspective—I thought the very best thing for these students would be to have a camera that would allow them to get good pictures in the dark venue. This would entail a camera that would allow them to set their own lighting settings or possibly would require them to take lights with them to light up areas too dark for filming. However, from a rhetorical perspective, I realized that what they needed most to capture the data they wanted was not expensive prosumer cameras and lighting equipment—what they needed was stealth. The product they needed to make would benefit from being raw and dark. They would benefit from using cameras that would allow them to be as inconspicuous as possible. Taking lights into this environment would be akin to showing up with their parents in tow. It would be rhetorical suicide. An *ethos* killer and, consequently, a project killer. The camera they chose to use for this truly fantastic project was the least expensive equipment to which we had access. Why? Because the "best" cameras were the biggest, most complicated, and most conspicuous cameras available to us. The images they would have been able to produce with these higher-end cameras would have been more "slick"—the antithesis of the image of the club my students were attempting to document. Even though these audio-visual authors would photograph as writers with an eye on editing and sharing their work, as ethnographers, in the scenes of collection, their handycam communicated that they were shooting a "home movie"—marking them not as outsiders but possibly as insiders. Furthermore, the grainy low-tech quality of their footage brought an authenticity to the experiences they documented that was consistent with the subject of their inquiry. *Lesson:* Sometimes "bad" cameras aren't so bad and sometimes "good" cameras aren't so good.

Rule #3: Audio-visual writers choose cameras according to their rhetorical purposes.

And vice versa.

If all you have available to you are handycams or video-equipped cell phones, you may not want to advise your students to go interview the Governor for a piece you hope to pitch to PBS. Then again, anything is possible with the right combination of appeals. I feel that much of Casey Miles's fabulous "The Gender Project" benefits from her use of low-resolution (low-res) video shot with the camera on her laptop. The low-res video seems to argue for the genuine nature of her footage—that it was captured absolutely as it happened, not as it was staged. That footage claims that she needed to capture the footage as it happened, by hook or by crook—*not* only after she got the tripod set and the lighting read and adjusted. However, if all of her footage looked this way we may lose this sense of rhetorical urgency; it is her overall mix of images across a broad range of quality that ultimately helps her amass her authority because we can see that the quality of her footage signifies *her* rhetorical choices, not simply the default grammatical choices of her video equipment. Just as we have been telling our writing students all along, it is best to demonstrate that we know the rules of grammar before we break them—or rather, before an audience who also knows those rules will likely allow us to break them.

Williams declares in her discussion of the grammar of visual design, "You must know what the rule is before you can break it" (49). The title of her book, *The Non-Designers Design Book*, indicates that Williams's advice is meant for novices. She's teaching what amounts to Visual Composition 101, and she draws our attention to grammatical concerns as we engage texts. In other words, she teaches grammar within the context of writing, not simply as a list of rules to be memorized before we begin designing but rather to be considered as we design. Her grammatical rules are consistent with Burke's discussion of form, which is all about expectations—about arousing and fulfilling "appetites" (*Counter-Statement* 31) and "desires" (124). That is, writers use grammar as a rhetorical device to satisfy audiences or to make them squirm. Writing teachers generally want their students to exercise these appeals as choices that help them fulfill their rhetorical purposes. Sometimes, such as with my students' use of low-res video to document the "scene" of an underground music and art venue, their purpose *is* to make the audience squirm. Or rather, to make some of the audience squirm—the outsiders, those who expect the grammar of slick production—and to satisfy the expectations of other members of the audience, the insiders, by making us other squares squirm.

Exactly how was it that I became a square? Probably when I decided that it was still cool to say *square*. Oh well, so it goes. Rock on!

Before you think I'm only endorsing the type of *ethos* that comes along with the use of low-res video and inexpensive cameras, allow me to discuss briefly a project undertaken by a different group of my students. Robert Busby was the owner and proprietor of another type of art gallery and music venue in Lansing: The Creole Gallery. Busby was known as the unofficial "mayor of Old Town," an area of Lansing that had fallen into disrepute, but that had been revitalized largely upon the ceaseless goodwill and hard work of Busby and his collaborators. In February of 2007, Busby was robbed and murdered by a vagrant he had been employing and sheltering at the gallery—a common practice for Busby. In the fall of 2008, a group of my students, despite never having made an audio-visual documentary, proposed to pursue a documentary project on Robert Busby. To do so, they first started collecting information about Busby from other Old Town merchants and immediately discovered just how beloved Busby remained within the community. While many key members of the community were enthusiastic about the project, they were also guarded, wanting to be certain that the project would be handled with great care. This project would need to have all of its procedural "t"s crossed and all of its audio-visual "i"s dotted. It would need to be both rhetorically/ethically responsible and grammatically correct. It would need to speak to a broad and well-educated audience of local artists, musicians, and patrons of art and jazz. In stark contrast to the documentary on the underground club, the Busby crew would need to signal their "insider" status by appearing to be as professional as possible. These shoots featured lighting gear, high quality microphones, and multiple high-definition video cameras. They also demanded a great deal of preparation and study.

The efforts paid off nicely. These students were welcomed into the community and their work has continued to profit from the contributions of the Old Town merchants and Busby's surviving family members long after our semester together ended. Their project lives on, and it does so largely to the credit of the *ethos* of those exceptional students—*ethos* earned by their careful conduct and concern for their subject matter, *ethos* earned and communicated, in part, by both the rhetorical and grammatical choices they made during filming and editing. In the words of director Noah Blon:

> In our piece, we brought together work about which we were initially frustrated and ashamed, and edited these bits into something that told a story. It was that twist that made us most proud of what we had done. This film taught us not just about the technicalities of film-making, but of the power of documentary to connect us as filmmakers to our surroundings and to communicate that connection to our audience. (Blon, Creighton, and Halbritter)

Let me be perfectly clear: In all of these productions to which I have referred above, the students made effective grammatical choices. All of these projects feature "good" grammar—good because it is consistent with the motives of their makers, and good because it does what they need it to do. Proper, because it communicates respect for the subjects of study and the appetites and expectations of their intended audiences. These grammatical successes were facilitated by some functional choices that allowed the projects to exist in the first place. As Selber has claimed, "the functional side of computer literacy" enriches critical and rhetorical literacy ("Reimagining" and *Multiliteracies*). We will limit our discussion to the functions of cameras as they participate in the operation of writing—a functional side of a form of computer literacy.

REIMAGINING THE FUNCTIONAL SIDE OF THE THREE CS

Writing teachers have three primary concerns about the functional capabilities of video cameras: Collection, Connection, Correction. The *other* three Cs.

I. Collection

- What are the *audio* capabilities? Will the video camera accommodate external microphones and headphones? (We have already discussed these concerns in Chapter Four.)
- How does the camera *store* the data it captures? Some digital video cameras store the audio-visual data they capture to some type of digital videotape (e.g., MiniDV). Others store their data to internal hard drives. Others to some sort of flash drive. In ten minutes, another technology will come along that will allow you to store audio-visual data in your dental fillings or something equally improbable. It's bound to happen. That's how it goes with this stuff. Our brief mission below will be to pay attention to two features of data storage: Possession and Backup.

Ia. Possession: Who has your data? Where is your project? These are questions I regularly ask my students. Imagine that a student who is doing a traditional, library-based research paper comes to you for advice after his project has crashed. He is in the final stages of his project and his hard drive has crashed, killing his access to all of his drafted work. Your first questions are probably about backup, and we'll get there in a moment, but for now let's just say that there is no backup of the draft. D'oh. OK, so next you may suggest that he go back to his sources and his notes and, knowing the choices he had made already (writing is epistemic, after all), he could rewrite his project. Sounds hard, but doable. However, he returned all of his library books and journals *and* he put all of his notes back into the books when he was done. Now all of those books, along with his notes, are checked out to other library patrons. This is a totally crashed project. Crash and burn.

Also absurd, right? I mean, who would do such a foolish thing? Well, let's keep this absurd situation in mind and imagine, instead, that the student had borrowed a digital video camera for the weekend from his university's media lab. He had set up a full schedule in advance to get all of his interviews and b-roll footage collected in his short window of time with the camera. Immediately after shooting his footage, he uploaded the footage into his computer—all of it. Then he returned the camera to the media lab, where it was quickly handed to another student. That all sounds reasonable, right? Nothing absurd in that. Now imagine that the video camera stores its data to an internal hard drive. It's one of those fancy, no-tape models. Who needs tape? The student's project is uploaded to his computer. Which is cool, until, as in the situation above, his computer crashes. Now what? The camera's hard drive storage was either wiped by the media lab prior to recirculating or rewritten by other users during subsequent video collection. Effectively, the student returned his books with all of his notes in them. No project. None. All of that hard work and careful planning results in no hard evidence.

Now, let's change one small but essential variable: The camera does not have an internal hard drive; it stores its data, instead, on some removable format (tape or disc or dental fillings). Now who has this data? The student does; he keeps it when he returns the camera. Where is his project? In his possession; it's still on those tapes (or discs or dental fillings).

Choices regarding storage format should be informed by advances in technological efficiency, but should ultimately be determined by the needs of writers. If we heed Taylor's advice and *keep people first*, then the technology, even as it inevitably changes, will suggest courses of action concerning both possession and preservation (backup). In terms of both, the cameras with hard drive storage suggest the necessity of an external storage device that the student would control—at least throughout the life of the project. Ensuring possession of writing data is essential for all writers.

1b. Backup: Preservation, or backup, is possession's partner. Backup anticipates the crisis at the heart of our hypothetical scenarios above and follows Taylor's seventh commandment for computers and composition: "expect the crash" (x). Not only do we need to possess the data, we also need to keep it preserved in a variety of locations. For audiovisual writers, it may be helpful to think of keeping many of the writer's "ingredients" as separate as possible. Even as we recommend that sounds are stored on separate tracks, raw data should be stored separately from data being edited, and from edited data. In other words, the raw data should be stored somewhere, e.g., on tapes, external hard drives, or dental fillings. The project itself (the uploaded footage and the editing program that controls it) should be stored somewhere else: on the computer's hard drive and backed up on an external hard drive. The final products (the final mixes) are the smallest and most portable files, but even these should be stored somewhere else: on the computer's hard drive and on thumb drives, email storage, or other storage media. All of these ingredients are integral to a project, and by keeping them separate and backed up separately, they may be more available to future uses. In other words, even though we make a lot of cookies, if we store all of our flour premixed as cookie mix, we won't be able to make bread or pie crust with that flour. The culture of remix has both a persistent hunger and a fickle palate. Consequently, storage of media items is critical.

Let me make what my students regularly call an "Uncle-Bump suggestion" here: because storage of media items is so important, and because media storage items tend to all look alike, efficient labeling of your media storage items is crucial. Imagine that the music files in your iPod were identifiable only by number (13456.aac, 13457.aac, etc.). How on earth would you be able to call up Radiohead's "High and Dry" in a moment when you really needed it if you didn't happen to remember the arbitrary number associated with your copy of the file? You probably wouldn't, and this would cost you either the time of searching or the opportunity to use something that you actually have—you just don't know where.

Rule #4: Label your storage media carefully and consistently.

II. Connection

- How does the camera *export* its data?
- How do the cameras *connect* to computers? To what computers will the cameras *not* connect?

Because writing teachers are concerned with teaching the operation of writing, audio-visual writing teachers must pay careful attention to the points of connection between the eyes (cameras) and the mind and memory (computers) of our looking/seeing system. How is information carried from the eyes to the mind and memory? Yup, you guessed it: tow trucks.

Anyone who suffered through the MacBook debacle of 2009 knows this rule well. In 2009, Apple removed firewire ports from its popular MacBook laptops: computers that *all* shipped with iMovie as part of its standard iLife software package. iMovie was a remix-only software on those MacBooks because there was no way to connect a video camera to the computer without the intervention of another intermediary computer. In the words of Casey Miles, one of the brilliant graduate students I have had the great fortune and incredible pleasure of working with: "f***in' firewire." I have no quarrel with firewire, or any other technology that works, *per se*. Similar to my position throughout, I endorse *no* particular writing technologies. Writing technologies are means to an end—they are Burkean "agency"—and, as such, they either enable our symbolic acts or they do not. Bad connections can be the means of failure for otherwise robust audio-visual writing systems. Without good connections, the best computers, the sweetest cameras and microphones, the best performances, and the smartest people are silenced.

Rule #5: Without proper means of connection, your assets are liabilities.

By the time this sentence—as I am writing it right now—is published and entering your consciousness, firewire may indeed be as dead as Aristotle: RIP. However, as long as there are components of any technological system—and that is what listening and looking systems are—there will be a need to pay careful attention to how all of those specific components connect. Be prepared.

III. Correction

- What is the recording *format* of the video camera? Can the format be changed?
- What are the processing capabilities of the computers that your students will use to edit this year? What are they likely to be in three years?
- Can the user easily adjust the *white balance* setting on the camera?

The last C of our triad, *correction*, is directed not at righting things that are wrong (for example, removing a car from a ditch) as much as it is dedicated to establishing and maintaining continuity, compatibility, and processing economy across an audio-visual project. This bit of correction is preventative rather than remedial care as it happens on the camera not in the computer. If correction were to be considered in the icy ditch scenario above, it would be the decision to stay home rather than risk driving on a country road in Michigan in February.

IIIa. Format: We want our video images to be as good as possible, right? Right. Therefore, we should always select the highest quality settings on our cameras, right? Wrong. High quality is almost always synonymous with large file size, and large file size is almost always synonymous with a correspondingly high demand for computer storage and processing power. In fact, while the high-definition camera you may be using may be both easy to operate and relatively inexpensive, finding a computer capable of rendering (reformatting), storing, and editing the video images it records may be quite difficult and costly. You and your students may have those computers, but, then again, you may not. If you do not, uploading high-definition video into a computer without ample RAM (minimum eight GB), ample hard drive space, and fast, multi-core processors is a recipe for producing foul language, heavy triage, and, often, project failure. Consequently, for most novice video projects (as of the fall of 2012), I recommend using low-definition settings on video cameras. The more versatile video cameras allow users to select the recording format. These are always preferable to high-definition video cameras that do not allow users to record in regular definition formats (e.g., DV or DV-Cam). A word of caution: When multiple cameras are being used on a single project, be certain to set all of the cameras to record in the same format. This will enable your students to upload all of their footage into a single editing project and will prevent inadvertently low-resolution footage from limiting the output of your high-definition footage.

As of 2012, most laptops and desktop computers (PCs and Macs alike) can handle short video projects (five to ten minutes, edited) recorded in regular definition. However, high-definition video requires hardware and software that exceeds the basic performance limits of most computers. Even if the software specifies that it is a high-definition software, the computer on which the software is installed may not actually be able to run the high-definition applications. This brings us to our next rule of Chapter 5:

Rule #6: Dream big, record small. Or, when in doubt, hi-def is out.

Doubt, here, refers to uncertainty about the capabilities of the computers to be used for editing. If, for example, your students will be using their own computers, always suggest using the lowest camera settings for entry-level projects. Smaller file sizes mean faster rendering and processing. Uploading video files from cameras to computers generally happens in real time—that is, thirty-five minutes of video takes thirty-five minutes to upload. Once uploaded, those files may need to be reformatted to perform some editing operations. All reformatting and processing procedures take time to perform. The smaller the files (and the faster the computer), the faster the process goes for the audio-visual author. So, dream big, record small.

IIIb. White Balance: Of all the possible settings to adjust on a video camera (exposure, manual focus, recording speed), why single out white balance? In fact, what is white balance? White balance is a setting that tells the camera, in any given light, what white is—and, consequently, what all the other colors are. If the photographer does not intervene in this process, the camera will still photograph in color. However, the colors of photographs taken in one type of lighting—let's say, in your living room at night—will appear as different colors than those photographed in other types of lighting—let's say, in your backyard at noon on a sunny day. Setting the white balance, manually when possible, will help create continuity across videotaping situations. Most dedicated video cameras (that is, video cameras that are not also cell phones, for example) will have automated scene settings (nighttime, indoor, outdoor, beach, snow, etc.) that approximate white balance settings for actual lighting conditions. Using these settings is usually better than ignoring white balance all together; however, white balance is generally pretty easy to adjust on dedicated video cameras, and it often involves pushing one button on the camera, aiming the camera at something white (e.g., a piece of white paper) in the same light as the thing you are planning to photograph, zooming in on that white item so that the camera sees only white, and pressing a button that registers the source as white. That's it. If this is done properly each time the camera is used, the camera should retain a high degree of continuity for the colors it reproduces.

Of course, the process of setting white balance is not flawless. Lighting changes for any variety of reasons from the time of day, to the motion of clouds, to the appearance of shadows due to a dynamic world. Not only does the world move, photographers move within it. Each location and each angle within a location alters the way the camera addresses the light. That does not immediately necessitate a new white balance setting for each shot; however, it may. Fig. 5.3a and Fig. 5.3b show two shots from a scene from LiteracyCorps Michigan. The photograph in Fig. 5.3a was taken with a camera that had been white balanced for the scene. The photograph in Fig. 5.3b was taken with a different camera that had not been white balanced for the scene. Notice how the photograph in Fig. 5.3b has much more yellow hue throughout all the colors of the photograph.

| Fig. 5.3a: White balance set for the lighting of the room. | Fig. 5.3b: White balance not set for the lighting of the room. |

White balancing allows multiple camera operators in a variety of scenes and settings to be able to contribute to a work that has a consistent authorial voice. Otherwise, what can emerge is multiple authorial voices revealed through the visual quality of different cameras and points of view. Also potentially compromised by conflicting white balance settings is the viewer's trust that any of the photographs have a high degree of *fidelity*. Documentary scholar Bill Nichols claims that "fidelity lies in the mind of the beholder as much as it lies in the relationship between a camera and what comes before it" (xiii). Nichols adds, "The documentary tradition relies heavily on being able to convey to us the impression of authenticity" (xiii). Consequently, when multiple cameras establish competing color relationships with what comes before them, the viewer's impression of authenticity can be compromised. When visual information is being presented as empirical evidence—that is, when it is evidentiary to the claims being advanced within the audio-visual text—the audio-visual writer's *ethos* depends largely on the viewer's impression of authenticity, especially since, as Nichols notes, "our belief in the authenticity of the image is a matter of trust to begin with" (xvi). While shaky photography, poor focus, unsteady zooming, inconsistent framing, and bad lighting may also compromise an audio-visual writer's authority by pointing to unskillful camera work—the interface with the world being photographed—variations in white balance can shake the very foundation of the authenticity of that world to begin with. This lesson has analogues to many familiar lessons about style and form in traditional writing instruction.

Rule #7: The white balance is the right balance.

Am I making too much of a big deal about white balance—a functional or formal concern—by connecting it to authorial *ethos*? Kress and van Leeuwen state, "Visual structures do not simply reproduce the structures of 'reality.' [. . .] They are ideological. Visual structures are never merely formal: they have a deeply important semantic dimension" (47). I am suggesting that photographs that demonstrate variation in the coloring of the world carry the deeply important semantic dimension of point of view and authorial voice. Where we demonstrate the obvious subjectivity of competing points of view, we lose the impression of objectivity and continuity—a lesson not far removed from an author's choice to avoid personal pronouns in scientific writing. Scientific texts are all written by subjective authors; however, the absence of personal pronouns and the use of passive voice can help facilitate a greater impression of objectivity—something valued highly in scientific texts. Kress and van Leeuwen write:

> Scientific and technical pictures, such as diagrams, maps and charts, usually encode an objective attitude. This tends to be done in one of two ways: by a directly frontal or perpendicular top-down angle. Such angles do not suggest viewer positions, but special and privileged ones, which neutralize the distortions that usually come with perspective, because they neutralize perspective itself. (143–44)

Consistency with regard to a *straight forward* or *straight down* point of view, while chosen by the author as a point of view, can disappear as a point of view in much the same way that passive voice can disappear as a point of view in scientific writing. Both are rhetorical strategies for featuring the object of study rather than the agent of study.

Kress and van Leeuwen discuss framing as a vehicle for authorial objectivity. They claim, "There are, [. . .], two kinds of images in Western cultures: subjective and objective images, images *with* (central) perspective (and hence with a 'built-in' point of view) and images *without* (central) perspective (and hence without a 'built-in' point of view)" (130). Kress and van Leeuwen follow, "Objective images, then, disregard the viewer. They say, as it were, 'I am this way, regardless of who or where or when you are'" (131), and claim, "By contrast, the point of view of the subjective, perspectival image has been selected *for* the viewer" (131). It would seem that uniform white balance similarly presents a built-in objective point of view and that variations in white balance present multiple subjective points of view. As we discussed earlier with backlighting, these variations, when selected, can provide powerful aesthetic contrast. However, when they are not selected— when they simply happen—they surface as grammatical errors that compromise authorial *ethos* in much the same way persistent grammatical errors compromise *ethos* in traditional forms of writing.

Poorly set white balance will not prevent your audio-visual writing students from making movies. However, talking about white balance can help you and your students to think about the ramifications of integrating multiple audio-visual media assets; and to think about not only what fills in the layers of an audio-visual composition but to think about how those layers talk to, with, and for each other; and, finally, to hear and see how the audio-visual writer's voice emerges from this integration. With each cut, each camera angle, each piece of non-diegetic music, the audio-visual author signals her presence to her audience. She says, in essence, "Hey, I'm doing this. It didn't simply *happen* this way. I made some choices. I made it happen *this way*. Notice me." Sometimes she will scream this announcement. Other times, she will whisper. At all times, we want her to control the volume and strength of her announcement. We want that to be her choice as well. Because white balance is a choice that most novice camera operators do not even know they have, calling your students' attention to the feature will serve as a first important step in considering the rhetorical ramifications for caring about this functional concern. In short, setting white balance moves the picture—the here and now event being photographed—into the *big picture*—the ongoing, multi-layered, re-mixed, and integrated operation of audio-visual writing.

THE RHETORICAL PRAGMATISM OF *ETHOS*

While we are on the topic of authorial *ethos*, and before we end our discussion of cameras, we need to discuss briefly two ethical concerns that have very practical outcomes in terms of rhetorical ends and means: copyright and IRB. In Chapter Six, we will explore a variety of audio-visual writing assignments and assignment sequences. Each of these, like each instance of writing itself, is driven by rhetorical aims even as it remains open to recognizing and following rhetorical aims that emerge through the act of writing. The push and pull between rhetorical aims and the epistemic process of pursuing them can lead audio-visual writers to choose means along the way that may be at odds with their original or emergent rhetorical aims. For example, a student in my audio-visual writing class wanted to experiment with making a documentary about a subject for which he had a great deal of passion: recycling. Like several of his classmates, he decided to publish early drafts of his documentary to YouTube to make it easy for his classmates and me to review his developing work. However, within minutes of posting his work, it was removed from YouTube because he did not have express permission from the copyright holder to use a piece of music that appeared in his documentary. Now, this piece of music was a favorite of his, and so he left it in his movie. During his final presentation of his work in class, he told us that it was his goal to inform as many people as possible about recycling. We had spent the semester using a variety of media assets, so I knew that this student was familiar with resources for finding music that would not compromise his ability to publish the project. I asked him, "Why are you letting one piece of music—one part of one layer of the multidimensional audio-visual text that you have spent eight weeks creating—stand in the way of realizing your pedagogical mission?" The next morning, with a new musical soundtrack, his documentary was posted to YouTube.

Rule #8: Component media should facilitate, not impede, the realization of your rhetorical mission.

The example above illustrates the importance of keeping aims and process in constant dialogue. Because he did so, and because we had anticipated this sort of ethical situation, my student was able to make one quick and deliberate move to realign the product of his audio-visual writing with the rhetorical purposes that had motivated its production. The catalyst in this instance was a piece of music; however, it could just as easily have been a photograph, a piece of remixed video, or an interviewee who decided to have her testimony removed from the project. In fact, shortly after successfully publishing his work, an interviewee did request that her portions of the work be withdrawn from the text. The work then came back down—this time removed by my student and not by the copyright-patrolling robots at YouTube. My student went back to the drawing board, this time with a bit less footage, but with even more resolve to get his message out. This student was glorying in both the successes and the problems—the unfinishedness—of his audio-visual writing, and, as all authors have experienced, some moments are more glorious than others.

That is the point here: If our mission is to produce specific kinds of texts for specific kinds of purposes, then we will want to teach the rules that govern those types of texts for those types of purposes so that our students may spend more time glorying in the finishedness of the texts they create. If, however, our mission is to help our students develop habits for aligning their rhetorical purposes, whatever they may be, with the audio-visual works they write in the service of those purposes, then we may want to allow our students to encounter the problems that emerge along the way and help them manage the problems that matter most—to them. We want to help our students make intelligent decisions, and we want to teach the rules of audio-visual writing according to the association model for teaching English grammar—within the context of instances of student writing.

That said, here is a rule you will want to teach first *and* follow up when it emerges: the *ethos* of conducting responsible research that involves human subjects. Your institution will likely have an *institutional review board (IRB)*—sometimes called an independent ethics committee (IEC) or ethical review board (ERB)—that will have policies for how research is to be conducted at your institution. In most instances, coursework-based undergraduate research is exempt from formal IRB review. However, graduate research most often is not—especially if the coursework-based project becomes part of a larger research project. Writing teachers should contact their institution's IRB office to discuss the institution's policies for students who conduct videotaped interviews. At many institutions, the IRB office will have online tutorials that students may complete to demonstrate that they are aware of the ethical risks of inquiry-based videotaping. If your students are going to pursue inquiry-based work with cameras and microphones—instruments of documenting the actions of identifiable individuals—your students should be aware of the ethical ramifications of doing so.

Rule #9: Make sure that your students have access to and experience with making ethical decisions as directed by your institution's IRB.

Peripherals Vision. Video cameras have a few functional partners, none more important than microphones, tripods, power supplies (batteries and battery chargers), and carrying cases. Some of you will be asked to help your departments or colleges make decisions about the camera equipment your students will need. Others of you, like me, may have to make all of these decisions yourselves. Remember, a writer teaches writing. What follows is what this audio-visual writer has learned about both audio-visual writing and what this teacher has learned about his students' needs. We have already discussed microphones in Chapter Four, so we will concentrate on the other three here, along with a brief recognition of the logic of brand loyalty.

Tripods. Tripods are absolutely essential pieces of equipment for students who will be working alone and/or will be conducting interviews. They may choose to not use tripods, but students should always have access to tripods so that they may produce the type of objective shots that Kress and van Leeuwen have described and that we have discussed above. When selecting tripods, choose tripods that come with extra connecting plates and carrying cases with shoulder straps. Why extra connecting plates? Tow trucks. Without a connecting plate, the tripod is useless.

Power Supplies. What happens when students are out in the field videotaping an interview, and their battery dies midway through the interview? Without a spare charged battery, nothing. However, if the cameras that students are using come equipped with spare batteries, they are a battery change away from being back in business. Furthermore, if the students have or can gain access to an electrical outlet, they can simply plug the camera in to both recharge the battery and power the camera. With each camera I lend, I include two batteries, a power supply for the camera, and an additional battery charger. Why? Because when the video camera has no power, neither does the audio-visual writer whose work depends upon it.

Carrying Cases. For years I had wondered why my mom bought such big purses. She has always maintained that they need to be so big to accommodate all the stuff she needs to lug around—everywhere—every day—always. I have argued that if her purses were smaller, she'd be forced to lug around less stuff: only five or six rolls of quarters, only one spare quart of skim milk, only one extra car battery. What seems to be at issue here is that my mom estimates the volume of items that she *may* need, and I assess what she *will likely* need. I'm more of a risk taker. Mom's more of a hunchback—er, I mean, pack mule—er, I mean, troubleshooter; but, as I've come to appreciate, Mom is always right (and wicked strong). When it comes to carrying cases, your students' video camera cases should be like my mom's purses: big enough to carry all of the things that they *may* need. They *will* need the cameras and the batteries, and the power supplies. Those are givens. What they *may* need is external microphones, microphone cables, interview permission forms, pens, wind covers for the microphones, and possibly adapters to make the microphones fit the camera. That's a lot of extra stuff. Make sure that those who are responsible for acquiring the cameras and the peripheral supplies that your students will use understand *how* your students will use that equipment so that your students may be able to carry *all that they may need* to the places where they must go. Retailers often suggest carrying cases for the cameras they sell, and these cases are most often suggested for their economy of size. For your students' potential concerns, follow Mom's example: Choose the big bag!

Brand Loyalty. I do not work for any camera manufacturing companies. Frankly, when it comes to all of the technology that I use and that I order for my students to use, I hate all of the gear equally. It all breaks. It all has pieces that get lost. It is all expensive—even the cheap stuff. However, I am a big fan of brand loyalty for the reasons that I have just listed above: for the peripheral concerns. Because batteries are so very important, ordering one type of camera can increase the likelihood that all of the cameras can share and swap batteries—something *never* possible across manufacturers. Never ever. Also, since tripod connector plates are both (1) absolutely necessary for connecting a video camera to a tripod, and (2) fantastically easy to lose, buying one brand of tripod, especially if each comes with an extra connector plate, will help ensure that your students can actually use the tripod that they schlepped to their video shoot once they get there.

I generally spend very little time on teaching my students how to use the equipment that they use in my classes. Instead, I like to use a series of low-stakes activities that demand that they use the gear, and I make the following tips sheet (Fig. 5.4) available to them as they pursue those activities. I also place links on our course website to the camera and peripherals manufacturers' websites and suggest that students search the Web and YouTube for tutorials that address the specific problems that arise as they use the equipment. This essentially eliminates the need to spend class time on lessons about camera operations.

Interview/Filming Tips

Cameras
- Set the white balance for your camera for each scene you shoot and re-set it each time the light changes.
- Keep a few sheets of white paper handy for setting white balance.
- Check that the lens is clean.
- Check that your camera has at least two batteries and a charger.
- Check that your camera has a power supply.
- **CHARGE YOUR BATTERIES OVERNIGHT PRIOR TO YOUR SHOOT (**& again before you return your camera)**!**
- Check that your camera has at least one microphone (either built in, or external)
- Check to see what type of microphone jack(s) your camera has & get adapters for your microphones if necessary.
- Have at least one spare tape per camera (mini DV format).
- **When shooting in High-Definition** (1080i) **on a Sony camera,** ALWAYS use Sony mini HDV tapes (rated specifically for High-Def) to prevent dropped frames during recording (trust me, you don't want dropped frames).
- Check that the recording setting is proper for your project & consistent on all cameras:
    - o   HDV 1080i (63 min)
    - o   DVCAM (43 min)
    - o   **DV SP (63 min)**

Audio
- **ALWAYS HAVE & USE HEADPHONES when recording audio!**
- When possible, use external microphones for interviews.
- When using two microphones into one camera, check to be sure you hear one microphone in only one ear and the other microphone only in the other ear.
- When using one microphone, make sure that you hear it in both ears.
- **Listen to the room before you set up microphones.** Move microphones away from sources of noise (unwanted sound): e.g., fans, machines, windows near traffic, TVs /radios, etc.

Interview/Filming Tips

- Match microphones to your need & to your camera(s).
- If your camera does not have phantom power (+48v) you will need (fresh or fully charged) AA batteries for any condenser microphones you will be using.
- Think about **audio B-roll**. You may want to roll the camera on location to target identifying sounds: e.g., party noises at a fraternity, the sound of someone typing at a computer, street noises, etc. (don't worry about the picture, you can edit that out).
- **Choose music carefully!** Keep in mind that the presence of music protected by copyright (virtually all music) will prevent you from publishing your documentary online or elsewhere. Use CC Mixter or music from my webpage for possible sources of CC-licensed music.

Timecode

- **When filming, always begin recording at least 20 seconds before your shot will begin & continue at least 20 seconds after your shot is done. Why? So you don't drop timecode.**
- When you begin recording, your camera lays down timecode. When you stop recording, the timecode stops too. If you begin recording at precisely the same spot you stopped (let's say @ 3:35), the timecode continues (e.g., @ 3:36 →). **If, however, your watch the footage you just filmed beyond the end of that footage (i.e., until the screen turns blue) & then begin recording again from there, the camera will start w/ brand new timecode (@ 0:00).** This will present problems to you when you attempt to upload your video into your computer.
- **So, that's why you always want to obey the first bullet point above—and when you watch back any footage on your camera, stop the tape before you reach the end of the footage (during that 20 seconds of extra time).** That way you won't lose anything important & you won't drop timecode.

Interview/Filming Tips

Permission Forms
- Have plenty printed out & on hand before you ever unpack your camera.
- Pack a few pens as well!

Shot Variety
- Vary placement of heads—avoid repetition of down the middle default
- Conduct some interviews indoors & some outdoors
- Avoid backing people up against a wall—allow more space in your shots
- Try to set the camera at different distances from interviewees
- Think about where your camera high should be—e.g., at or below eye-level.
- Where should your cameras be placed? What camera(s) should remain mobile?

Image Movement
- **Zooming** (lens movement): Zooming will increase "jiggle," so avoid zooming when not using a tripod
- **Panning** (camera movement): Avoid fast movements with the camera, whether on or off a tripod.
- **Use a tripod** for all of your interviews unless you're going specifically for that "MTV" style, shaky shot.
- **Check that your tripod has a connector plate!** Without a connector plate, you do not have a tripod.

Lighting
- Light source should be from the front or from a side
- **Avoid back lighting**—i.e., light sources behind the subject
- Try to use natural light (sunlight) when possible

Video B-Roll
- Mix motion & still photography
- Use to set the scene of the interview and/or the topic of discussion
- Evidentiary editing: use as evidence to support interviews or voice-over narration

Interview/Filming Tips

Practice
- Interview yourselves on film before interviewing others
- Conduct a few low-stakes interviews first
- Allow ample time for set-up and tear-down
- Scout a good location or two
- Ask for suggestions re: interview location

Interviewing
- Whenever possible, **arrive at least one hour early to set up your interview scene** (and allow at least 30 minutes for tear-down).
- **Always plan to use more than one camera for filming interviews.**
- Try to have interviewees repeat the question in her/his answer when possible—this will give you the greatest flexibility when editing.
- Ask questions that seek substantive answers (e.g., Questions that contain the words What or How: What do you see to be the biggest threat of global warming? How could or should sororities initiate pledges in a safe manner?).
- Avoid asking questions that seek Yes/No answers (e.g., Questions that begin w/ the words Is/Are, Do/Does, or Will/Would: Do you believe in global warming? Is the minimum drinking age fair? Would you join a fraternity?).
- When possible, send interviewees questions you will be asking in advance. Allow your interviewees to prepare for your interview session.
- Try asking interviewees to bring **artifacts** (items that they can talk about)—things that may be relevant to your concerns (e.g., you may ask a professor to bring something especially representative of her PW class—a book, a sample of student work, an external hard drive, a box of crayons, whatever). These things will help your interviewee both tell you and show you something that they already think is important to them—they come w/ stories already attached to them.

Fig. 5.4: A tips sheet for audio-visual writing students who will be using video cameras.

CONCLUSION

I will end this chapter where it began, by reminding us, again, that we teach writing, not photography. However, I am fond of saying to my students, especially in my parting words at the end of a semester, "whatever it is that you are doing, do *that*." In other words, you may not *be* a photographer; however, if you are taking pictures (motion or still)—if you are *doing* photography—then you should *do* that determinedly and reflectively—intelligently. In short, you should do that *rhetorically*. In this section, I have offered a very brief discussion of some of the do and don't rules of using cameras. However, I have offered these as heuristics for encountering lessons about writing, not as hortatory commandments that must not be broken. Since I am a writing teacher, I don't mind my students making the types of mistakes—that is, finding their way to the sorts of *problems*—that occasion the application of the do and don't rules. In fact, I invite them to go looking for these sorts of problems. Because problems are the stimulus to thinking, the rules become far more valuable when they may be used to prevent or solve problems—*experienced* problems, not just those rumored to occur. I will amend Williams's sage advice, "You must know what the rule is before you can break it" (49), as follows to articulate our final rule of Chapter Five:

Rule #10: Sometimes you must first break the rule in order to learn the value of the rule.

The value of *this* rule is that it becomes a product of *thinking*, not of rote memory—a direct descendent of the association model for grammar instruction. If you allow students to find these problems, the rules can emerge as lessons, and the problems can become rhetorically situated—that is, features of interactions between people, not simply features of cameras. Lindemann reminds us that "Student writers don't need to 'know' grammar in the same way that linguists and teachers do" (4th ed. 85). Of course, this claim suggests that writing teachers *do* need to know the principles of grammar, since, as Williams claims, "*naming* these principles is the key to having power over them" (11). I invite *you* to find your way into the problems of audio-visual writing, to experience them for yourself, and to allow them to stimulate your thinking about why these rules may have value for you as a writer and as a teacher. Teachers must foresee many problems—more than we have time to experience. A writer teaches writing. However, as we know, a teacher of writing must be more than just a writer. Teachers must know more rules than they use. Writers know that they obey rules that they never memorized—that they learned because they found a need for the rules. Audio-visual writing teachers must be both and must seek both experiential and theoretical knowledge. With that disclaimer, I offer a collection of the ten rules that have emerged throughout our discussion of what audio-visual writing teachers must know about video—the Code of Audio-Visual Writers, if you will:

Rule #1:	*Remember where you are going.*
Rule #2:	*Video cameras are the shoes of your audio-visual wardrobe.*
Rule #3:	*Audio-visual writers choose cameras according to their rhetorical purposes.*
Rule #4:	*Label your storage media carefully and consistently.*
Rule #5:	*Without proper means of connection, your assets are liabilities.*
Rule #6:	*Dream big, record small.*
Rule #7:	*The white balance is the right balance.*
Rule #8:	*Component media should facilitate, not impede, the realization of your rhetorical mission.*
Rule #9:	*Make sure that your students have access to and experience with making ethical decisions as directed by your institution's IRB.*
Rule #10:	*Sometimes you must first break the rule in order to learn the value of the rule.*

Now that I have assembled "The Code," I will end this chapter by remixing the words of Captain Barbossa, from *The Pirates of the Caribbean: The Curse of the Black Pearl*, when Elizabeth attempted to invoke a particular rule of the Pirate's Code: "The code is more what you'd call 'guidelines' than actual rules. Welcome aboard the Black Pearl, Miss Turner."

6 Teaching Twenty-First Century Writing as Symbolic Action

> *[P]roblems are the stimulus to thinking. That the conditions found in present experience should be used as sources of problems is a characteristic which differentiates education based upon experience from traditional education.*
>
> —John Dewey

> *An important goal of any writing teacher is to help students gain confidence in their ability to use the code effectively, perhaps even to find pleasure in manipulating its symbols.*
>
> —Erika Lindemann

When you assign a research paper, when are your students writing it? Are they writing it when they get the assignment and try to imagine how they may begin to respond to it? Are they writing it when they pick up, consider, and either take or put back books and journals in the library? Are they writing it when they type words and phrases into a search engine or database? Are they writing when they sit down at their computer and transfer notes from their notebooks into their computers? Are they writing when they leave their desks to go for a coffee, or to the gym, or to the shower, or to bed? Are they writing when they pick and choose which suggestions to accept and which to reject following a draft workshop in class or after meeting with a writing center tutor? Are they writing when they decide not to revise the work, again, for a higher grade?

Yes.

Writing is the realization of a writer's writerly decisions. At all stages of a writer's process the writer dances between invention and revision, between exploration and arrangement, between guessing and

197

knowing, between seeking and finding, between accepting and reject-
ing. Each step of this dance is a step of writing—even if each step,
when frozen in time and abstracted from the dance, does not look
much like a prototypical *dance step*. Importantly, the dance would not
be complete without each step, and even more importantly, the dance,
and all of its steps, is itself a contradiction. It is both fixed and ever
changing, an operation and a process, entitled and defined, all there
at once and sequential. It is both the dance of *a* research paper and the
dance of *this* research paper—a type of symbolic act fitted to a particular scene. The experience of having performed the dance of *a* research
paper will inform the next particular rendition of the dance, even if
it does not dictate it. The next scene will present new problems, and
the process will need to respond to those new particulars. Some of the
steps of that process will be permanent. Others will be held in place
with duct tape. Duct tape is used to correct infrastructures and protocols—scenes—that were not designed for emergent actions. Duct tape
is used to fix problems.

This chapter will look for duct tape in order to see problems. Unlike the actual duct tape that fixed (i.e., corrected) the problem in the
preface of this book by fixing (i.e., adhering) a makeshift movie screen
to the wall, the duct tape we will look for in this chapter is metaphoric
duct tape. What does metaphoric duct tape look like? Well, in this
chapter, the duct tape will appear in the form of writing assignments,
and the problems these writing assignments will be attempting to fix
will be learning goals for writing students—problematic learning goals
that have resisted being addressed successfully by way of traditional
writing assignments. Our problems.

This chapter moves our discussions, thus far, into the design of
writing assignments and writing courses. It begins with problems that
are filtered through theory to expose learning goals. The contents of
this chapter ask us to accept that a writing assignment is a vehicle for
realizing learning goals—it is not merely a recipe for producing a type
of writing, even though it will do that along the way. Again, producing
and perfecting particular types of writing is, indeed, a perfectly legitimate problem. However, it is not the only legitimate problem—nor
is it even a common problem. Most students who take a writing class
will rarely if ever again write a book review or a literacy narrative or
even a research essay. Some will. Some will become like us. Most will
not. This chapter attempts to meet the needs of a wide variety of writ-

ers: those with goals similar to ours and those with goals less familiar to us. Consequently, the assignments we consider will not be aimed at producing the book review, or the literacy narrative, or the research essay. The assignments we will discuss are aimed at realizing learning goals—at invoking the habits and awareness of writers. It builds people, not stuff—even though it does so by asking people to build stuff. The thing that will be assessed is not the artifact of writing as much as the realization of the lesson, and if we have designed our assignments as obstacle courses—as a series of problems that will stimulate students' thinking—the very act of doing the assignments—of negotiating the course—will deliver the lessons.

In this chapter, we will consider three problems—problems that I have confronted in my teaching, and problems that I have found to be common among many of the writing teachers I know and whose teaching I have observed. While these three problems are similar in that they are common to many writing teachers, they are different in kind in that they have led me to the expression of different learning goals and to different assignments designed to help my students realize those learning goals. You may have faced similar problems, and, if you have, I hope that the steps I outline will help you and your students convert these problems into productive catalysts to thinking and writing. However, my intention is not to prescribe means but to model a problem-based method for designing a variety of assignments: a non-graded invention workshop; a stand-alone audio-visual writing assignment; and a sequence of writing assignments.

Here is the important feature of this approach: It looks for and responds to existing problems—problems that have resisted being ameliorated by way of traditional writing assignments. Rather than presenting the problem of prescribing new forms of writing, it looks to new forms of writing as a means for addressing existing, emergent, or persistent problems. Each problem we consider will move through a similar sequence of considerations: Problem → Theory → Lesson/ Learning Goal(s) → Assignment → Delivery → Assessment. The problems we identify will be filtered through theory that will claim the way we are to understand the problems—how to claim the problems not only as ours as teachers but as ours within a field of academics. These filtered problems will then be converted to lessons or learning goals, and the assignments that we will consider will be aimed at helping students realize these learning goals by way of *play-intensive* audio-visual writing activities. Next, we will discuss how we can go about delivering the assignments: the Burkean *agency* or means of delivery, the time required to pursue and complete the assignment, the material and social infrastructures necessary for implementing the assignments, and the ethical and practical constraints that affect the delivery of the assignments—in short, the scenes and means that will impact how we may or may not implement the assignment. Finally, we will consider how to assess the outcomes of these assignments.

Here's the secret of this approach to assessment: Assess the lesson/learning goal(s), not the assignment. This approach emerges from Murray's advice that drives the entirety of the book you are reading: to glory in the unfinishedness of student writing. The movies your students make do not need to be publishable—we are not teaching moviemaking. We are using moviemaking as a means to teach writing and, especially, to teach writers. As long as our learning goals are met, our assignments are working. Consequently, the products of our students' efforts do not need to be scrutinized under the rubric of audience expectations for professional or publishable moviemaking.

Let me say that again.

As long as our learning goals are met, our assignments are working. Consequently, the products of our students' efforts do not need to be scrutinized under the rubric of audience expectations for professional or publishable moviemaking.

This approach may be difficult for many of you to adopt and possibly even to accept. We are a field steeped in the tradition of crafting traditional forms of academic writing: forms we read, write, and know well. We see the strengths and the weaknesses of student writing and we compare and contrast that with what we know of the spectrum of academic writing: the best, the worst, and all points between. We also know the uses of these products and, consequently, have become accustomed to seeing the products themselves as goals. We know the use(s) of the research essay. We know the practical applications of annotated bibliographies. We believe in the pedagogical value of the revelations that define the literacy narrative. As such, the realization of the form is the goal. We teach the book review, we teach the literacy narrative, we teach the research essay, and if we apply Dewey's logic regarding problems, the solipsistic problems we often assign are the forms themselves. Problem: Students need to learn to write research essays → Learning Goal: Students learn to write a research essay →

Assignment: Write a research essay. The goal, throughout, is the realization of a form.

Let's reimagine this.

First, a caveat. The assignments I will present are robust in that, *like all writing assignments*, they will address far more problems and learning goals than the few that I will identify (i.e., *entitle*). Also, I do not imagine that the specific problems that I will name here are truly common. Consequently, these assignments are not plug and play; that is, they do not look like assignments that you can photocopy and plug into your assignment sequence. That would be antithetical to the entire enterprise we have undertaken here. The problems may be ours, but the learning goals and the assignments must be yours. I invite you to study the process of moving problem to assignment in order to imagine other problems and/or learning goals that may be developed through this process. What will ultimately guide your selection of assignment and assessment? In short, that's your problem. (☺)

PROBLEM #1: METAPHOR

Problem: Students have problems using metaphor in their writing to shape and express their perspectives. Notice the difference between this problem and the one identified above. It identifies a problem across writing forms; consequently, it may look across writing forms for ways to address the problem—especially, if the problem is persistent within traditional forms of writing.

Theory: In Chapter Two we asserted the pedagogical importance of metaphor. In essence, metaphors present problems to be solved because they take two obviously different things and assert their sameness. Love is war. Red is the new black. Filmmaking is writing. Let's recall, also from Chapter Two, that Burke writes, "Every perspective requires a metaphor, implicit or explicit, for its organizational base" (*Philosophy* 152). Burke's own organizational metaphor for his *A Grammar of Motives* is the drama. The things people do are *acts*. These acts are shaped by the *scenes* in which they are performed. Burke's dramatistic metaphor shapes his rhetorical perspectives for analyzing human motives, so it follows that we may address perspective expressed in student writing as a function of identifying and utilizing analogical extension realized by way of effective, perspective-directing metaphor.

Students may have trouble approaching their beliefs about language or education or writing as *beliefs*—things that exist as we believe or will them to be—and not as facts—things that exist outside of our beliefs or those of others. However, helping them identify foundational metaphors through which they entitle their beliefs may help them understand and potentially alter or strengthen their existing perspectives. For example, students may not see the power of metaphor in the title of the educational policy, "No Child Left Behind." At the heart of the idealistic mission claimed by its title, No Child Left Behind is a metaphor that states something like the following: No student is a substandard student—or, expressed in the positive plural, all students are standard students. Now, as we know, an effective metaphor needs to assert the sameness of very different things, and these are two very different things: all = some. Exposing the metaphor allows us to posit both where the metaphor is productive and where it is not rather than simply accepting or dismissing the claim as a statement of truth. However, this bit of metaphoric wordplay may be hard for students to adopt and possibly even to accept. Helping them equate symbolic *things* that are clearly different in kind may serve as a bridge to the symbolic action of linguistic metaphor. For example, common is extraordinary.

Lesson/Learning Goal: To help students experience the pedagogical and perspective-shaping value of metaphor in their writing.

Assignment #1, "Moving Meaning through Metaphor": This learning goal identifies itself as a supporting lesson—one that serves a variety of forms of writing. Consequently, the assignment I have used to realize the learning goal is a supporting lesson for other assignments. I have situated it, most often, as a lesson of invention, one that asks students to play—to experiment—to try to find something that they do not already have. The assignment chooses for its perspective the metaphor I mentioned above: Common is extraordinary. The means the assignment chooses to pursue its perspective are movie cameras. Here's what I ask of my students:

1. Take a video camera and a tripod and go for a walk.
2. As you walk, look and listen for the most common items you can find. These should be things that you walk by without ever

consciously noticing. Your job on this walk is to see and hear the things you do not normally see and hear.

3. As you identify candidates for this study, stop and videotape these common artifacts and/or activities.

    - Cigarette butts outside a building
    - Piles of mulch
    - The sounds of university vehicles backing up
    - Graffiti spray painted on sidewalks
    - The *sounds* of people getting on and off of elevators
    - The dancing of bees in a flowerbed
    - The sounds of campus life: people congregating and/or moving about—auto, bike, and foot traffic

4. Study the artifacts or activities that catch your eye or ear by regarding them from multiple perspectives—points of view or points of audition.

    - Close-ups: filming with the camera very close to the visual object, sound, or action under study.
    - Reverse perspective: i.e., filming from "behind" the visual object, sound, or action —as though from its point of view or audition.
    - Zoomed shots: filming with the camera far from the visual object, sound, or action under study but using the camera's lens to create a close-up by way of "zooming in."
    - Establishing or distance shots: filming with the camera far enough away from the visual object, sound, or action under study to place it in context with its immediate surroundings.

5. Review your videotape and/or upload your videotape into the editing software on a computer.
    - If *not* using editing software: proceed directly to the questions below.
    - If using editing software: create a two-to-three-minute video that combines the footage you shot, music, and text or narration to help us see and/or hear the visual object, sound, or action under study in a new way or context.

- In a text document (e.g., MS Word) or presentational document (e.g., PowerPoint or Prezi) respond to the following questions:
    1. What surprises you?
    2. What do you see or hear that you have never seen or heard before?
    3. What do these surprises suggest to you? What do they remind you of? What do they mean?
    4. What was so common about the objects you chose to study?
    5. What was extraordinary about the common objects you studied?
    6. How might you use your footage to help others notice the extraordinary qualities of the common things you have observed?
    7. How did using the (audio-)video camera change your perspective about the things you have encountered and recorded?
    8. Are the things you have recorded *still* common? How so? How not?
  6. Restrictions:
     - No visual studies of identifiable people.
     - Other than music, all sights and sounds must be captured by way of your video camera.
     - Collect at least two visual studies and two audio studies.
     - Shoot no more than fifteen minutes of footage overall.

Delivery: There are many ways to approach the delivery of this assignment. I am considering only two: one that captures and edits video and reflects on the process of doing so and one that captures video and reflects on the process. Choosing between them or other options may be facilitated by considering our four delivery concerns.

- *Agency* (means of delivery):

  Capturing Video/Cameras: To do this assignment, students will need to have access to video cameras of some sort. Many students carry video cameras to class each and every day in the form of their personal communication devices (PCDs: phones, iPads/tablets, laptops, and who-knows-what by the time you are reading this). PCDs have the great advantage of access and availability; however, they also tend to record very poor quality audio and often need special adapters to connect with computers. However, PCDs most often connect directly to the Internet, which can serve as an intermediary warehouse—a satellite storehouse for transferring data from the PCD to the computer. Furthermore, PCDs, despite their ability to capture video data, may not have the memory to store or the RAM to process a full video project—especially the cell phones. Imagine that a three-minute edited video will likely require sixty minutes of raw video. This is most often far beyond the storage capabilities of cell phones. Supplying students with identical video cameras or cameras with similar features, limitations, and connections can streamline the delivery of this assignment. Laptop cameras have the advantage of big playback screens, large memory banks, and immediate access to editing software; however, their size and the position of the camera lens on the same surface as the view screen make laptops poor video cameras for this assignment.

Capturing Audio/Microphones: The microphones and sound capturing software of PCDs most often make them very bad devices for recording sounds that will later be scrutinized in detail. Devices designed specifically for sound recording and video cameras that accept external microphones make the very best choices for doing the listening portions of this assignment. If those materials are unavailable, you may want to limit the assignment to visual observations.

Audio-Visual Playback: While PCDs have the ability to capture audio and video, they must play it through tiny speakers or headphones and display it on pocket-sized screens. Uploading the content from the cameras onto a computer—whether or not you intend for your students to actually edit that material—is ideal as it will greatly improve your students' ability to study the audio-visual content they've captured. Consequently, if you are supplying cameras, it is best to supply both cameras and compatible computers to ensure that students will be able to upload the content on the cameras to computers.

Additionally, if many students are working in the same space, headphones are critical for preventing the cacophony of sound that results from many projects playing simultaneously.

Editing/Computer Hardware and Software: Essentially every desktop and laptop computer now comes pre-equipped with entry-level video editing software. While that ensures that we can edit video, it does not ensure that the computer will have the connection ports necessary for connecting all types of video cameras. That makes students' laptops potentially very bad choices for this assignment; however, we will exploit this potential limitation to our advantage in Assignment #3 below.

- *Time:* Depending on how much time you have to do this assignment and the potential limits placed on time by institutional infrastructure for circulating video recording equipment and/or computer lab access, this assignment can be done in as few as one or two, two-hour class periods. It can also be assigned as homework in order to give students more time to collect footage, more access to a variety of spaces for filming, and more time to upload footage at a lab. Obviously, the more time you have available will allow you and your students to do more with the editing of these pieces. However, not having a great deal of editing time does not necessarily impoverish the exercise. The lesson is aimed at making metaphorical connections between things in the world. As long as students have the experience of re-seeing and re-hearing items and actions in the world, the lesson has been delivered. Of course, getting to further develop these metaphors and the perspectives they reveal in the edited work will enrich students' experience with the lesson.
- *Material and Social Infrastructures:* Does your institution have video cameras that your students can access? If so, do you and your students have access to computers that are compatible with those cameras? Is it reasonable, for your class, to require students to purchase a video camera or the cables required to connect their PCDs to their own laptops (possibly instead of a textbook)? Should students work individually or in small groups? These are the types of questions I ask regularly, and when my institutions did not have the resources I needed to

help me address my learning goals, I went about finding the means to acquire those resources—a task that was always infinitely easier when I could describe not only what I needed but why I needed it and how I intended to employ it—answers informed by way of both my experience as a audio-visual writer and the process described here.

- *Ethical and Practical Constraints:* It is important here not to forget your learning goals. Students will shoot video footage that may look pretty bad. Then again, it also may look surprisingly good. Within a pedagogy that selects student work as the texts for a class, students may serve as models for what is more effective and what is less effective. Consequently, among all of these novice moviemakers are your emerging experts. The reward of performing well comes at little expense to performing poorly since our expectations for high-quality photography and audio recording are very low. This can help your students accept the mission of play involved in this assignment, an assignment that asks that they take chances, look in ways they are unaccustomed to looking, and listen in ways they are unaccustomed to listening. The restriction above that students may not study people is motivated by an ethical concern about the treatment of individuals and their identities. By eliminating people as subjects, we can virtually eliminate the need for prior training in research methods, and by requiring students to capture all of their own footage, we dramatically reduce the opportunity for copyright infringement and/or intellectual property concerns. Copyright concerns, however, may surface if students incorporate music into the edited versions of the assignment—or if students videotape photographs, works of art, or scenes where music is paying in the background. In fact, copyright may indeed be a problem that could realize its learning goals by way of this assignment as well.

Assessment: Assess the lesson, not the assignment. Because this assignment is a support assignment, you may deem it appropriate to be exempt from formal assessment. I have always employed this as an ungraded assignment. Furthermore, my interaction with the text is primarily formative during the capturing and editing of the footage. I troubleshoot students' problems using the hardware and software. During in-class screenings, my role is to take notes on the edited movies or raw footage—notes regarding the metaphors in the works and looking for both outstanding moments and common audio-visual problems (audio-visual grammar and usage). My goals in doing so are to glory in the unfinishedness of the products of the assignment—to stimulate conversation about the work in class and to create a record to be placed into conversation with the traditionally mediated reflections. My goal for that response is, again, not summative but formative—one that moves students to think more about their use of the *common is extraordinary* metaphor as signaled in their dialogue between what they have videotaped and studied and the surprises that they discuss in their reflections. In other words, I attempt throughout to avoid treating the text(s) as finished in order to glory in where it is going, not critique what it is.

Final Thoughts about Assignment #1, "Moving Meaning through Metaphor": There are so many potential problems and learning goals that versions of this assignment may address. It may be used to introduce students to the capabilities and limitations of their own computers or PCDs. In short, the limitations of PCDs may be used to point out the importance of sound in many forms of moviemaking—a lesson that is delivered not through success but by failure. Please look and listen for opportunities for your students to learn through failure—to use failure as a motivator—a reward that comes at the cost of effort and attention, but not at the cost of a bad grade. This work depends heavily on experimentation—on play—on taking risk. Be sure that your assessment rubric rewards risk. The assignment is an obstacle course. Simply negotiating it delivers the lesson—a lesson that you will put to further use elsewhere in your curriculum.

PROBLEM #2: INQUIRY

Problem: Here's a problem I have encountered repeatedly over the years: When I ask students to select topics of interest for their research projects, they often select, against my insistence, topics on which they feel they are already experts. Their research efforts tend toward reporting and toward acquiring references that support their preformed theses; consequently, these students have trouble approaching research as a method of inquiry—as a method that helps them answer real questions and as a method that helps them arrive at a thesis.

Theory: In Chapter Two, Murray advised us of the importance of Co-operative Learning, of student choice and ownership of the projects pursued in a process-oriented writing pedagogy. Dewey's "doctrine of interest" also warned us "to furnish conditions such that the natural impulses and acquired habits, as far as they are desirable, *shall obtain subject-matter and modes of skill* in order to develop to their natural ends of achievement and efficiency" (*Interest* 95). Because, as Dewey reminds us, "problems are the stimulus to thinking" (*Experience* 79), it is important that we give our students more than opportunity to pursue topics of interest. In the service of inquiry-based projects, it is imperative that we give our students the opportunity to pursue *problems* of interest—that is, *real* problems—problems that will demand that students *obtain subject-matter and modes of skill* in order to attempt to *solve them.* Our problems—the ones that help us define learning goals—are slightly different from the ones we ask our students to identify. Our problems help us build assignments for our students. Their problems help them fulfill our assignments. In doing so, they get a two-fer: They realize both their and our learning goals. Win. Win.

Lesson/Learning Goal: For students to conduct inquiry-based research, to lead with questions—things they need to learn—instead of assertions—things they want to tell.

Assignment #2, "Ask and Ye Shall Receive": I love this one—mostly because it works. That, plus the name rocks! Right, so let's get to it. Here's what I ask my students to do:

- Each student proposes a topic for an interview-based documentary movie project that s/he thinks would be interesting, informative, and doable on or near campus. The topic of the documentary should be something the student finds interesting but does not know much about. For example, what happens to all of the plastic drink bottles on campus after a football game?

- All students shop their ideas to the rest of their classmates, who then vote in order to determine the top four or five proposed topics.
- Students sign on to be members of these top four or five inquiry-based project production teams.
- In their new inquiry teams, students begin the project by making lists of things they would want to know about their topics.
- Based on their questions, students then begin to make lists of people to interview and choose their top candidates and adjust their questions as necessary for each person they want to interview.
- Production teams present their production plans to the rest of class. Their presentations must indicate all of the following information:
  - A topic and angle or perspective.
  - A brief explanation about what makes this such an attractive and problematic topic, and possible/probable audiences of concern. Students ask about their topics: Who cares and why? What is at stake?
  - At least five guiding questions.
  - A list of interview candidates and explanations of why they are appropriate for the project.
  - Roles and responsibilities for each team member.
  - A timeline for each phase of the project.
- Students arrange and conduct the interviews, making sure to get each participant to sign a permission form that each team prepares to inform participants of their project and what they intend to do with the results.
- Students make movies from the footage they collect and screen their movies in class.
- Each student writes a three hundred- to five hundred-word reflection about his or her experience with the project.
- Restrictions:
  - Students MUST film their own interviews. They may not repurpose interviews found elsewhere.
  - All participants must sign releases and all participants' full names must appear in the list of credits at the end of the movie.
  - Movies should be five to seven minutes in length.

- Each movie must include at least one interview and at least one piece of music suitable for publishing online.

Delivery: There are many concerns for this project that will likely span five to six weeks of the class. Because this interview-based project relies on group work and the involvement of people from outside the class, I always place these assignments in the middle third of the semester to allow a cushion of time to accommodate expected but specifically unforeseen setbacks.

- *Agency* (means of delivery):

    Capturing Video/Cameras: Unlike Assignment #1, students' PCDs are out for this assignment. This project demands more dedicated audio-visual gear.

Table 6.1

video cameras	tripods
headphones	external microphones

Consequently, you will need four or five documentary kits for each class of twenty to thirty students. Students will need some very basic training with the audio-visual gear (discussed in Chapter Five) and some low-stakes practice sessions in order to feel comfortable enough to concentrate on the interviews themselves. This most often takes a remarkably short time— thirty to sixty minutes of class time at the most. Assignment #1 above can also act as a good low-stakes primer for teaching students the basics of camera operation. Most important for students to learn, beyond the very basics of camera operation, is how to set up the shot: How to avoid back-lighting, how to choose a location for the interview, how to create shot variety across interviews, and how to set or select the appropriate white balance setting on the camera (see Fig. 5.4 for a sample hand-out with these types of tips for students). Aside from those few things, I actually prefer to allow students to shoot interviews that may have technical problems because these often create incentive to learn how to prevent those grammatical errors in the future. For example, nothing teaches about the importance of avoiding backlighting like a very good interview in which it is impossible to see the speaker's face due to backlighting—an approach that follows the association model of grammar instruction discussed in Chapter Two. These grammatical lessons are situated in works of student writing and consequently have more value to students than abstract camera lessons that are technical, as they apply to cameras, and *not* grammatical, as they do *not* apply to acts of writing—yet. So the lesson for us—for teachers—is to allow students to make mistakes—to find problems. Problems are the stimulus to thinking and to learning. Let them make mistakes. Let them identify the problems that emerge in their work. Then, let them fix the mistakes that they cannot live with—the ones that their classmates have learned to fix or avoid. Let your students play. If you do, they will learn. However, let me stress the importance of *not* punishing students for taking chances. That is, be certain that your assessment rubric will not punish students for making these valuable mistakes. These mistakes should fuel formative—learning—suggestions, not summative deductions.

Capturing Audio/Microphones: Encouraging students to use external microphones may seem like a technical lesson—and in part it is; however, it is also a lesson in rhetoric masquerading as a technical lesson. It asks students to take control of the audio—to consider the most important information at the heart of the movies they are making: the things that people say. As we discussed in Chapter Four, students will quickly learn that bad audio in an interview situation is a potential project killer. Interviews, especially high-stakes interviews with people with whom students may have only one chance to speak, demand that students get good audio. Consequently, lavalier, shotgun, and/or handheld microphones become material indicators of the rhetorical value of the audio tracks.

Table 6.2

video cameras	tripods
headphones	external microphones

That said, the most important piece of audio gear on an interview shoot is a good pair of headphones. I have experienced student movies that employed external microphones that were turned up too loud or that had dead batteries or that were simply not plugged in (or that were being bludgeoned by a delicate string of rogue pearls!). Headphones, plugged into the camera, will let your students know if the camera is receiving the audio signal and will allow them to make adjustments to the signal if there is a problem. When it comes to audio, junk in = junk out. Unlike the grammatical lessons of backlighting and camera positioning, students will not be able to cover bad audio in an interview with b-roll footage. The lessons of bad audio have been some of the most powerful lessons I have learned and that I have witnessed students learn; however, they most often come at a dramatically high cost. So tell your students, shout it from the rooftops, WEAR HEADPHONES WHILE FILMING INTERVIEWS! That is all.

Editing/Computers and Software: Many of your students may have laptops with software capable of editing their movies. These movies do not demand sophisticated high-end editing software. The standard-issue software on their computers and/or software that students may download for free or at low cost will do just fine. Their laptops will need to be able to connect to the type of video cameras you are using. If some of your students have appropriate laptops, they should serve as anchors for each of the groups. Now, here's the good part of using student laptops: Editing is usually the most time-intensive part of any video project. Students' laptops can keep the same work schedule as their owners. So, students can edit all night long on their own laptops—something they likely cannot do in a campus computer lab. Also, students can control access to their own laptops, preventing other users or regular maintenance from moving or deleting files, etc. Finally, laptops can go anywhere that students can go, which greatly facilitates how, when, and where groups can meet to make their movie. OK, that's the good. The bad thing about laptops is that they live with a single owner, an owner who can potentially hold the project ransom or prevent, for good or bad reasons, the rest of the group from working on the project. Students may, understandably, be reluctant to allow group mates to borrow the laptop or even to work on the computer. These will be decisions that you—teachers—will need to confront when planning and delivering video-based group writing projects.

Computer labs have some really good selling points: They are communal, and they put everyone in the same room. Groups can look over their shoulders at the work that other groups are doing. This can foster a culture of creative sharing and competition. It can give students peer resources for solving problems when things go wrong. It can level the playing field for software and hardware because everyone in the class will use similar gear. It can also foster a more inclusive group editing dynamic—one that begins with much less of a proprietary lease on the computer by any one group member. I must say, however, that in my experience, one or two students usually surface as the primary editors. I must also say, however, that in my experience, the group members who are not the primary editors, almost without exception, say in their reflections that should they have another chance to make a movie that they want to do the editing, that they want to do the hard work, that they want to put in all of those hours. Imagine that. OK, that's the good. The bad thing about computer labs is that they are fixed in time (hours of operation) and space (location).

In terms of software, during what I hope may be a reasonable run for this book, editing software will come and go. I have published a chapter elsewhere that featured screen captures of specific software that was no longer available for purchase at the time of publication. True. This book, in an attempt to remain relevant at least through its initial publishing cycle, has taken a nonspecific approach to software and hardware. Therefore, this is what I can say about software here: If you have a choice, choose editing software that gives you the greatest amount of audio control. Ideally, you want software that features no fewer than three audio tracks: one for voice-over narration and audio b-roll, one for music, and the audio track that is embedded in the video track. Even more ideal, you want software that will allow independent volume control of each audio track at any point in the track. It is also ideal for the software to give you the ability to control panning (left and right speakers) and tone (bass, midrange, and treble). These controls may help students make basic, post-production (performed during editing) fixes of common audio problems that occur during recording.

Fig. 6.1: Screen capture of multiple audio tracks (green) from Apple's Final Cut software. This figure shows six tracks of audio grouped as three stereo (Left and Right) audio track pairs. The pink lines and nodes (running horizontally through the length of each track) represent volume levels. Notice that where volume levels decrease in Track One (L and R), they increase in Track Two (L and R) or Track Three (L and R).

Beyond the audio tracks, the ideal editing software will allow students to layer at least two tracks of video. The most common move of documentary is something Nichols calls "evidentiary editing," a technique that "organizes cuts within a scene to present the impression of a single, convincing argument supported by a logic" (30). Being able to easily layer at least two video tracks enables student editors to use the interview videotape as a base track for their movie and to drop in b-roll and evidentiary clips where necessary. It also allows students to hide edits that help them streamline things that interviewees say. In other words, they can cover up the choppy video track that corresponds to the edited audio track. An interviewee at a Recycling Center may say, for example, "I have worked here for, geez, what is it, five years now. No, six. Six years. Wow. And I've been director for the past two years." The editors may decide to streamline the interviewee's statement as follows: "I have worked here for [cut] Six years. [cut] And I've been director for the past two years." That edit will create two noticeable jump cuts in the video track. However, the editors may decide to overlay b-roll they have shot of the Recycling Center in order to mask their edits (Fig. 6.2). This is an absolutely common move of documentary work—one that should be easy to perform with the software you use. If it is not easy, you may want to look for other software. For example, some software has only one video track; however, the software will allow editors to extract the audio from a video clip and replace the video portion with another video clip. I call this *evidentiary hole digging* (Figs. 6.3–6.6). This technique is far less elegant than a multitrack approach, but it is also entirely manageable. However, if it is not possible to perform evidentiary video edits in the software you are using, then you *must* find other software. Period.

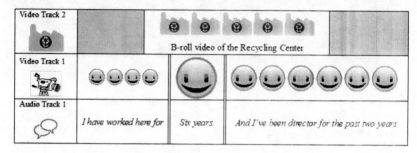

Fig. 6.2: A stacked or overlaid video track. Video Track 2 will play instead of the Video Track (1) that it is covering.

Fig. 6.3: Evidentiary Hole Digging Step 1: Three video clips with embedded audio.

Fig. 6.4: Evidentiary Hole Digging Step 2: Three video clips with corresponding detached audio.

Fig. 6.5: Evidentiary Hole Digging Step 3: The video content to be replaced has been eliminated.

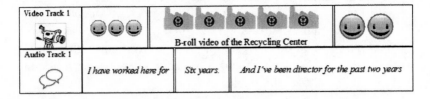

| Video Track 1 | | | B-roll video of the Recycling Center | | |
| Audio Track 1 | *I have worked here for* | *Six years.* | *And I've been director for the past two years* | | |

Fig 6.6: Evidentiary Hole Digging Step 4: The video b-roll has been inserted into the hole created in Step 3.

- *Time:* The assignment should require five to six weeks from initial proposals to final edits. Like teaching itself, editing can take as many hours as anyone has to give it. That said, the learning goal driving this project is not to create a perfect documentary, it is to facilitate inquiry-based writing. Consequently, even rough edits can allow us to realize our learning goal. That said, by situating the assignment in the middle of the semester, students who are motivated to improve the final form of the movie will have time to do so. A wonderful motivator for these final revisions could be a public screening of the documentaries closer to the end of the semester.

Week 1	Students propose and select topics, form groups, and begin to plan the projects. Initial training with equipment in class. Students take IRB training modules available through your institution (homework). Review documentary models in class.
Week 2	Students present final project proposals to class. Students begin filming. Students draft permission forms and learn where to look for open source and Creative Commons licensed music. Continue reviewing documentary models in class.
Week 3	Students film during this week. Students begin playing with editing software and practicing the basic moves of evidentiary editing in class in preparation for editing their movies.
Week 4	Students continue filming during this week, and begin editing. Students should help create the first draft of grading/evaluating rubric this week.

Week 5	Students finish all filming. Draft workshops for movies in progress. "Final" drafts of movies should be uploaded to the web by the end of this week. Students should revise grading/evaluating rubric in class this week.
Week 6	Students screen movies in class. Students write and submit final reflections. Students contribute to grading/evaluating and response to peer movies.

Fig. 6.7: Six-week schedule for Assignment #2.

- *Material and Social Infrastructures:* Much of this assignment relies on audio-visual hardware and software that will need to be provided by your institution. As you look around your institution, you may learn, as I have learned in the past, that your institution is ill-equipped or possibly completely unequipped to allow you and your students to pursue an assignment such as this one. It is my hope that the earlier sections of this book and the method of building assignments in this chapter will help you present compelling arguments to your chair, dean, or provost for the funds to acquire the equipment you and your students will need. Programs that claim to value multimedia and/or audio-visual writing must make their values materially evident. If programs and the institutions that house those programs do not invest in the infrastructure to make good on their expressed values, then everyone, students included, will recognize the conspicuous absence of material evidence to back those claims. This conspicuous absence is as good as a neon sign that reads, "audio-visual writing is not our work." The more thoroughly these types of assignments are integrated into the writing curricula, the stronger the argument becomes that this kind of writing is important to your institution and program, and the more social resources you and your students will have.
- *Ethical and Practical Constraints: Copyright.* Students must learn to collaborate effectively to pull off this assignment. They will need to organize not only the content of their movies but also their schedules and the human and technological assets that they will need to complete the assignment. They will also need to understand where to find music and possibly other

supporting media that are available for them to not only use in class but also to publish for public access. This will require very basic introductions to Creative Commons and to Copyright Law. It should also include a brief discussion of Fair Use. There are a variety of sources for this information; however, Copyright Law and the availability of media that carry predetermined terms of use are in nearly continual flux as audio-visual writing technologies and audio-visual publishing venues become more and more common. The most important law for you and your students to know is that since 1978, the moment any content (texts, movies, photographs, art) is created by U.S. citizens, the authors of that content are automatically granted full protection under Copyright Law for ninety-five years. Furthermore, as of 1992, any content protected by copyright as of 1978 was automatically renewed to the maximum term (Lessig, *Free Culture* 134–35). What does this mean for us? According to Lessig, "the public domain is presumptive only for content from before the Great Depression" (25). This means that if we find a piece of media made after 1930, it is safe to assume that the media remains protected by copyright. Therefore, finding resources for media with clear terms of use and collections of media that are in the public domain (that is, no longer protected by copyright) is increasingly important— especially for students whose work in our classes may qualify as Fair Use, but whose work when posted to the Web is no longer in the classroom and is consequently no longer being used fairly. Your students need no instruction about where to find media. They do, however, need instruction about where to find media available for safe, fair, and legal use. Familiarize yourself with Fair Use recommendations from the U.S. Copyright Office and from current publications specializing in copyright and intellectual property.

Assessment: Assess the lesson, not the assignment. Unlike Assignment #1 above, this assignment is a major graded assignment. I recommend wholeheartedly that you let your students participate in the creation of the grading rubric that you and they will use to evaluate the results of their work. My students regularly decide that the final scores will be determined by first averaging the scores awarded by their peers and then averaging those outcomes with the scores I award. Each class is different though, and each class should decide. By weeks four and five, your students will be deep into the work of the assignment and will be situated well to help you determine how to evaluate their work. At this point, the assignment's thin requirements of one interview and one piece of music will explode, informed by the students' need to use far more than one interview and likely more than one piece of music to make a compelling movie. They will determine what is possible, what is impossible, and what is exceptional by way of doing the work of the assignment—that is, by negotiating the obstacles of the course. Furthermore, involving students in assessment is something that they will likely resist—because it is very difficult to do and because they have likely rarely, if ever, been asked to participate in assessment. In other words, assessment presents them with yet another problem. However, this is a problem you *want* them to have as it forces them to begin to articulate the criteria for success. Their movies won't be simply good or not so good. They will be evaluated by way of writerly criteria, not just by way of readerly appreciation. Fig. 6.8 shows an example of a scoring sheet that my students and I created for evaluating a version of Assignment #2. Notice that half of the possible total points are awarded for criteria related to the primary learning goal of the lesson: inquiry. The first four criteria evaluate the story and the evidence used in support of the overall message of the movie—a message that is born of the questions used to solicit the evidence. The other four criteria are specific to the text: criteria that break apart the all-there-at-onceness of the final product. These criteria ask students to recognize and evaluate the writerly moves within the works, not only the works themselves. In fact, only one of the eight total criteria, the last one, is devoted to the kind of readerly evaluation that students are most familiar making: the overall "SWEET" or "WOW" factor. Furthermore, with each section of each class, each semester, this scoring sheet changes. However, the first four criteria are pretty stable across sections because these are the criteria that serve as the foundation of the work that students do throughout not only this assignment but the entire semester.

Documentary Scoring Rubric:

Filmmakers:

Title:	Points				
	1	2	3	4	5
Message: ○ It tells a story	1	2	3	4	5

Compelling
  ○ It tells a story WORTH TELLING
  ○ Revealing
  ○ Purposeful
	1	2	3	4	5

Convincing ○ Evidence supports claim(s)	1	2	3	4	5

Credible
  ○ Evidence is credible
  ○ It seems like a legitimate documentary
     ○ Real & compelling issue
     ○ Carefully investigated
     ○ Carefully composed
	1	2	3	4	5

Editing:
  ○ Sequence
  ○ Shot selection & variety
  ○ Transitions
  ○ Titles
  ○ Sound levels
  ○ Photography
	1	2	3	4	5

Music:
  ○ Music adds positively to the overall argument of the film
  ○ Music adds positively to the overall effect of the film
	1	2	3	4	5

Credits:
  ○ All participants
  ○ Music
  ○ Who made the movie
  ○ Photos/Media
	1	2	3	4	5

Overall SWEET! Factor	1	2	3	4	5
TOTAL	/ 40				

Comments: Identify something in the movie that made you say

1. **"SWEET!"**

2. **"How'd you do THAT?"**

3. **"Yeah, but . . ."**

4. **"Who knew?**

5. **"So what."**

Fig. 6.8: Sample scoring sheet for Assignment #2.

Final Thoughts about Assignment #2, "Ask and Ye Shall Receive": I have run versions of this assignment many times and I am always surprised by the time and effort my students invest into this assignment. Best of all, these movies become texts of our class—models of not only inquiry but of collaborative authoring, of creative approaches to research, of *ethos* (credibility), *pathos* (compelling), and *logos* (convincing), and of citation. We can use these texts to discuss not only their strengths but also their limits for moving opinion and for providing evidence. When this assignment precedes an individual research project, students enter the project with a perspective informed by their recent experience of identifying and addressing problems by way of collaborative, question-based research. This leads us to our final problem, which will be addressed by not one assignment, but by a full assignment sequence.

PROBLEM #3: WRITING IS EPISTEMIC

Problem: In a book devoted to the epistemic nature of writing, one that chooses for its central mantra that a writer teaches writing, how is it that the epistemic quality of writing can be a problem? Well, it's really a matter of sequencing—the arranging of horses and carts and all. When I began teaching courses dedicated specifically to audio-visual writing, I did so as an audio-visual writer. You know, a writer teaches writing and all. The students in these classes were a mix of undergraduates and graduate students, mostly senior, professional writing majors and a variety of MA and PhD candidates. Being a writing teacher, I was committed to allowing my students to propose their own projects—ones that were fitted to their interests and possibly even to their research programs. I know, I've read this book too. The trouble was, I began to realize that I was seeing potential projects for my students that they were not seeing. When I asked them what they wanted to do, they had trouble responding, and I wondered how this could be. How could these advanced students not have projects? How could they not have questions that they wanted to see and hear anew by way of audio-visual writing projects? Then it hit me: the problem was that audio-visual writing is epistemic, and since these students had not yet known audio-visual writing through the experience of *doing* audio-visual writing, they were having trouble, frankly and understandably, projecting what an audio-visual project may enable them *to do*. That became the problem that was the stimulus to my thinking. How could students imagine ends for new forms of writing until they had actually attempted to write in these forms? No wonder I was feeling, at the end of the assignment, as though students were at the right place to actually begin the assignment—but by then, it was over. What next? Problem #3 is a problem and lesson of what next.

Theory: I have repeated, several times, this chapter's first epigraph from John Dewey about problems and thinking and experience, so I won't repeat it again here, though I could. However, I will repeat this chapter's second epigraph from my mentor Erika Lindemann: "An important goal of any writing teacher is to help students gain confidence in their ability to use the code effectively, perhaps even to find pleasure in manipulating its symbols" (4th ed. 16–18). Lindemann, here, asks us to allow our students to play—not simply *to* play, but *to learn to* play. Confidence and pleasure are developed through the mastery that is born of doing: experience. Lindemann also calls our attention to what Selber calls *functional literacy*: a knowledge of the code and how it behaves—how to work the machine, so to speak. Selber claims that knowing how to work the machines of digital writing and even knowing how the machines themselves work can help inform and improve critical literacy and rhetorical literacy. Let's, then, also return to Selber's tripartite rubric for literacy from Chapter Two. Selber claims, "I do not necessarily place a higher value on it [rhetorical literacy]: There will be times when an attention to functional or critical concerns should be paramount" (*Multiliteracies* 25). However, here we confront what may seem to be a paradox: functional literacy assumes an external end, and it is also a means. Much as the association model for grammar instruction, grammar becomes a lesson in the service of rhetorical ends. It solves a problem. How do we *value* functional instruction if we do not yet *value* rhetorical ends for the functional literacy?

Dewey claims there are two types of educational values: intrinsic and instrumental. "Intrinsic values," he says, "are not objects of judgment, they cannot (as intrinsic) be compared, or regarded as greater or less, better or worse. They are invaluable; and if a thing is invaluable, it is neither more nor less so than any other invaluable" (*Democracy* 238). Relational values, things that help us make judgments such as better or worse, Dewey calls instrumental. Dewey states, "Things judged or passed upon have to be estimated in relation to some third thing, some further end. With respect to that, they are means, or instrumental values" (238–39). Dewey continues,

It is true of arithmetic as it is of poetry that in some place and at some time it ought to be a good to be appreciated on its own account—just as an enjoyable experience, in short. If it is not, then when the time and place come for it to be used as a means or instrumentality, it will be in just that much handicapped. Never having been realized or appreciated for itself, one will miss something of its capacity as a resource for other ends.

[. . .] The way to enable a student to apprehend the instrumental value or arithmetic is not to lecture him upon the benefit it will be to him in some remote and uncertain future, but to let him discover that success in something he is interested in doing depends upon ability to use number. (240)

In short, the trick is to allow students to gain a tool that they don't think of as a tool but as a prize and then to allow them to find a problem that will ask them to reconsider their prize as a tool for addressing that problem. The key, it seems, is to use play—an intrinsic good, some invaluable thing done to its own ends—to *emerge* as instrumentally valuable, to allow the functional knowledge acquired through play to be put to a future use once it is owned and appreciated as being intrinsically valuable, once the student gains confidence in manipulating the code, once she can seek pleasure in doing so, once she can see how it works. Only then will she likely imagine using it as a tool.

Thus, we will address Problem #3, getting students to use new audio-visual writing skills as instrumental skills for addressing their own valued intellectual problems as a sequence of lessons and assignments.

Lesson/Learning Goal: For students to imagine and pursue problem solving by way of multiple forms of writing—specifically, for students to use audio-visual writing as a means of discovery and expression and not only as a means of production.

Assignment #3, "Multimediated, Audio-Visual Writing Is Multi-Epistemic": I will describe two assignment sequences here—however, not in the same depth as the first two assignments. Instead, I will talk about how I move toward similar learning goals situated in very different kinds of classes. The first, in many ways, is the easier of the two: the audio-visual writing course I mentioned above. The second is a version of the course that I imagine most of the readers of this book will be teaching, first-year writing, the harder of the two. I will use the same learning goal for each class; however, for the first, it will be the primary goal and for the second it will be a subordinate goal.

Course 3.1: Audio-Visual Writing: There is nothing *easy* about this course, as my students are fond of telling me. However, in terms of having to justify the presence of multiple audio-visual writing projects in the span of a single semester, it's a no brainer: that's what we're there to do, after all. In terms of reaching our final destination, preparing students to imagine and pursue problem solving by way of forms of audio-visual writing, we have a lot of ground to cover in one semester. My mantra for this course is "bite off more than you can chew." I encourage students to think big—to imagine projects that they really want to pursue, even if they imagine that they will not possibly be able to finish those projects in the span of the semester. The audio-visual writing products they create are in the service of their learning goals, even if they do not deliver *finished* works. We glory in the unfinishedness of their writing and concentrate on their developing audio-visual writing skills as vehicles that will help carry them to the destinations they value, eventually, once they are able to recognize their values. Because my students will need to learn to imagine academic ends for writing that they do not yet control, we begin the sequence by playing around with editing.

- Assignment 3.1.1: The Remix
- Assignment 3.1.2: The Remix
- Assignment 3.1.3: The Low-Stakes Interview-Based Documentary
- Assignment 3.1.4: The Bite-Off-More-Than-You-Can-Chew Project

It doesn't look like that much, really. Just four assignments in fifteen weeks—and the first two are nearly identical. Nearly, but not exactly, because even though they produce similar types of texts, they aim at much different goals.

The first remix is a no-holds-barred audio-visual remix. I require my students to use their own computers because my students all must have a computer as a condition of being a student at our institution.

However, this assignment can easily be performed in a computer lab. I prefer to have my students use their own laptops for a number of reasons. First, I know that editing can be extremely time-consuming—especially as students learn their way around a new editing software. By using their own computers, students can take the time they need to learn, not just the time available to them during lab hours. Also, they can begin to learn the affordances and limits of their own hardware and software. So my students often say things such as, "I've had this software on my computer for a few years and I've never, ever used it before." The first Remix helps them know their gear and teaches them to learn the basics of audio-visual editing. Another goal for the first remix is to get folks to learn how to get media online and how to break that media up in order to make something new from it. Critically, we do not publish these remixes outside of our class, so our uses are clearly for educational purposes only and are consequently fair. I expressly tell students in my prompts for Remix 1, "the sky's the limit. Play. Have fun."

Remix 2 allows us to build upon our new skills and knowledge. Now our learning goal is to move toward understanding the ethical parameters of remix in general. For Remix 2, students may use only media assets that they know they have permission to use and publish (i.e., assets in the public domain, assets licensed through Creative Commons, or assets they have obtained express permission from the copyright holder to use). It follows that Remix 2 has some restrictions that Remix 1 does not because students must honor the conditions of all Creative Commons (CC) licenses that limit their uses of CC-licensed material. For example, the license in Fig. 6.9 requires remixers both to attribute the author of the artifact (signified by the "BY" symbol) and that remixers share-alike ("SA"), i.e., that they share their remix with a license identical to the one on the media asset they are remixing. Licenses that require "SA" can make things pretty tricky whenever remixers attempt to use multiple pieces with different types of licenses.

Fig. 6.9: Creative Commons License

That is a problem that drives the learning goals of this lesson, a lesson that uses a remix assignment hot on the heels of another remix assignment to move emerging skills toward new learning goals, goals that help the student writers grow as editors who both gain experience in editing and build ethical knowledge about a variety of uses for their new skills—because audio-visual writing is epistemic. Importantly, the express goal of Remix 2, aside from the additional restrictions, remains "the sky's the limit. Play. Have fun." Students learn to find new toy boxes that may later function as toolboxes. The two-remix sequence spans the first three to four weeks of the semester.

After the remixes, each and every student has a growing grasp on what editing can do—on the layers that we discussed in Chapters Two and Three. Now, in the third assignment of the sequence (3.1.3) these audio-visual authors begin to create content: They make the media they will edit. This assignment introduces students to the concepts, skills, and tools we discussed in Chapters Four and Five. For this assignment, I often prescribe the topic so that students have a common problem. A topic I have found to be productive is to have students make two- to three-minute videos that supplement course descriptions for the courses of the program. These work quite nicely within the learning objectives of our professional writing program. The program becomes the client and the students themselves are the end users of the products they create. For this project we need to learn to use cameras and microphones and often lighting equipment. Students need to learn to plan and conduct interviews with teachers and students. Students learn to use more professional editing software in our media lab, and, working alongside each other in the labs, the students teach each other how to make the movies. They swap tips about using the gear. They troubleshoot the editing software together. They teach each other because they are emerging as audio-visual writers, and audio-visual writers teach audio-visual writing. This assignment spans five or six weeks; however, because it relies on the schedules of other teachers and students, its placement in the middle of the semester allows for a rolling completion date to accommodate the variety of scheduling difficulties that may arise.

As they pursue the third assignment, my students propose their final projects. Some are individual projects. Some are group projects. Now that I've been doing this for a while, some of my students elect to glory in the unfinishedness of projects begun in previous versions of my class—projects that were bites too big for my previous students to chew completely. This is fine because the course goal is for students to use audio-visual writing as a means for solving problems they value. Students make these choices. Some are ready to make the imaginative leap to propose their own projects, others are not. Either way, they collaborate to develop their skills and their experiences working through problems with audio-visual writing media. Students who bite off more than they can chew propose deliverables that will come due at the end of the semester, often a making-of-the-project-so-far type of video (for example, see Noah Blon's discussion of his team's making-of-the-project-so-far video in Blon, Creighton, and Halbritter). In Chapter Five, I referred to Casey Miles's "The Gender Project," a project that was born in the class I am describing here. Casey's project represents a bite too big for the semester, and is a project that students in subsequent sections of my class have taken on as their own projects—following Casey's lead and joining the conversation with their own questions, approaches, skills, limitations, and voices. The final assignment of the sequence involves a proposal presentation to the class, a final project, a presentation of that project to the class, and a traditionally-mediated meta-reflection about the process of coming to know their project and themselves as audio-visual writers. In terms of the four-part final assignment, I weight the grade of the reflection equal to the project itself. For the final project, students must propose not only what they want to do but how they intend to do it; in other words, they present to the class the very same delivery rubric I have been using in this chapter: accounting for agency, time, material and social infrastructures, and ethical and practical constraints. In short, they define problems and use those problems to write their own assignments, and their proposals become the articulations of the expectations that we will have for the products they generate. Any differences in what they make and what they proposed to make must be addressed during their presentations of their final projects and in their meta-reflections. Consequently, students not only write the assignments, they participate in assessing them as well—because audio-visual writers teach audio-visual writing.

This assignment sequence attempts to move students with little or no experience making audio-visual texts toward being able to imagine outcomes for audio-visual writing in their lives. It does not attempt, in fifteen weeks, to make movie makers of them. That would be impossible. It does, however, ask them to begin thinking like movie makers by first engaging play in order to recognize intrinsic values in audio-visual writing, values and interests they can and do put to later instrumental ends. In all, the aim is not to make movies, even though that is what we do. The aim is to make audio-visual writers. Making movies is the means by which we accomplish that aim.

Course 3.2: First-Year Writing: Before we proceed, let's recall the learning goal that is driving this assignment sequence: To move students to imagine and pursue problem solving by way of multiple forms of writing—specifically, for students to use audio-visual writing as a means of discovery and expression, not only as a means of production. The first part of this learning goal graphs perfectly well onto the missions of many, if not most, first-year writing programs. The second part focuses on a subset of the first, and while that has been our focus in this book, it is only one form of writing that the general writing curriculum must consider. That said, it is a potentially legitimate form for first-year writing to consider. Why am I hedging? Why is it a *potentially* legitimate form? Because the form is not the learning goal. The form is a means to realizing a learning goal. Consequently, the form must be integrated into a learning sequence that, unlike Course 3.1 above, will look to multiple forms of writing in order to help students develop as writers. The course that I will describe will employ multiple audio-visual writing assignments, a decision that may seem antithetical to the goal of giving students experience with *multiple* forms of writing. Well, it is antithetical only if by *multiple* we mean *as many different forms as possible*, and if it is the latter that we mean, then what we are teaching is the forms, not the writers. Lindemann claims, "All writing courses share a common goal: giving students enough guided practice in composing that they become more fluent, effective writers at the end of the course than they were at the beginning" (4th ed. 254). Notice that Lindemann's common goal is about people, and not about a particular form of writing. It is "they," the writers, who become more fluent and effective, not the products *per se*. When exploring and employing multiple forms of writing with the goal of developing writers, the lessons must select forms, not vice versa. The forms are the means. The students—the writers—are the goals. Consequently, *multiple* forms means just that: multiple, more than one.

I am not about to reinvent the wheel here. In each of the institutions where I have taught, the mission of the first-year writing course is something akin to the goal we pursued in Assignment #2 above: for students to learn the conventions of inquiry-based writing. In other words, to pursue writing projects that are led by questions—things students need to learn—instead of assertions—things they want to tell. Thus, this assignment sequence will employ Assignment #2 as detailed above. That documentary assignment, a collaboratively-authored project, will be followed by an individual research project. That way, students can take what they have learned about inquiry, authoritative references, and making their own arguments through the statements of others—all lessons from the documentary project—and put this knowledge to use on the final research essay. Why an essay? Because an essay will allow students to quote in a different way—to quote sparingly, not liberally, as they do in the documentary; to explore the difference between writing in time and writing in linear space; to experience the differences in scope of argument and depth of evidence between time-based audio-visual writing and space-based traditional writing with alphabetic text; to dance two different forms of inquiry-based rhetorical dances.

That is where the documentary assignment will lead. The documentary project will span six weeks. The final research project will span at least five weeks. Even with a week of overlap, those two assignments will span at least two-thirds of the semester, which means we need a four-week assignment to lead the semester. This assignment, as we saw in Assignment 3.1 above, must create a need for what will follow. It will need to help students identify an intrinsic interest that they will be able to reimagine as instrumental: tools to help them solve the problems that emerge later in the semester. The first assignment will need to exploit the confidence-building and the latent lessons of play.

Furthermore, the first assignment needs to take some of the technological pressure off of the documentary assignment so that, when we get to the documentary assignment, we can really concentrate on the inquiry aspects—the lessons we will lean on in the final project—rather than the functional aspects of learning to use the gear. Plus, our first assignment will need to help students learn how to work in groups—to be collaborative authors. If we are really lucky, it will also teach us something about the genre of documentary so that we don't have to do that too even as we are making the documentaries. Our first assignment, then, will be to propose and create several group-authored mockumentaries: a four-to-five-week project.

The mockumentary assignment will select restrictions that stem from the learning goals mentioned just above:

- It must be funny.
- It must do the things a documentary does.
- It must contain at least one interview.
- It must have at least one piece of music.
- The topic must be approved by the class.

That's it. The model texts we will study in class in order to identify common features of documentary, such as evidentiary editing, voice-over narration, and behind-the-scenes footage, will be found in mockumentary films such as *This Is Spinal Tap* and *Waiting for Guffman*. We will have fun. We will play. We will gain confidence in our abilities to use audio-visual code effectively, and we will strive to find pleasure in manipulating its symbols. We will develop functional literacies immediately in the service of making the mockumentary and others that will later prove to be functional in the service of both the documentary and the research-based essay. We will play, and we will learn.

Of course, along the way, we will write traditional alphabetic texts that articulate our proposals, and we will share our proposals and the works that emerge from them in live audio-visual presentations. We will reflect in traditional writing on what we have been learning. We will develop assessment criteria. We will assess our work together. We will respond to our readings in a variety of ways: in traditional writing—with pen and paper and electronic text—and in video logs (vlogs). We will imagine and pursue problem solving by way of multiple forms of writing.

Final Thoughts about Assignment Sequence #3, "Multimediated Audio-Visual Writing is Multi-Epistemic": I remember going to my son's first beginning hockey lessons. The kids were all decked out in hockey gear: helmets, pads, sticks, and gloves. The whole nine yards (of hockey ice). Sorry, bad metaphor. Anyhow, the thing that defined these lessons as hockey lessons were largely the uniforms. These lessons were really lessons in skating fundamentals—the very basic functional skills of the sport—lessons that my son would have refused to attend had they been called what they were. The thing of it was, the teachers decided that the whole fundamentals of skating thing must have sounded pretty much like drudgery as well because these folks found the coolest ways to get the kids to learn to skate—all dressed up like hockey players. They ran on the ice. They jumped on the ice. They chased each other. They fell down—a lot. They saw how much "snow" they could make by scraping their skates across the ice. I wanted to strap on skates and put on all of those layers of cool (and terribly expensive) gear and get out there with them. I found myself in the queue of other envious parents, with our noses pressed up against the Plexiglas, wishing that I could take these fundamental skating lessons—not because I wanted to learn to skate but because I wanted to have that much fun. I wanted to play. They played, and, in so doing, they learned how to skate—and that skating is the consequential prize of skating the obstacle course of those beginners' hockey lessons. That skating, that prize, that toy will become a tool put to instrumental ends in future lessons and games.

The assignments of this chapter all rely on the foundational role of play because it is through play that functional knowledge is developed—knowledge necessary to help students not only accomplish critical and rhetorical ends but reveal those ends as possibilities. The play fosters intrinsic value in the hard, hard work of authoring—because that is what it is: hard, hard work, work that often involves both stamina and tremendous flourishes of herculean effort. I tell my students some version of these words each semester: "I could never assign all of the work that you will elect to do in this class," and those words are among the truest I've ever uttered. Right up there with "Thanks, Mom" and "I hope I'll never have to go on the job market again. Ever." How do I get my students to do the work they do? I give them problems and I ask them to play. When play is addressed toward a problem, it becomes work—the work of learning. I set up an obstacle course of writing tasks that ask my students to use the toys of Assignment #1 as the tools of Assignment #2, and I reward their play by assessing the lesson and not the assignment. I am able to recognize the obstacles, the lessons, and the play because I know the work—because I am an audio-visual writer who teaches audio-visual writing; because I have faced those problems; because I have done that work; because I have had that fun.

Multimediated audio-visual writing tasks are fantastically complex with layers and layers of rhetorical elements and layers and layers of technical skills and practical concerns and interpersonal negotiations. These writing tasks are most often overtly collaborative in that they involve several or many people in their production. As such, these writing tasks can help writing teachers reveal things about traditional writing that are often hard to see and hear: the crowd of people with whom the solitary author is communicating, the conversations she is joining, the conversations and other authors she is referencing, the tropes and grammatical architectures built by others that behave as though they are hers. The intersubjectivity of writing. And so, at the end of this book, let's go back to the beginning—back to Chapter One, where Berlin claimed that "The epistemic position implies that knowledge is not discovered by reason alone, that cognitive and affective processes are not separate, that intersubjectivity is a condition of all knowledge, and that the contact of minds affects knowledge" (165). Audio-visual writing—the acts of writing, not the products of writing—is so powerfully epistemic because it asks students to confront, head on, the cognitive and affective processes of writing. They make knowledge because they deliver on the foundational metaphor of Dewey's doctrine of interest: Work is play.

> The doctrine of interest [. . .] is a warning to furnish conditions such that the natural impulses and acquired habits, as far as they are desirable, *shall obtain subject-matter and modes of skill* in order to develop to their natural ends of achievement and efficiency. Interest, the identification of mind with the material and methods of a developing activity, is the inevitable result of the presence of such situations. (*Interest* 95)

Like any productive metaphor, the two elements, the vehicle and the tenor, must be different enough to be productive. They are. They must be. Work is not play—as we have all experienced. Yet we seem to work hardest when our work *is* play. Even though I said above that

I wouldn't do it, I'm going to repeat this chapter's opening epigraph from Dewey—just this one last time:

> [P]roblems are the stimulus to thinking. That the conditions found in present experience should be used as sources of problems is a characteristic which differentiates education based upon experience from traditional education. (*Experience* 79)

The answer to ensuring that work does not simply become play—or, rather, that work is not simply replaced by play—is to be found in the foundational metaphor of Dewey's educational filter: Problems are solutions.

Audio-visual writing assignments, such as the ones offered above, will introduce new problems to your institution, to your department, to your pedagogy, to your classes, to your assignment sequences, to your students, to you—to your writing—to your life.

Now, go have some fun.

Afterword

If the preceding pages have done their job, you're probably saying something akin to the following to yourself right about now: "Great, but there's so much I still don't know! I'm going to need to know film theory, I'll need to know more about photography, about specific camera and microphone models, about sound files, about movie editing and specific editing software! What do I buy? How much do I/we need to run a class? A department? Where do I turn in my institution for help?"

Yes. Those are some of the right questions. You and your students will pursue answers to those questions guided by your local needs—according to your learning goals for your classes. Some of you will never need to worry with lighting or advanced camera operations. Some will. Some of you will need to build resources and infrastructures for putting lots of equipment into the hands of your students. Some of you will not. Some of you will teach classes devoted to audio-visual writing. Some of you will employ audio-visual writing assignments only once or twice in a semester. Some of you work at institutions that already have considerable audio-visual resources. Some have limited resources. So it goes.

This book and its author can offer you—that is, *all* of you—no specific answers to these questions and no specific suggestions for addressing these inevitable concerns. Our project here has not been to attend to the multitude of our local processes. Rather, our aim here has been to proclaim our unity by way of identifying our operational concerns—those that enable us to see beyond our applied lessons to the learning goals—our motives—that fit acts to scenes and scenes to acts. If this is how *we* can approach *our* work, how can *you* approach *your* work? What will guide you through your specific concerns? For that, I offer a mantra.

Repeat after me: I am a writing teacher; I teach writers.

As I was finishing the revisions of this book, I spoke with a colleague and dear friend who had just moved to a new institution. Audio-visual writing has played an important role in her teaching; however, upon her arrival, she found that her new institution had only one video camera available for her students to use. "So," she said to me, "I can't do my video-writing lesson." I agreed, she couldn't do her lesson—as it was; however, that didn't mean, necessarily, that she and her students could not make good use of that single camera. Together, we conceived a project that could divide her thirty students into five groups who would each complete a nongraded project over the course of the semester: five groups, each with two weeks of access to the camera. As the semester would progress, the first groups would create movies that subsequent groups could use as models. Along the way, the class could chart the progress of these successive efforts and build a list of formative, audio-visual writing lessons compiled from their collective efforts.

The learning goals driving this assignment would be to help each student in the class engage all three of Selber's literacies applied to audio-visual writing: functional, critical, and rhetorical. The assignment would not place all students on the same calendar nor would all groups begin at the same level of development; however, it would use these potential shortcomings as strengths by shifting the emphasis from marking a summative assessment of students' finished work to charting formative criteria for assessment of their *unfinished* work. Students who go last profit from those who go first—and vice versa. This lesson would be unfair if student learning were not reciprocal, and this lesson would likely be unfair if students were graded on the finishedness of the texts they create. However, this lesson could be a remarkable example of a tenet that drives the pedagogy at work in this book: Audio-visual writing is epistemic. Students will write and use that writing as a source of learning. Be creative. Fit your acts of teaching to the scenes of your teaching efforts. Look to learning goals to help you reimagine your assignments. Look to learning goals to help you identify opportunity in what at first may seem to be infrastructural limitations.

Repeat after me: I am a writing teacher; I teach writers.

This book asks you not only to glory in the unfinishedness of audio-visual writing, it asks that you glory in the unfinishedness of the teaching of audio-visual writing. This book hopes to help you get started. However, you will each need to assess how you may approach getting finished. We have not talked much here about film theory. If you find, in your efforts, that you and your students may profit from such study, then I highly encourage you to pursue that. I have found the work of documentary film scholar Bill Nichols to be especially helpful because his terminology and analysis hinges on the language of rhetorical study, and I have found Michel Chion's discussion of "point of audition" to be especially helpful for locating the audio-visual writer's voice in the layers of the soundtrack. Even as our multidisciplinary field of writing teachers emerges from myriad academic histories, the development of our audio-visual writing theories will be directed by our multifaceted intellectual predilections, interests, and experiences. So read, study, search, practice, and discuss your work and your students' work. Be reflective practitioners and seek to address the emerging needs of your expanding audio-visual pedagogy and practice.

Repeat after me: I am a writing teacher; I teach writers.

Finally, for now, accept that the technologies and infrastructures of creating and sharing audio-visual writing are in constant and rapid flux. From semester to semester, it may be nearly impossible to keep up with all of the changes. Resist the urge to try to be responsible for all of the content your students will need to access. Even as you may assign a handbook in your class to help your students address writing issues as they emerge for each student, direct your students to search the Internet for blogs, video tutorials, and user manuals for the audio-visual equipment and software they will use. My students regularly Google their way to answers about lighting and camera operations and learning how to perform special effects and post-production fixes in specific editing software and specific operating systems. Directing your students to these resources is not passing the buck for learning this information yourself; it recognizes that audio-visual writers need to learn more than how to make an audio-visual project in our classes; they need to be able to pursue audio-visual projects after they leave our classes. In short, in their lives as audio-visual writers, they will need to learn again and again how to solve software- and hardware-specific problems. Asking them to do so in your class can help them develop sustainable audio-visual writing practices.

Repeat after me: I am a writing teacher; I teach writers.

Notes

1. For Burke, meanings that adhere to our orientations are *pious* and meanings that alter of our orientations are *impious*. Piety and impiety are equally codependent. Burke states, "piety is a system-builder, impelling one to go farther and farther in search of appropriate materials that will go with his concerns" (*Permanence* 246). In other words, one must pursue impious means to perfect one's pious perspective. Terministic catharsis is all about moving piety by way of impiety.

2. Welch refers to Ong's *Orality and Literacy* (11).

3. Diogenes and Lunsford refer to Ong's *Interfaces of the Word* (289).

4. I assume that *multimodal* here refers to multiple modes of rhetorical delivery (e.g., exposition, argumentation, description, and narration); however, their use could also refer to modes of reception, much like Dunn's use of the term.

5. In Chapter Two, we will focus on writing as symbolic action, and Burke's dramatistic hexad (agent, act, agency, scene, purpose, and attitude) as a rubric for discussing a variety of symbolic acts.

Works Cited

Alten, Stanley R. *Audio in Media*. 9th ed. Boston, MA: Wadsworth Cengage Learning, 2011. Print.

"American Stories, American Solutions." YouTube . BarackObama.com. 2008. Video. 30 Sept. 2012.

Axelrod, Jim. "Kodachrome: The Legendary Film's Last Days." *CBS, Sunday Morning*. 26 December 2010. Web. 8 July 2012.

Bartholomae, David. "Inventing the University." *Cross-Talk in Comp Theory: A Reader*. Ed. Victor Villanueva, Jr. Urbana, IL: NCTE, 1997. 589–619. Print.

The Beatles. *Sgt. Pepper's Lonely Hearts Club Band*. Capitol/EMI Records, 1967. LP.

Berlin, James A. *Rhetoric and Reality: Writing Instruction in American Colleges, 1900–1985*. Carbondale: Southern Illinois UP, 1987. Print.

Blon, Noah, Caron Creighton, and Bump Halbritter. "Big Questions, Small Works, Lots of Layers: Documentary Video Production and the Teaching of Academic Research and Writing." *Kairos: A Journal of Rhetoric, Technology, and Pedagogy* 16.1: n. pag. Web. 15 August 2011.

Born Into Brothels: Calcutta's Red Light Kids. Dir. Zana Briski and Ross Kauffman. Perf. Kochi, Avijit Halder, and Shanti Das. Red Light Films, 2004. Film.

Bowie, David. "Modern Love." *Let's Dance*. EMI Records, 1983. CD.

Bowling for Columbine. Dir. Michael Moore. Perf. Michael Moore, Charlton Heston, and Marilyn Manson. Dog Eat Dog Films, 2002. Film.

Burke, Kenneth. *Counter-Statement*. 1931. Berkeley: U of California P, 1968. Print.

—. *Permanence and Change: An Anatomy of Purpose*. 3rd ed. Berkeley: U of California P, 1984. Print.

—. *The Philosophy of Literary Form*. 3rd ed. Berkeley: U of California P, 1973. Print.

—. *A Grammar of Motives*. 1945. Berkeley: U of California P, 1969. Print.

—. *A Rhetoric of Motives*. 1950. Berkeley: U of California P, 1969. Print.

—. "What Are the Signs of What?: A Theory of 'Entitlement'." *Anthropological Linguistics* 4.6 (June 1962): 1–23. JSTOR. Web. 15 August 2010.

—. *Language as Symbolic Action: Essays on Life, Literature, and Method.* Berkeley: U of California P, 1966. Print.

—. "(Nonsymbolic) Motion/(Symbolic) Action." *Critical Inquiry* 4.4 (Summer 1978): 809–38. Print.

Citizen Kane. Dir. Orson Welles. Perf. Orson Welles, Joseph Cotten, and Dorothy Comingore. Mercury Productions, 1941. Film.

Conference on College Composition and Communication. "Students' Rights to Their Own Language." 1974 and 2003. Web. 8 July 2012.

Chion, Michel. *Audio-Vision: Sound on Screen.* New York: Columbia UP, 1994. Print.

DeJoy, Nancy. *Process This: Undergraduate Writing in Composition Studies.* Logan: Utah State UP, 2004. Print.

Dewey, John. *Democracy and Education: An Introduction to the Philosophy of Education.* New York: The Free Press, 1916. Print.

—. *Experience and Education.* 1938. New York: Touchstone, 1997. Print.

—. *Interest and Effort in Education.* Boston, MA: Houghton Mifflin, 1913. Print.

—. *The Quest for Certainty: A Study of the Relation of Knowledge and Action.* New York: J. J. Little and Ives Co., 1929. Print.

Diogenes, Marvin, and Andrea Lunsford. "Toward Delivering New Definitions of Writing." *Delivering College Composition: The Fifth Canon.* Ed. Kathleen Blake Yancey. Portsmouth, NH: Boynton/Cook, 2006. 141–54. Print.

Dobrin, Sidney I. "Paralogic Hermeneutic Theories, Power, and the Possibility for Liberating Pedagogies." *Post-Process Theory: New Directions for Composition Research.* Ed. Thomas Kent. Carbondale: Southern Illinois UP, 1999. 132–48. Print.

Dunn, Patricia A. *Learning Re-Abled: The Learning Disability Controversy and Composition Studies.* Portsmouth, NH: Boynton/Cook, 1995. Print.

Ede, Lisa, and Andrea Lunsford. "Audience Addressed/Audience Invoked: The Role of Audience in Composition Theory and Pedagogy." *College Composition and Communication* 35.2 (May 1984): 155–71. Print.

Elias, Nina, and Bethany Tomaszewski. "Phoenix—Lisztomania//Michigan State Brat Pack Mashup." *YouTube.* 13 December 2010. Web. 8 July 2012.

Fahrenheit 9/11. Dir. Michael Moore. Perf. Michael Moore, George W. Bush, and Ben Affleck. Dog Eat Dog Films, 2004. Film.

Fantasia. Dir. James Algar, Gaëtan Brizzi. Perf. Leopold Stokowski and Deems Taylor. Walt Disney Studios, 1940. Film.

Freire, Paulo. *Pedagogy of the Oppressed.* Trans. Myra Bergman Ramos. New York: Continuum, 1997. Print.

Garner, Ken. "'Would You Like to Hear Some Music?' Music in-and-out-of-control in the Films of Quentin Tarantino." *Film Music: Critical Ap-*

proaches. Ed. K. J. Donnelly. New York: Continuum International, 2001. 188–205. Print.

Hairston, Maxine. "The Winds of Change: Thomas Kuhn and the Revolution in the Teaching of Writing." *College Composition and Communication* 33.1 (1982): 76-88.

Halbritter, Bump, and Todd Taylor. "Remembering Composition." *JAC: A Journal of Composition Theory* 26.3–4 (2006). DVD.

Haven, Cynthia. "The New Literacy: Stanford Study Finds Richness and Complexity in Students' Writing." 12 October 2009. Web. 8 July 2012.

Hocks, Mary E. "Understanding Visual Rhetoric in Digital Writing Environments." *College Composition and Communication* 54.4 (June 2003): 629–56. Print.

Ihde, Don. *Listening and Voice: A Phenomenology of Sound.* Athens: Ohio UP, 1976. Print.

Jackson, Michael. *Thriller.* Epic, 1982. LP.

Jenkins, Henry T. *Convergence Culture: Where Old and New Media Collide.* New York: New York UP, 2006. Print.

The Jimi Hendrix Experience. "Little Wing." *Axis: Bold as Love.* MCA, 1967. LP.

Kent, Thomas, ed. *Post-Process Theory: Beyond the Writing-Process Paradigm.* Carbondale: Southern Illinois UP, 1999. Print.

Kress, Gunther, and Theo van Leeuwen. *Reading Images: The Grammar of Visual Design.* 2nd ed. New York: Routledge, 2006. Print.

Lady Gaga. "Bad Romance." *The Fame Monster.* Streamline, 2009. CD.

Lessig, Lawrence. *Free Culture: How Big Media Uses Technology and the Law to Lock Down Culture and Control Creativity.* New York: Penguin, 2004. Print.

—. *Remix: Making Art and Commerce Thrive in the Hybrid Economy.* New York: Penguin, 2008. Print.

Lindemann, Erika. *A Rhetoric for Writing Teachers.* 4th ed. New York: Oxford UP, 2001. Print.

—. *A Rhetoric for Writing Teachers.* 3rd ed. New York: Oxford UP, 1995. Print.

Mannheim, Karl. *Essays on the Sociology of Knowledge.* Ed. Paul Kecskemeti. New York: Oxford UP, 1952. Print.

March of the Penguins. Dir. Luc Jacquet. Perf. Morgan Freeman, Charles Berling, and Jules Sitruk. Bonne Pioche, 2005. Film.

Miles, Casey. "The Gender Project." *Vimeo.* 27 December 2012. Web. 8 July 2012.

Murray, Donald. "Teach Writing as a Process Not Product." *Cross-Talk in Comp Theory: A Reader.* Ed. Victor Villanueva, Jr. Urbana, IL: NCTE, 1997. 3–6. Print.

—. *A Writer Teaches Writing: A Complete Revision*. 2nd ed. Boston, MA: Houghton Mifflin College Divison, 1985. Print.

National Council of Teachers of English. "Resolution on Composing with Nonprint Media." 2003. Web. 13 May 2012.

—. "Resolution on Students' Right of Expression." 2004. Web. 13 May 2012.

—. "Teaching Composition: A Position Statement." 1985. Web. 13 May 2012.

—. "NCTE Beliefs about the Teaching of Writing." 2004. Web. 13 May 2012.

Nichols, Bill. *Introduction to Documentary*. Bloomington: Indiana UP, 2001. Print.

North, Stephen M. *The Making of Knowledge in Composition: Portrait of an Emerging Field*. Portsmouth, NH: Boynton/Cook, 1987. Print.

O Brother, Where Art Thou? Dir. Ethan and Joel Coen. Perf. George Clooney, John Turturro, and Tim Blake Nelson. Touchstone Pictures, 2000. Film.

Olson, Gary A. "Toward a Post-Process Composition: Abandoning the Rhetoric of Assertion." *Post-Process Theory: New Directions for Composition Research*. Ed. Thomas Kent. Carbondale: Southern Illinois UP. 1999. 7–15. Print.

Ong, Walter J. *Interfaces of the Word*. Ithaca, NY: Cornell UP, 1977. Print.

—. *Orality and Literacy: The Technologizing of the Word*. London: Methuen, 1982. Print.

Peirce, Charles S. "Deduction, Induction, and Hypothesis." *The Essential Peirce: Selected Philosophical Writings (1867–1893)*. Vol. 1. Ed. N. Houser and C. Kloesel. Bloomington: Indiana UP, 1992. 186–99. Print.

—. *Pragmatism as a Principle and Method of Right Thinking: The 1903 Harvard Lectures on Pragmatism*. 1903. Albany: SUNYP, 1997. Print.

Pirates of the Caribbean: The Curse of the Black Pearl. Dir. Gore Verbinski. Walt Disney Pictures, 2003. Film.

Pulp Fiction. Dir. Quentin Tarantino. Perf. John Travolta, Uma Thurman, and Samuel L. Jackson. Miramax Films, 1994. Film.

Raising Arizona. Dir. Ethan and Joel Coen. Perf. Nicholas Cage, Holly Hunter, and Trey Wilson. Circle Films, 1987. Film.

Richards, I. A. *The Philosophy of Rhetoric*. New York: Oxford UP, 1936. Print.

Roger & Me. Dir. Michael Moore. Perf. Michael Moore, James Blanchard, and James Bond. Dog Eat Dog Films, 1989. Film.

Riordan, Rick. *Percy Jackson and the Olympians*. Series. New York: Hyperion Books CH, 2006–2011. Print.

Selber, Stuart A. *Multiliteracies for a Digital Age*. Carbondale: Southern Illinois UP, 2004. Print.

—. "Reimagining the Functional Side of Computer Literacy." *CCC* 55.3 (2004): 470– 503. Print.

Sid & Nancy. Dir. Alex Cox. Perf. Gary Oldman, Chloe Webb, and David Hayman. New Line Cinema, 1986. Film.

Simon, Paul. "You Can Call Me Al." *YouTube*. 16 June 2011. Web. 8 July 2012.

Sonnenschein, David. *Sound Design: The Expressive Power of Music, Voice, and Sound Effects in Cinema*. Studio City, CA: Michael Wiese Productions, 2001. Print.

This Is Spinal Tap. Dir. Rob Reiner. Perf. Rob Reiner, Michael McKean, and Christopher Guest. MGM, 1984. Film.

Stuckey, J. Elspeth. *The Violence of Literacy*. Portsmouth, NH: Boynton/Cook, 1991. Print.

Taylor, Todd. "Design, Delivery, And Narcolepsy." *Delivering College Composition*. Ed. Kathleen Yancey. Portsmouth, NH: Boynton/Cook, 2006. 127–40. Print.

—. "Ten Commandments for Computers and Composition." *The Allyn & Bacon Sourcebook for Writing Program Administrators*. Ed. Irene Ward and William Carpenter. New York: Allyn & Bacon, 2001. 228–42. Print.

—. *Take 20: Teaching Writing*. Bedford/St. Martin's, 2007. DVD.

Torres, Carlos Alberto, ed. *Education, Power, and Personal Biography: Dialogues with Critical Educators*. New York: Routledge, 1998. Print.

VH-1. "Artists A-Z: Biography, Dusty Springfield." 2003. Web. 21 July 2003.

Welch, Kathleen E. *Electric Rhetoric: Classical Rhetoric, Oralism, and a New Literacy*. Cambridge: MIT Press, 1999. Print.

Williams, Robin. *The Non-Designer's Design Book: Design and Typographic Principles for the Visual Novice*. 3rd ed. Berkeley, CA: Peachpit, 2008. Print.

Yancey, Kathleen Blake. "Made Not Only in Words: Composition in a New Key." *College Composition and Communication* 56:2 (December 2004): 297–328. Print.

—. "Writing in the 21st Century: A Report from the National Council of Teachers of English." Urbana, IL: NCTE. 2009. Web. 1 March 2009.

Index

abductive logic, 51

act, vii, x-xi, xiii-xiv, 3-8, 12, 16-18, 23, 26, 34-40, 43-44, 46, 48-49, 52-53, 71, 76, 84-85, 97, 108, 113, 115-116, 123, 139, 166, 170, 199, 201, 211, 235, 239; of collecting, 168; of revision, 149; of teaching, 236; of writing, 172, 187, 212, 233

actor, xiii, 17, 89-90, 92, 163

agency, xi, xiii-xvi, 24, 33, 37, 39, 71, 181, 200, 228, 239

agent, xi, 17, 33, 36-37, 38-39, 53, 71, 84, 110, 114, 170, 185, 239

alignment, 62, 98, 98-100, 105, 107, 114

all-there-at-onceness, 62, 82, 83, 85, 87, 96, 97, 107, 108, 160, 220

alphabetic text, 18, 24-25, 51, 54, 230-231

Alten, Stanley R., 132

analysis, vii, xiii, 17, 32, 36, 101, 104, 109, 113, 116, 171, 237

assessment, 14, 18-19, 56, 58, 63-64, 72, 119-201, 207-208, 212, 220, 231, 236

assignment, xii-xiii, 46-50, 65-66, 68-71, 159, 186, 197-202, 204-209, 211, 217-219, 222-230, 232, 234, 236; audio-visual project, 181, 222, 237; audio-visual remix, 59, 99, 225; audio-visual writing, xi, 20, 173, 186, 222, 225, 229, 235; documentary, 54, 66-67, 164, 176, 230; inquiry-based project, 50, 209; interview-based project, 164, 211; mockumentary, 231; movie, 67; moviemaking, xvii; reflection, xvi, 33, 39, 66, 69, 167, 210, 228; remix, 68, 98, 227; sequence, 66, 68, 186, 201, 222, 224, 229-230, 234; traditional writing assignments, 198-199; writing, 70, 198-199, 201, 234

attitude, xiii, 3, 12-13, 25, 38-40, 43-44, 64-65, 71, 84, 87, 110, 113, 169, 185, 239

audio mixer, 153-156

audio studies, 204

audio tracks, 140-143, 147, 149-150, 152, 155, 157, 212, 214-215; independent, 141, 145; layers of, 140; separate, 140, 143

audio visual: playback, 205

audio-visual, 101, 173-174, 176, 178, 180, 183, 196, 205, 231; assets, 88; author, xiv-xv, 44, 74-75, 89, 91-93, 107, 111, 170, 174, 183, 186, 227; composition, 88, 92, 94, 107, 116, 186; design, 98; editing, 65, 168, 226; functional literacy, 150; gear, 211; grammar, 60-61, 208; information, 6, 39, 107; materials, 152; media, ix-x, 65, 186; multidimensional, 109, 116, 187;

About the Author

Bump Halbritter is Associate Professor of Rhetoric and Writing at Michigan State University, and is Editor of *CCC Online*, the audio-visual sister publication of *College Composition and Communication* (2010–2015). His work on aural rhetoric and audio-visual writing pedagogy has appeared in *Kairos, Enculturation, Computers and Composition*, and in the edited collection, *Digital Tools*. Bump, along with his MSU colleague, Julie Lindquist, is the co-principal investigator of the research project LiteracyCorps Michigan (LCM), a long-term, multiphase research project that uses digital video to drive the investigation and documentation of the literate lives of first-generation college students at MSU. Julie and Bump have presented video products generated through this study at the *Conference on College Composition and Communication, Writing Research Across Borders, Computers and Writing, Rhetoric Society of America, the National Council of Teachers of English*, and many invited talks. A discussion of the methodology they have created for LCM, "Time, Lives, and Videotape: Operationalizing Discovery in Scenes of Literacy Sponsorship," appears in *College English* (November 2012).

Bump Halbritter

CPSIA information can be obtained at www.ICGtesting.com
Printed in the USA
LVOW132007180213

320647LV00001B/27/P